Francesco Aquilar
Mauro Galluccio

Psychological Processes in International Negotiations

Theoretical and Practical Perspectives

Springer

Francesco Aquilar, Psy.D.
Director
Center for Cognitive Psychology and Psychotherapy
Naples, Italy
francescoaquilar@tiscali.it

Mauro Galluccio, Ph.D.
Political Coordinator
Directorate General for Development and Relations with African, Caribbean and Pacific States
The European Commission of the European Union
Brussels, Belgium
galluccio@moverim.eu

ISBN: 978-0-387-71378-6 e-ISBN: 978-0-387-71380-9

Library of Congress Control Number: 2007925689

Printed on acid-free paper.

9 8 7 6 5 4 3 2 1

springer.com

To Raffaela and Michele
My beloved parents
Mauro Galluccio

To our children
with the active hope
that they will be able to live
in a better world
Francesco Aquilar
Mauro Galluccio

Foreword

International Negotiation: A New Challenge for Cognitive Therapy is well edited by Francesco Aquilar and Mauro Galluccio and follows some of the main principles that I outlined in my article "Rational-emotive behavioral approaches to peace and negotiation" (Ellis, 1992). I said in that article that peace negotiators can choose, if they will, to select peaceful negotiation or combative methods to try for solving national and international Yes, select. Most nations and individuals choose to select fighting—with predictable results. The editors and their collaborators choose REBT approaches and ably teach readers how to effect it. A much better choice! Try it and follow it!

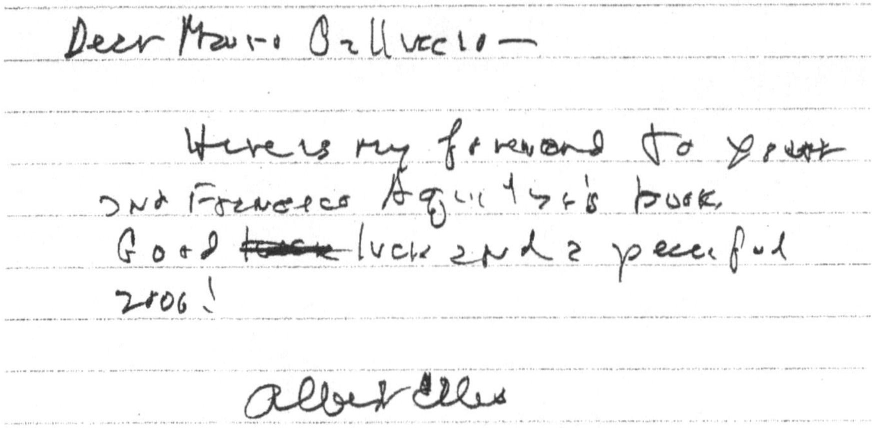
Dear Mauro Galluccio —

Here is my foreword to your and Francesco Aquilar's book. Good luck and a peaceful 2006!

Albert Ellis

Psychological Processes in International Negotiations: Theoretical and Practical Prespectives is well edited by Francesco Aquilar and Mauro Galluccio and follows some of the main principles that I outlined in my article "Rational-Emotive Behavioral Approaches to Peace" through Negotiation" (Ellis, 1992). I said in that article that peace negotiators can *choose*, if they will, to select peaceful negotiation or combative methods to try for solving national and international conflict. Yes, select. Most nations and individuals choose to select fighting – with predictable results. The editor and their contributors choose also REBT approaches and ably teach readers how to effect it. A much better choice! Try it and follow it!

Albert Ellis,
New York, NY

Note: *International Negotiation: A New Challenge for Cognitive Therapy* as written in the Foreword by Albert Ellis was originally chosen for the title of this book.

Francesco Aquilar
Mauro Galluccio
March 2007

Preface

In this historical period, the difficult issue of international negotiation appears even more problematic than in the past, given the new, and in many ways unpredictable, developments of world politics. The numerous political, economic and anthropological problems underlining the world equilibrium could be better faced using the contribution of psychology of training and of cognitive psychotherapy (individual and of group). This is not because these disciplines offer magic solutions, but rather because of the positive operational consequences that the knowledge and the techniques set up in these sectors may provoke. Three sectors in particular could benefit from the interaction between psychology of training, cognitive psychotherapy and political science, and these are:

A) The training of negotiators (actual and future), with the purpose of reducing the difficulties of negotiation deriving not from structural factors difficult to eliminate, but rather from cognitive errors, from a reduced ability to manage destructive emotions, from dangerous misinterpretation, from subconscious, auto - and hetero – destructive, habits;
B) The analysis and the redefinition of cognitive and emotional processes underlining conflicts (between people and between governments), with the purpose of finding new and creative solutions, if possible "without losers";
C) The social spreading of a cooperative attitude and the most peaceful possible, through the operation of "social psychotherapy" (Aquilar, 1996, 2006) founded upon the respect of different cultural anthropologies, that could also bring as a consequence a cooperative involvement of public opinion toward a reduction of conflicts, in the Western World and in the rest of the world as well.

Numerous studies have been carried out in the last years on this specific matter, and a review of the principal contributions will be presented in the text. Nevertheless, it seems we are able to observe two limits in the texts and in the articles that we have examined:

a) The publications in the two spheres still seem too distinct from one another. This means that there are very important observations and theories in the area of political science and very important research and theories in the area of psychology applied to international negotiations. But the gap between the two spheres still seems too wide;

b) The consequences of this in-depth work of study and research seem to be too abstract and nebulous for the moment, for it is not yet carried out in a precise project of training; and there seems to be missing a sufficiently articulated description of a step-by-step project that would concern not only the training of operators but also the development of the cognitive-emotional abilities of governors and a (framework) for a social psychotherapy leading to peace in a non-utopian way.

In order to establish a more solid bridge between the two spheres (political science and cognitive psychotherapy training) this book is the product of a collaboration of a psychotherapist (Aquilar) and of a political scientist with in—depth knowledge of cognitive psychology and psychotherapy (Galluccio): together we have examined the specialist literature on the topic, and unifying the two competencies we have tried to formulate an account of the "state of the art", and to outline possible features of development of the other two topics involved.

Numerous anthropological-cultural questions are, sometimes tragically, subtended to the problems which are the object of our work. And these variables often greatly influence the ways of thinking of people who are inevitably distant from the desirable "neutrality" of the researcher. In this sense we hope that being Italian ourselves has allowed us to refer to a point of observation of the world reality that, even if it is a solid expression of Western culture, has been, since always, from a cultural point of view, very close to the Eastern World and to its people.

For the reasons described above, the structure of the book includes not only a description of the cognitive and emotional processes involved in the issue of international negotiation but also an operational guide for the training of negotiators. In the first section of the volume we discuss the theoretical matters and describe the cognitive and emotional processes hitherto identified by researchers; in the second section, an operational model is introduced, surely still premature and in need of further elaboration, for the initial psychologically oriented training of negotiators. However, so that the two sections do not seem untied and so that the motives, for which, from determinate observations, one can derive determinate modalities of training, are clear, a paragraph of "connection" (called "practical guide") is presented at the end of every chapter of the first part which links the treated arguments and the practice of the negotiators' training, that is instead introduced in detail in the second part of the volume.

Particular mention must be made of a research project on international negotiation effected and developed by one of us (Galluccio), conducted by interviewing a consistent sample, composed of senior and junior officials of the European Union, with a strong background in negotiation practice on the international stage (described in the fifth chapter of the first section).

Such research has the purpose to investigate the characteristics and opinions of a rather wide sample (120 subjects) of professional negotiators. Their experiences and the conclusions they draw from their profession have been passed through a sieve of nineteen open questions considering seventeen characteristics of personality, trying then to draw from the answers some general information on the concepts linked to negotiation. This research is an initial attempt to understand the reality of negotiation as it is perceived by the negotiators themselves, in a way to favour a three-dimensional vision of the object of our study, which merges the perspectives of the political scientist, the social psychotherapist and the negotiator. For greater clarity, some graphs that can better illustrate the presented research are also included in an appendix.

In the second section of the book, some hypotheses formulated by the other one of us (Aquilar) are introduced in the general framework, regarding a possible practical modality for a cognitive-oriented training of negotiators, with some elements described in a step-by-step fashion.

In order to build a training program for negotiators that is effective, rapid, easy to memorize, and operationally useful, it was necessary to imagine a scenario in which the participants themselves could experiment with the skills that they had been acquiring during the training. For this the proposed model, to be developed in three weeks, foresees four hours of theoretical lessons a day in the morning; and four hours of laboratory practice a day, in the afternoon. In the part "practice" indirect learning techniques were proposed, easy and amusing for the participants, and which aim at not only favouring the acquisition of information but above all at fostering personal growth and the "mastery" of cognitive, emotional, communicative (verbal and nonverbal), meta-cognitive (conceptual and meta-representational) and meta-communicative functions. In three weeks, we aim to "condense" the operational knowledge of leading teachers/psychotherapists, to apply to themselves and to use it in order to decode and to positively influence other people's behaviour and opinions.

What has been brought to your attention until this point, is introduced in this book in an easy and, we hope, comprehensible way, also for the lay reader, who is culturally interested but does not have a specific professional background in both fields of interest: This objective has compelled us not to weigh the "practical" discourse down with too many quotations, to reduce to a minimum references to any documentation for which determined maneuvers or strategies are proposed, and also not to exaggeratedly detail the explanation of proposed techniques. In fact, as with every "experiential" learning, from the "menu" it is possible to imagine its characteristics, but to fully appreciate it, one should "taste it."

Therefore, the structure of the book tries to provide an answer to the limits of the specialist literature on the topic, as described above. To contribute to building a common ground between political science and cognitive psychotherapy training, to introduce a hypothesis of a structured training program (to be validated and improved in the future), and to exemplify with pilot research a modality of assessment of what is observed in the area of study.

We are aware that our proposal, besides resuming the development of a new operational discipline of study, presents limits and is susceptible to criticisms and improvements. We hope nevertheless that it can represent a meaningful heuristic contribution, both theoretical and practical.

Acknowledgements

We would like to thank all those who have helped us to conceive and carry forward this project, the subject of which is the application of cognitive psychotherapy to international negotiations. In the first place, we thank the author who has mainly influenced our work with his complex and comprehensive theoretical framework, Giovanni Liotti. We would also like to thank all those colleagues at the Italian Society of Behavioural and Cognitive Therapy (SITCC) who were supportive in our approach. A special thank-you also to the colleagues of the European Association for Behavioural and Cognitive Therapies (EABCT) and of the International Association for Cognitive Psychotherapy (IACP) who have spurred us on to do our work with their input and ideas.

We would like to thank Aaron Beck for his suggestions and insights. A particular thanks is reserved for Howard Gardner, Paul Gilbert, Aimée Karam, Robert Leahy, Donald Meichenbaum, Jeremy Safran, and Olivera Zikic who have so appreciated and cared about our project that they are joining us in continuing the study of the interaction between international negotiation and cognitive psychotherapy and who are already working on a follow-up to the project.

We are also very grateful for the incisive comments contributed by officials from the European Commission in the research project we conducted with key EU actors involved in the ACP-EU negotiation process. A special thanks goes to Stefano Manservisi and Koos Richelle, from two of the External relations departments, who enthusiastically have been backing our research project since the beginning. Our thanks also go to individual European Commissioners. We are similarly grateful to officials and Members of the European Parliament, the Council of Ministers and other non-state actors, who provided equally valuable insights.

A very special thank you goes to Sharon Panulla from Springer who, from the beginning of this exciting adventure, has shown a continuing interest in our work, accompanying us with efficiency and professionalism throughout by providing enlightening suggestions and observations.

And finally, our heartfelt thanks goes to all our relatives and friends who have been supportive and loving during the preparation of this work and, indeed, on all other occasions, giving us the energy and strength to carry on. Without their support and affection this book would never had been written.

Contents

1 Introduction: Theoretical and Psychological Aspects of International Negotiation

It is better to know some of the questions than all of the answers.
James Thurber

1.1 Introduction

Human psychology is an important factor to take into the highest consideration when analysing international negotiation contexts. Cognitive psychologists and psychotherapists emphasise examination of the thoughts and beliefs connected to our emotions, moods, physical experiences, behaviours, and the events in our lives. A central idea in cognitive psychotherapy is that our perception of an event or experience powerfully affects our physiological, emotional, and behavioural responses to it (Beck, 1988; Ellis, 1994). For how people think, feel, and behave toward other individuals and groups is one essence of their warring with each other (Beck, 1999; Ellis, 1992).

Negotiation, mediation, and the ability to feel potential disputes even before they show up in order to prevent them are essential skills in this rapidly changing and complex global environment. This book is meant to analyse the field of international negotiation through cognitive psychology and a cognitive psychotherapy approach. The word 'cognitive', derived from the Latin word for thinking, refers to the ways in which people make judgements and decisions, and the way in which they interpret – or misinterpret – one another's actions (Greenberger & Padesky, 1995). The cognitive revolution has provided a new focus on how people use their minds to solve problems, or to create, or aggravate them (Mahoney, 1991; Semerari, 2000). How we think shapes a path we will follow and determines whether we will succeed and enjoy life, or even survive. These goals will be reached more easily if we have a modality of thinking that is clear-cut and simple. If instead our thinking is caught up by distorted symbolic meanings, illogical reasoning, and erroneous interpretations and consequential emotional disorders, we become in effect deaf and blind (Beck, 1988; Guidano & Liotti, 1983).

This book explores the interaction among cognition and emotion and negotiation practice which in a certain way and with different modalities and degree, is always affected by cognition and emotion. The objective is to set up an integrated theoretical framework of the psychological dimension of international negotiation based on cognitive, motivational, emotional, and behavioural aspects which influence the negotiation processes as a whole. The research project, which is briefly explained (for reasons of space) in Chapter 5, represents an essay to identify and analyse the importance attributed to some traits of negotiators in generating a climate of confidence and establishing a negotiation working relationship.

We think the application of this approach on cognitive bases to the realm of international negotiation is of potentially great importance. Foreign policy decision makers and their collaborators and advisors are frequently placed in the position of having to make judgements about a set of issues, the nature of a conflict, and the negotiators on the other side of the table before sitting down to engage in the work of negotiation. The burgeoning area of research on cognitive biases has made eminently clear that the kinds of judgements such policymakers are likely to make may well be affected, often adversely, by the baggage that they carry along with them in the form of various biases and perceptual predisposition (Goldstein & Keohane, 1993; Herrman, 2003; Jervis, 1976; Jones, 1997; Lau, 2003; Levy, 2003; Sears, Huddy, & Jervis, 2003 b; Van den Assem, 2000).

Moreover, the social-cognitive-psychological approach to the negotiation has been criticised for the lack of contextual data analysis. Sometimes an inappropriate and confident use of this approach has brought into the story of this interdisciplinary sector the feeling of incorrect evaluation of the context (Bazerman et al., 2000). It is true, however, that we cannot state in a definite and precise way how best to view and examine the relationships among cognition, motivation, and emotion as a whole, as well as in our particular field of international negotiation, because of the absence of suitable research paradigms and of the difficulties of measuring the variables. Certainty does not belong to the realm of international negotiation!

Needless to say, we hope in the near future to collect more contextual data in order to continue to improve our theoretical and practical approach to the study of the particular interdisciplinary field represented by international negotiation and mediation studies. However, we have some doubts that the debate can be resolved solely by research data. Therefore, we are forced to rely largely on psychology, logic, and theory, while keeping an eye out for observations that could help us evaluate the tenability of our assumptions, propositions, and hypotheses.

Meetings, interviews, discussions, and exchange of ideas with the most influential psychologists, political scientists, and negotiators all over the world, who have been characterized by a certain amount of time deployed for the study of international negotiation and mediation, have been accompanying our work from the start of our project all along this exciting experience of trying to set up our own theoretical framework for international negotiation. Needless to say, very long and never-ending discussions with different eminent scientists have given us food for our thoughts and we would certainly be hiding something from you if we did not admit that our book also reflects our experience derived from having had the chance to interact with those famous and very available psychologists, psychotherapists, politicians, and negotiators with whom we have been having thoughtful conversations. We really thank them for the passion and the example they have been giving us on human change processes and for still encouraging us every day to "keep up the good work" (personal exchange of e-mails with Albert Ellis, 2004).

1.2 International Cooperation

A little less than two decades ago, most world leaders and citizens were celebrating the end of the Cold War and looking forward to a more secure future without the divisions of the world in a bipolar one and the threat of an imminent mutual assured destruction threat suspended over their heads. Instead, the fall of Berlin Wall has not transformed the world of international relations into a far less complex world. On the contrary, it has provoked a dangerous fragmentation of the focal points of tension and violence all over the world. This global geopolitical upheaval has consequently been pushing the major international powers to negotiate an increased (maybe forced) cooperation for defining new roles and new competencies on the international stage through a multilateral tool. In fact, however strong a nation is, even if it is a superpower, it cannot do everything on its own. As remarkably underlined by the former President of the United States, Jimmy Carter, in his Nobel lecture (2002):

> Instead of entering a millennium of peace, the world is now, in many ways, a more dangerous place. The greater ease of travel and communication has not been matched by equal understanding and mutual respect. There is a plethora of civil wars, unrestrained by rules of the Geneva Convention, within which an overwhelming portion of the casualties are unarmed civilians, who have no ability to defend themselves. And recent appalling acts of terrorism have reminded us that no nations, even superpowers, are invulnerable. It is clear that global challenges must be met with an emphasis on peace, in harmony with others, with strong alliances and international consensus.

Nowadays, it is extremely difficult to make a separation between national interest and international interests: the demands and the imperatives of international cooperation. There are international problems and opportunities generated by increasing globalisation that require international handling and, hence, co-ordinated international policy responses. Modern science and technology bring with them benefits for all those that can be touched by them; the same holds true for goods and for a human concept as communication is reduced to an abstract concept, or an improved well-being that could be brought to people by international free trade (obviously not an equal one).

But there is also the dark side of this globalisation process from the speeding up of environmental pollution to the drug trade, from terrorism and the proliferation of weapons of mass destruction, together with loss of control of them and their consequential spreading around the globe, to transnational crime and communicable diseases. This mix of problems and opportunities reminds us that stability and prosperity (we could say the capacity to enjoy life in a decent way at least) – the goal of foreign policy in almost all nations – can only be achieved if international subjects can act together in pursuit of interests that transcend their boundaries.

The way they will negotiate these common pathways will have an enormous influence on world peace. All the leaders have good intentions (especially those from the so-called civilised world), but as we all know: "the road to the hell is paved with good intentions." Could they be helped by serious professionals to put into practice their legitimate good intentions in a more straightforward and clear way? The world in which we live nowadays, where lethal weapons and technological know-how may easily "travel" around the globe and where a few fanatics may soon be able to destroy lives and things in the name of some ideologies, needs a more prosocial, compassionate, and empathic attitude by the people in order to build up hope for a better future for ourselves and our children. As matter of fact, intrapersonal and interpersonal peace acquires a vital importance all at once, in order to be able to negotiate international peace.

1.3 A Few Questions

The field of international relations as a whole, and that of international negotiation in particular, is not a closed world populated by abstract figures or rational agents. Actors from these worlds are first of all human beings with their good or bad attitudes toward themselves and the external environment that surrounds them. This world undoubtedly is enriched with psychological problems. Sometimes because of "dangerous politeness" we are unable to ask questions even of ourselves in order for a deeper understanding of those human dynamics. We could have many questions that spring to our mind, and be prepared for a breakthrough in negotiation attitude. The freedom to ask stimulates brains to investigate these psychological dimensions and it could enrich our knowledge of the complexity of the interdependence of behaviours.

A few of them could be:

1. How do the inner world and related cognitive schemata of important leaders influence their own countries' foreign policy behaviour?
2. Does leadership matter?
3. Do leaders' psychological reasoning and attitudes cause some of them to become more conflict-prone, or more obstinate in conflict prevention and conflict resolution favouring negotiations and compromises?
4. Do arms races escalate because of rational political necessities or rather for political necessities assessed through the lens of thinking errors and consequential negative emotions/moods (hate, fear, anxiety, anguish, disgust, surprise)?

5. Does aggressive pre-emptive deterrence work in order to bring peace in the world?
6. Is it sustainable to refuse to negotiate from a position of power?
7. Could leaders face in an emotionally competent way other leaders that think they have to put across their own view, must get others to agree, and have got to fulfil their personal desires in provoking often negative chain reactions in response?
8. Do diplomats/negotiators have certain attitudes in common?
9. Do diplomats/negotiators have enough confidence in their emotions and moods?
10. Do diplomats/negotiators have the skills to achieve a state of mind over mood?
11. What are the conditions that produce terrorism?
12. Does terrorism exist because of people born already bad or also because of objective and prolific economic, social, and psychological background contexts?
13. To effectively prevent terrorism should great powers also pay attention to their actions and words on the thinking, beliefs, and goals of so-called (disrespectfully according to some authors and commentators especially in Europe) rogue states and militant groups?
14. Do mass media deeply influence foreign affairs, negotiations, and decision-making processes?
15. How do leaders' declarations affect perceptions and misperceptions of direct and indirect audiences?
16. How do the emotions of hate, fear, anxiety, and anguish affect the information processing and a sense-making of certain situations?

The first sensation we can have after being invested by this Niagara Falls of questioning is certainly that of confusion, breathlessness. The second one is to honestly admit that there are not very many ready, precise, and serious answers to such questions. The third one would be the hope that more than answering all the questions it is rather "smart" to understand a part of them. In the past, few psychologists have concerned themselves with group conflicts or with international relations. Such problems were regarded by most psychologists as far too broad and amorphous, too much in the macrodomain. Later, with the cognitive revolution of the 1960s a new consciousness of the psychological aspects of international negotiation came to the fore. Moreover, the belief spread, also between actors of international negotiation, that the bulk of the topic, generally speaking, should be scientific and quantitative in its approach, using laboratory methods under controlled conditions or conducting large-scale social surveys; in practice, there was a huge amount of difficulty in appraising the issues proposed by the realm of international relations because such issues were too general, intangible, and hence unresearchable (Oppenheim, 1984).

However, the excitement of the early 1960s and the emergence of peace research as a field of study in its own right brought about some changes in this situation. Scholars in international relations became more interested in behavioural approaches and quantitative methods, and so began to investigate the psychological scenarios with a new quality (Bazerman et al., 2000). On the other hand, social psychologists, aware of the dangers of nuclear warfare and stimulated by the hope of making a contribution to the solution of the problems of humankind, were tempted to lend their skills and theoretical outlook to this important new field. At that time, some useful advances were made in the area of game theory, considerable simulation programs were undertaken jointly with strategists or international relations and international negotiation scholars, crisis gaming was developed, and various content-analytic methods led to an improved understanding of historical events (Avenhaus, 2002; Axelrod, 1984; Kahn, 1991, 2002; Raiffa, 1982, 2002; Sebenius, 2002; Tetlock, 1996). We also saw the first effort to develop the problem-solving workshop as a method of conflict resolution (Rubin, 2002; Kelman & Fisher, 2003).

1.4 International Negotiation

International negotiation could be defined as an interdisciplinary tool that facilitates international activity in an effort to manage the interdependence between international subjects in a peaceful manner through compromises and agreements that have the capability of mutually satisfying all main interested actors. It is a joint decision-making process through which negotiating parties accommodate their conflicting interests into a mutually acceptable settlement (Faure & Sjostedt, 1993). It involves at least two parties but may, in the multilateral case, engage several hundred actors representing governments and governmental or nongovernmental organisations.

Typically, the purpose of negotiation is to find a cooperative formula for the distribution of a set of values under discussion between the negotiating parties. The profiles of particular negotiation processes may vary considerably, depending on the actors involved, the nature of the issue at stake, and the setting of the negotiation. There is the importance and difficulty of winning public support, identifying the vital interest, identifying the other side's perceived interests, and how to prepare for the future (Gallucci, 2002). It should be made clear that negotiation does not mean agreeing. It means conveying your interests and why, and trying to understand the others' interests and why they want them. The central element in these definitions and others that resemble them is the assumption of interdependence of interests, actual, potential, or perceived between the negotiating parties. The negotiation process is then an attempt to reach agreement on how that interdependence shall be managed (Kahn, 1991). In the simplest and most optimistic cases, the alternative to reaching agreement is a separation. If two negotiators are unable to reach an agreement on a certain issue, one of them leaves, and there is no continuing interdependence. On the other hand, if two nations cannot successfully negotiate a boundary dispute, their geographically determined interdependence is not lessened; it is simply unmanaged (Zartman, 2003).

In pessimistic cases the results of failed negotiation may easily bring one or both parties to aggressive and dangerous behaviours.

1.5 Value Claiming/Creating Strategies and the Interpersonal Dimension

Economic theory and games theory show through logic–mathematical experiments that cooperation is the best rational and most efficient strategy if parties at the negotiating table jointly take into account the utility of cooperation for both of them. Unfortunately, in reality parties do not adopt the cooperative solution automatically. It is rather a long process exercise in which situational as well as cognitive, emotional-motivational, and relational factors come into play.

Moreover, the negotiation process has often been described as a process of exchange, or a division of resources (Pruitt, 2002). It is useful to think of the negotiation process as a linked and consequential sequence of four core tasks fundamental to achieving breakthroughs (Zartman, 2003; Watkins & Rosegrant, 2001):

- Diagnosing the structure (the architecture of the whole situation: parties identify and negotiate the problem they want to settle; the interdependence of issues; the interpersonal dimension of the negotiation process).
- Identifying barriers to agreement.
- Managing conflict.
- Building momentum.

Most negotiations involve both dimensions of claiming value and creating value and this provokes a tension between these two strategies and the interpersonal dimension of the negotiation process. You do not usually have a negotiation, which is totally competitive, because then there will be no outcome/agreement. On the other hand, there is no negotiation that is totally cooperative. There is always some kind of slight competition at least. Most of all because you need to set up priorities and objectives that obviously could be different from your counterpart's priorities and objectives. As remarked by Dr. Gallucci[1] in an interview given in February 2002: "So the first word is get the priorities right, understand what the vital interest is, if there is one, understand what the objectives are. It's nice to know what your context is in the international system, who could be on your side, who not. That's the most important thing."

It could be interesting to understand how competitive and cooperative behaviours come to the fore and analyse cognition and emotions involved in the different interpersonal phases during the negotiation process and the

[1] During the North Korean nuclear crisis of 1994, Dr. Gallucci was the chief U.S. negotiator.

disclaiming of different strategies. Fisher and colleagues, in their fundamental book, *Getting to Yes,* published for the first time in 1981, summarised three negotiation styles: soft, hard, and principled negotiation. Obviously they particularly prefer and lay down the elements of a principled negotiation to be applied in different negotiation contexts because in their words "every negotiation is different, but the basic elements do not change" (Fisher, Ury, & Patton, 1991). Principled negotiators are cooperative problem solvers that have as their main aim wise outcomes. This magic result according to the above-mentioned authors could be obtained following these wise suggestions: separating people from problems; exploring interests and not dragging feet to defend one's own interests; avoiding the bottom line; enlarging pies through a creating-options process; trying to reach results based on standards; and yielding to principle not pressure. This is wise advice, but are we sure people just reading and trying to retain such words and intrinsic messages may change and begin to negotiate in a principled way if they do not already have a basic personal balance?

1.6 Negotiating a Working Relationship

In practice, international negotiation should aim at disciplining, modulating, and managing interdependence between acting subjects in a peaceful and skilful manner through shared communication, problem solving, and compromises. This may be seen as an integrated interpersonal process that nurtures and fosters (or harms and disheartens) relationships in the international arena, allowing (or not) negotiators to reach agreements that have the capability of mutually satisfying all main actors involved. This intrapersonal and interpersonal process should be construed as preserving relationships during the negotiation. However, the realm of international negotiation is prone to unforeseen and ambiguous situations. To negotiate also means to tolerate a certain degree of ambiguity and uncertainty and the capacity to manage a series of potential (or perceived) conflicts that could be resolved without harming the negotiation working relationship. Information processing can become more easily biased if there is a high degree of ambiguity in the perceived message. The more ambiguous the information is, the greater will be the receiver's commitment to the established view (Jervis, 1976).

The specialised literature, on the specific topic of international negotiation, has analysed the issue of relationship preservation in the negotiation process (Druckman, 2002; Fisher, Ury, & Patton, 1991). Their experience has brought us the awareness that the ability to effectively negotiate ensues from the creation and maintenance of a relationship with the counterpart. Personal relationships create a degree of confidence and openness between negotiators which decreases anxiety, and facilitates communication (Pruitt, 2002). The capacity to manage a series of potential (or perceived) conflicts in being concentrated on the problem and not the person that is in front of her is a major resource the negotiator has to preserve the working relationship (Fisher, Ury, & Patton, 1991).

Personal relationships create a degree of confidence and openness between negotiators, which facilitates communication between actors in helping to master normal anxiety and frustration for uncertainty and ambiguity in the negotiation process. Unfortunately, the dominant perspective in research papers about negotiation published in the last decade focuses its attention on the decision processes, devaluing the traits and skills of the negotiator as a determining factor in the outcome (Bazerman et al., 2000). Instead, the interaction between human beings always involves the building of perceptions about others, which can influence the outcome of this interaction. In a negotiating process, depending on the degree of complexity of the negotiation, personal individual traits can be decisive in building favourable or unfavourable perceptions to the positive development of a relationship of trust between the involved parties (see our research project described in Chapter 5). Without some level of interpersonal trust, representatives are unlikely to be able to cooperate tacitly or explicitly to manage their dispute (Watkins & Rosegrant, 2001).

The competitive process narrows perceptions because it stimulates the view that the solution of a conflict can only be imposed by one side on the other, which in turn, leads to using all sort of tactics in order to get the desired outcome. The negative chain reaction may "push" each side (if they can do it) forward to look for superiority in power and legitimacy. Consequentially, the issues in conflict assume a dramatic importance. The conflict may become a power struggle or a matter of moral value if not a mirror in which the parts project all their frustrations and negative emotions. Hence, the counterpart may be identified with the issue and for a magic touch, the issue at stake does not have any more definite time and place.

Escalating the conflict increases its motivational significance to the participants and could make a limited defeat less acceptable and more humiliating than a mutual disaster (Deutsch, 2002). In fact, the conflict is not a tangible and objective phenomenon. It exists in the minds of persons who are involved in it (Beck, 2003; Ellis, 2002). Negotiators do not act in an objective negotiation context. Rather they act in their interpretation of the context[2] (Rumiati & Pietroni, 2001). Needless to say, we think that the analysis of rational elements (i.e., game theory, strategies, tactics, etc.) would be better complemented with psychological approaches and in particular with a cognitive approach (Galluccio, 2005).

It is advisable for people to not forget that the negotiation process for many people could be one of the most stressful aspects of a relationship. What occurs during this process may well have a major impact on the long-term relationship that is being established. Therefore, it is important always to look ahead and focus not only on the current negotiation but also on future interactions as well. People who adopt a competitive attitude play a "zero-sum game" in which the gain of a part will be associated automatically to the loss of the counterpart.

Negotiations, in which stronger actors adopt strategies to gain the best part of resources, while giving the illusion to the counterpart of mutual gain, are

---

[2] The intersubjective observation is solely a physical manifestation of the conflict (i.e., discussions, aggressiveness, international rules or procedures, etc.).

also extremely dangerous for the relationship's sustainability. Cooperation is rather an outcome of a complex never-ending process of cognition, motivation, emotions, and communication, to set up first of all a sustainable and lasting relationship during the negotiation process. The cooperative process of working out an agreement may produce a psychological commitment to a mutually satisfactory outcome (Druckman, 2002), and perhaps if we understand the process better, we can use our foresight to speed up the evolution of cooperation (Axelrod, 1984).

Working relationships, where trust, understanding, respect, and friendship are built up over time tend to maximize the long-run mutual benefit and can make each new negotiation smoother and more efficient (Fisher, Ury, & Patten, 1991; Pruitt, 2002). In fact, a negotiation is certainly about issues, but it is also about feelings and personal relationships. Trust, credibility, satisfaction, and positive emotions as a whole, or alternatively, anger, hostility, distrust, and negative emotions as a whole are intrinsically linked to the negotiation outcome. The relationship that is established, for better or for worse, surrounds and profoundly affects the outcome of the ongoing and future negotiations.

One must constantly work at managing relationships during the negotiation. It is possible to be hard-nosed and tough, and still establish a good relationship with high levels of credibility (Fisher, Ury, & Patten, 1991). The key could be to separate the conflict elements, which are political/diplomatic/business-driven, from personal elements, which relate to you and the other party as people. One can have real power if able to get the outcomes one wants without having to force people to change their behaviour through threats or payments. The ability to share information – and personal credibility – become an important source of attraction and power. It is important that negotiators in the international arena show consistency in their contingent stances and decisions regarding democracy, human rights, openness, and respect for the counterpart's opinions. Unfortunately, there is a thin red line between those "healing" attitudes and the destruction of these values through arrogance or, in extent, *rapports de force* (balance of power).

In all negotiations it is important to combine our assertiveness with flexible and empathic tools: a good mix of hard and soft skills. The Iraq war in 2003 is a good example of how a controversial action undertaken on a false and weak basis, instead of rational and more sustainable diplomatic negotiations, can bring pain, local political chaos, confusion between allies and their constituencies, and reduce the attractiveness of the American image in other countries (even allies' countries). Negative behaviours and actions can soften or sharpen hard structural edges, and they can affect the ratio of love to hate in complex love–hate relationships (Nye, 2002). It would be of the utmost importance to bear in mind that all the actors in the negotiation process play an active role in shaping relationships. Believing that relationships improve without individual effort is mere wishful thinking. Believing that relationships can exclusively deteriorate because of the counterpart is a demonstration of emotional incompetence (Galluccio, 2005d). A normal citizen (a "man in the street") can have this belief. A man of state and his advisors have the duty, at least, to try to think about it in a different way.

1.7 Cognition-Emotion Eliciting in International Negotiation

Cognition is intended as either the process through which an individual constitutes representations of his environment, portions of it or himself, or the product of this process. Main cognitive processes instead consist of perception, consciousness, attention, learning, memory, and language. The integrated cognitive motivational model which is analysed in this book takes into account the importance of cognition, emotion, communication, and behaviour. Emotions typically arise because of the evaluations of events in relation to a person's individual concerns and expectations. They provide information about the self in interaction with the environment and they come out from the relationship and continuously go back to the relationship: then it appears as an intrinsically intersubjective process (Liotti, 2001). People who have to negotiate, even before they take a seat and prior to becoming fully aware of all necessary steps of the real negotiation, are often in a particular predisposition from which they have to judge a subsequent determination of facts, the nature of the conflict, past disputes, and, last but not least, the negotiators that sit on the other side of the table.

The crux of the negotiation resides in the principal social functional role cognition and emotions play in the dynamic of human interaction, communication, and relationships. A sense of vital stake – or even less dramatic scenarios – can make the negotiation so crucial to a party that negotiators because of their internal schemes may lead the negotiation toward dysfunctional cognitive cycles (Safran, 2002; Galluccio, 2004, 2005a). However, not all negotiations may be in potential danger, or may break down, when instead a good deal would have been possible, because of negative emotional arousals. Sometimes, it simply happens that the outcome does not match the minimum acceptable agreement a party was supposed to achieve (having political instructions from her hierarchy) on pure technical or political levels. Unfortunately, as often brilliantly remarked by Albert Ellis (1992: 98),

> The forces and conditions that impel people to resort to feuds and wars are hardly entirely psychological but also include many important social, political, ecological, economic, and other important factors. These may easily overwhelm the intentions and goals of even the most peace-loving individuals and induce them, albeit reluctantly, to back military action.

1.8 Communication and Negotiation Process

The mastery of emotional communication in conflict interaction is an important tool in order to improve performance during the negotiation process. In fact, the style of human communication throughout the negotiation process affects the interpersonal relationship development amongst the actors involved. This is important because if the international negotiator does not take into account that what he deems as nonaggressive (his normally acceptable communication style and behaviour in his accustomed environment) may be deemed aggressive from his counterpart, it may lead to wrong perceptions that draw the negotiation down the wrong path. Essentially, negotiators should also play close attention to the impact of their words and actions on the thinking of the counterpart. Otherwise the communication may not have the intended impact and thus the negotiation end in an impasse rather than a resolution of the issues at hand.

The capacity to identify our mental states and our counterpart's mental states, in being conscious of the awareness of the interdependence of this consciousness process is an important ability that could be helpful in the negotiation context. Leaders/negotiators could be able to follow the negotiation process in a more psychologically active, directive, and positive way in order to be present and conscious actors in this process. They should be aware of mental traps and habits and be ready to develop new tools and perform new skills able to give them the possibility of thinking about their own and their counterpart's thoughts in a way to give their part of active contribution to transform the negotiation arena in a more liveable environment as a catalyst for further social changes.

It is important that negotiators and mediators be trained to improve their awareness of psychological intrapersonal and interpersonal dynamics. Moreover, awareness and mastery of the emotional history of the negotiation process are really useful tools a negotiator/mediator should manage in order to achieve positive and sustainable results. Negotiators and mediators should then learn how to identify, express, and modulate emotions which have been generated and acquire meaning because of the interpersonal process that binds negotiators and negotiators and mediators together. This process could facilitate an acquisition of a high flexibility of responses based on the particular history of negotiators' interactions with the environment. Emotional competence, a self-efficacy in emotion-eliciting encounters (Saarni, 1999), could be a compass to improve the negotiation process as a whole and at the same time aid in building up a human relational way for working together in order to reach a common shared positive final outcome.

1.9 A Research Project

This book provides a small picture of a research project conceived and operationally conducted by one of us (Galluccio) on the European Commission of the European Union (EC) negotiation thinking in the specific political field represented by European Union (EU) external relations. Attention has been focused for the most part on the EC–ACP relationship and the related daily negotiation process. In 2000 the 78 African, Caribbean, and Pacific (ACP) countries and the EU signed the Cotonou Partnership Agreement. The agreement was the achievement of a comprehensive, structured, and thorough negotiation process between the ACP and EU over a number of years. Our aim is primarily to try to understand better civil servants', politicians', and diplomats' thinking in its evolution, to provide a benchmark for future comparison and discussion. We used the tools of interviews and questionnaires with distinguished European Commission civil servants (international officials).

1.10 Practical Guide: Necessary Awareness for Negotiators

The awareness that is necessary to operators of international negotiations (and also to the governments that they represent) could be listed in a series of factors:

a) Every human being, rather than living "in the reality," lives in his "representation of the reality" that could more or less correspond to the reality commonly perceived.
b) This "representation of the reality" is influenced by biological-evolutionistic, anthropological-social, and psychological-individual aspects.
c) From this "representation" could originate powerful emotions that could determine inadequate behaviours in a wide sense.
d) Part of the "representation" can be unconscious and many methods exist in order to acquire a greater consciousness of one's own thought and emotional processes, and the thought and emotional processes of the "other" with whom one enters a relationship (or conflict).
e) These "representations" come into contact through the codes of communication (and of the metacommunication, that is, to communicate on what we have communicated).

From this state of the art could derive many implications, beginning with the following.

a) Negotiator training could reveal an effective specific group training, similar to group psychotherapy, for a limited time, with learning and experience "modules" to be based on different levels of complexity (basic, intermediary, superior).
b) More than simply explaining the theory of cognitive and emotional processes which enter into the play of the negotiation, it could be useful to allow the participants to "see" the differences of mental organization among individuals as they happen (live), through exercises that would allow one "to personally experiment/test" not only the presence of beliefs and emotional systems (organized in different forms however referable to some recurrent and well-known forms from the experts), but also the modifiability of these systems of beliefs and emotions.
c) Particularly, problem-solving strategies should be observed and, if possible, they should be widened.
d) All mental content regarding the identity (both individual and social) appears as strongly capable of activating powerful emotions, among which

the emotion of anger tightly connected to the process of aggressiveness (which defuses the ability to negotiate): Particularly, the processes connected to anger, to territoriality, and to dominance–submission would require particular attention.

e) Some of the rules of communication and metacommunication cannot be directly known by "naïve" observers; in the training programmes for negotiators it could be necessary to implement the acquisition and mastery of these communicative abilities as well as those cognitive, emotional, and relational abilities.

2 Peace Psychology, War Prevention: Coping with Psychological Elements

2.1 Psychological Insight in the Study of International Crisis

Psychological insights into the study of foreign policy have largely been ignored during past years and only recently have they been gaining importance. This cold and avoidant attitude could have been due to various reasons such as: scepticism regarding the relevance of psychological theories and/or evidence; the feeling that it would not lead to a much more substantial understanding of foreign policy; the problem of linking beliefs to foreign policy actions; and, obviously, various methodological problems. In fact, it has been argued by different parties that the relevant literature in psychology has emerged from the artificial setting of a laboratory using subjects who, in some respects, are quite unlike foreign policy officials (Geva & Skorick, 2003). There has been a belief that approaches centring on cognitions and perceptions (not to talk about emotions) of even the highest-ranking leaders are unlikely to extend our understanding of foreign policy in any significant way. Bureaucratic politics model literature emphasises the notion that intragovernmental dispute arises from parochial interests and not from genuine intellectual differences (Oppenheim, 1984).

The theory of domestic influence, for example, considers psychological concerns as cues of little interest because they are merely the agents of the system and faithfully reflect the needs of the dominant ruling class (Houghton, 1998). Homogeneity of beliefs is assumed because the processes of political recruitment and political socialisation effectively suppress all but the most trivial differences in politically relevant beliefs (Jervis, 1976). Moreover, many theorists agree that it is wrong to assume a direct linkage between beliefs and actions because the role that beliefs and attitudes may play in policy making is subtle, indeed. Beliefs form one of several clusters of factors that may shape and constrain behaviour. It is necessary to distinguish between decisions in foreign policy and actions (Van den Assem, 2000) because there has been evidence showing a slippage between some executive decisions and implementation (probably due to the means–ends relationship). Finally, there could be problems related to research, as for example:

- *Access to data*: It is true that those interested in the beliefs of decision makers have no guidebooks to which they can refer for comparable evidence, quantitative data, or even categories of data. Those interested in economic aspects are more likely to find data regarding GNP of a nation, or other relevant data.
- *Interpretation of available data*: There is also difficulty in transforming available biographies and other types of evidence into data that are directly relevant to the theoretical question at hand. Different persons will get different results from the same data.

2.2 Leadership Matters

Negotiators are always representative of parties in the negotiating context: constituencies, heads of states and governments, ministries, presidents, corporations, firms, NGOs, and so on. Hence, negotiators could be seen as catalysts in order to improve leaders' attitude changes. Then, we think it would be interesting to better analyse the way leaders and their direct advisers perceive and interpret information, events, and constraints in their international and domestic environments in order to start to collect samples of these processes. How they make decisions and choices in foreign policy in managing internal and external political pressures could be an interesting insight to better understand international complex figures.

State leaders have the not so easy task of making a political synthesis of international and domestic problems. Also, if in the end they try to define their international and domestic priorities, leaders, as do all human beings, have their own cognition, emotions, expectations, and interpretation of events through the lens of their inner representations, perceptions, and belief systems[1] (Goldstein & Keohane, 1993; Van den Assem, 2000). Leaders' personal experiences, belief system, cognition, emotions, and behaviours may influence the political context. Their vision of the world may shape goals and perceptions, judgement of events, crises, and other leaders' behaviour interpretations (Beck, 1999; Jervis, 1985). Leaders and their close advisers, according to these internal schema and personal judgements (entwined with a supreme aim to be confirmed in office by their constituencies), may plan strategies and launch actions.

---

[1] In 1957, Leon Festinger advanced his classic theory of cognitive dissonance, which describes how people manage conflicting cognitions about themselves, their behaviour, or their environment. Festinger posited that conflict among such cognitions (which he termed dissonance) will make people uncomfortable enough to actually modify one of the conflicting beliefs to bring it into line with the other belief.

It is true, however, that there are also national and international political and constitutional constraints that soften or exacerbate a decision-making process. To give a very simplified picture for the first case, we can think about the constitutional Chinese system in which leaders may face a longer internal decision-making process due to the coalition-building process. On the other hand, we may think of the United States in which it seems there is the opposite problem known as the groupthink phenomenon, in which group members may develop rationalizations supporting a shared illusion of their own infallibility and invulnerability within the institution (Colman, 2003).

2.3 Groupthink

To analyse this social and political phenomenon, we require a two-part analysis: one dealing with the environment in which the decision is to be made (to discern whether groupthink is a factor), and another dealing with the process of decision making itself (to see how the theory may play a part in the decision-making process). Before discussing the definition of *groupthink*, we must first attempt to define the group involved. What type of group is most likely to be susceptible to this decision-making tribulation? Although Janis, the major expert of these studies, does not directly deal with this question, it is necessary to raise certain points: namely, does the phenomenon occur only in democratic structures, and if so, why does the structure appear to be prone to groupthink?

The answer, we believe, lies in the nature of the democratic structure, for inherent in this type of structure is the importance of committees. On the other hand, dictatorship structures, for instance, are more hierarchical (cohesive leadership) and therefore stress individual leadership, rather than that of groups (Huddy, 2003; Quaglino, 1999). Finally, within a democratic system of government, the committee in charge of foreign policy is normally composed of the top position-holders of the department of foreign affairs and linked departments: the Foreign Office of Britain, or the United States, for example. It is not the matter of our current studies but such a definition of groupthink could be also applied in group decision making in different civil organisations.

Groupthink is a term derived by Janis from the "newspeak" in George Orwell's futuristic novel, *1984*. As described by Janis (1982: 9), groupthink is the product of

> a mode of thinking that people engage in when they are deeply involved in a cohesive in-group, when the members' strivings for unanimity override their motivation to realistically appraise alternative courses of action. ... *Groupthink* refers to the deterioration of mental efficacy, reliability testing, and moral judgment that results from in-group pressures.

According to the *Oxford Dictionary of Psychology* (Colman, 2003: 318), groupthink is defined as "a collective pattern of defensive avoidance, characteristic of group decision making in organisations in which group members develop rationalisations supporting shared illusions of their own infallibility and invulnerability within the organisation."

2.4 Symptoms of Groupthink

Janis (1982) has documented the following symptoms of groupthink.

1. Illusion of invulnerability: Creates excessive optimism that encourages taking extreme risks.
2. Collective rationalisation: Members discount warnings and do not reconsider their assumptions.
3. Belief in inherent morality: Members believe in the rightness of their cause and therefore ignore the ethical or moral consequences of their decisions.
4. Stereotyped views of out-groups: Negative views of the "enemy" make effective responses to conflict seem unnecessary.
5. Direct pressure on dissenters: Members are under pressure not to express arguments against any of the group's views.
6. Self-censorship: Doubts and deviations from the perceived group consensus are not expressed.
7. Illusion of unanimity: The majority view and judgements are assumed to be unanimous.
8. Self-appointed *mindguards*: Members protect the group and the leader from information that is problematic or contradictory to the group's cohesiveness, view, and/or decisions.

When the above symptoms exist in a group that is trying to make a decision, there is a reasonable chance that groupthink will happen, although it is not necessarily so. Groupthink occurs when groups are highly cohesive and when they are under considerable pressure to make a quality decision. When pressures for unanimity seem overwhelming, members are less motivated to appraise realistically the alternative courses of action available to them. These group pressures lead to carelessness and irrational thinking because groups experiencing groupthink fail to consider all alternatives and seek to maintain unanimity. Decisions shaped by groupthink have a low probability of achieving successful outcomes.

Examples of groupthink "fiascos" studied by Janis include U.S. failures to anticipate the attack on Pearl Harbour, the Bay of Pigs invasion, the escalation of the Vietnam War, and the ill-fated hostage rescue in Iran by President Carter's administration. Current examples of groupthink could be found, according to numerous professionals and commentators, in the decisions of President George W. Bush's administration to pursue an invasion of Iraq based on a policy of "pre-emptive use of military force against terrorists and rogue nations." It seems that the decision to rush to war in Iraq in 2003, before a broad-based coalition of allies could have been built, and apparently with inadequate support or contingency plans, has placed the United States in an unenviable military situation in Iraq that has been costly in terms of military deaths and casualties, diplomatic standing in the world, and economically.

2.5 Groupthink Consequences

Janis (1982) lists eight possible consequences which may lead to low probability of a successful outcome.[2] These are:

1. In complete survey of alternatives
2. Incomplete survey of objectives
3. Failure to re-examine the course of action initially preferred by the majority of the members from the standpoint of nonobvious risks and drawbacks that had not been considered when it was originally evaluated
4. Failure to reappraise initially rejected alternatives
5. Poor information search
6. Selective bias in processing information at hand
7. Failure to work out contingency plans
8. Low probability of successful outcome

Moreover, in the process of decision making, other effects such as secrecy to the point of excluding experts, mass media, outside critics, and the self-appointing of "mindguards" may derive from the group members' attempt to retain unity and *esprit de corps*. Lastly, Janis describes his central theme: the more amiability among the members of a policy-making in-group, the more danger that independent critical thinking will be overcome by group-think, which is likely to result in irrational and dehumanising actions directed against out-groups.[3]

Janis points out the various losses that ensue from this kind of group process. Decision making may be defective, because there is an incomplete survey of alternative courses of action. The group may also fail to appreciate the risks involved in a chosen plain and to reappraise the plan after setbacks. Group-think also limits exploration of all channels of information and produces biased judgements of the information that is obtained. McCauley (1998) argues that in his 1982 essay of the formulation of the theory Janis had offered the rudiments of a theoretical account of the model in terms of self-esteem. He reports that the stress of an external threat is the anticipation of the loss of social self-esteem if the group does not respond successfully to the threat and the group is more likely to anticipate failure when the current decision is perceived as difficult or morally ambiguous or follows recent group failures. He further argues that the symptoms of groupthink have in common the fact that they all contribute to forming and maintaining consensus that the group and its premature decision are reasonable, right, and likely to succeed against an external threat from a person or people who are unreasonable, wrong, and likely to fail.

---

[2] It is interesting to review the following consequences of groupthink and to consider how many of them apply to the Bush administration's handling of the "war on terrorism" and the issues related to Iraq and Saddam Hussein.

[3] When forming an ad hoc decision-making committee, most leaders select an advisory group of like-minded people. This element seems to add to the feeling of *esprit de corps*.

However, after having analysed Janis' theory on groupthink, McCauley (1989) points out that despite the obvious hazards associated with groupthink, it may sometimes be an efficient mode of solving problems: when there is ample available information and when the circumstances are clear-cut, groupthink has proven to be successful. He considered the impact of conformity and compliance pressures in distinguishing two influence processes by which groupthink could operate: compliance and internalisation. Any theory of how decision-making can fail must contain the seeds of the theory of how decision-making can succeed (McCauley 1998). The groupthink model does in fact offer a stronger specification of what the ideal model should or could look like.

McCauley continues in affirming that if groupthink is a disease of an insufficient search for information, or alternatives, and modes of failure, the "cure" could be represented by a better search for procedures that would involve, (1) impartial leadership that encourages the airing of doubts and objections within the group, and searches for information and evaluation from sources outside the group, (2) procedural norms that support systematic consideration of alternatives, (3) second-chance meetings after preliminary consensus, and (4) special attention to the motives and communications of threatening competitors.

Thus, ideal decision-making emerges as the inverse of the definition of groupthink and the specification of failings of groupthink. The essence of the ideal is a maximisation of search and evaluation procedures. The group must be better than the average individual within the group if group procedures ensure that information and ideas are pooled, and that evaluation averages away individual biases (e.g., change for the appearance of sake of change, or keeping things as they are to maintain stability and/or invisibility).

Although Janis (1982) and McCauley (1989, 1998), have applied the term "groupthink" to decision makers, it is applicable as well to the more or less uniform thinking of any cohesive group engaged in intergroup conflict with other groups (Beck, 1999). Groupthink can result in irrational and dehumanising actions directed against the opposition, based on such implicit assumptions as: "We are a good group, so any deceitful actions that we perpetrate are fully justified." Furthermore, "Anyone who is unwilling to go along with our version of the truth is disloyal."

When overt conflict breaks out between groups, further psychological transformations occur within both sides. Internal cohesion increases; a two-sided worldview develops in which "we" represent truth and justice, desire only security and self-respect, and respond reasonably to provocation, whereas "they" are dehumanised and vilified and their aggressive conduct seen as the result of flawed and even evil dispositions. These attitudes discourage contact, and any communication is treated as a concession; a blackout of communication often follows rapidly. The perceived need for solidarity in the face of external threats suppresses internal dissent, partly through pressure to conform but more perniciously through self-censorship. Moderate leaders get pushed aside by more radical ones. Individual inclinations toward overconfidence get magnified, and the illusion of invulnerability takes hold (Watkins & Rosegrant, 2001).

2.6 How Group Membership May Influence the Individual

What happens to the individual when in a group? Researchers claim that the members seek to conform to a group norm. But do all members conform in the same way in any type of group? Is this conformity advantageous or disadvantageous? What are the cognitive and motivational mechanisms by which strong group identifiers maintain positive feelings for their group and fellow group members? The concept of group polarisation was studied deeply for the first time in 1969 by Moscovici and Zavalloni, two social psychologists, who provided evidence that favourable or hostile attitudes may become more positive or more hostile, on average, following group discussions (Moscovici & Zavalloni, 1969).

Solomon Asch (1952) demonstrated that a great deal of illogical conformity occurred even when the correct decision was obvious. People tend to "modulate" their perceptions and evaluations under influence of in-group members. Asch was able to show through his experiments that subjects tended to shift from a previous judgement considered wrong after having assumed conformity to the judgements of others. Obviously, such in-group general thinking helps to bind a group together, but it represents a fertile ground for the growth of cognitive distortions and dysfunctional beliefs. The biases and cognitive prejudices leading to cognitive distortions such as arbitrary inference and overgeneralisation are similar in interpersonal conflict or with members of another group (Beck, 1988, 1999) and interpersonal emotions are based on some of the same psychological processes in group actions. In a group there is a mix of beliefs: individual beliefs and group beliefs. The "meeting" and "integration" of these beliefs could act as a fuel on the fire provoking an explosion of ethnic conflict and acts of prejudice, persecution, and war (Beck, 2002).

Group members are bound together and mutually influenced by their verbal and especially nonverbal communication; group members experience a similar emotion because they attach the same meaning to their perceptions. The thinking, feeling, and acting (behaviours) of an individual in a group have a double meaning to be explained satisfyingly. We need to understand interpersonal dynamics and the context of the group. Group behaviour and action relate to the communication, not always direct, of beliefs, images, and interpretations across the group. Individuals in the group are attuned on other group members' consciousness and particular meaning assigned to certain special events affects all members. They may readily accept opinions and policies advocated by the leader (Beck, 1999). Once again, Janis (1982) has already shown how members of a cohesive group become victims through the striving for unanimity.

2.7 Leaders' Interpretation of Events

Sometimes, leaders are smashed like potatoes between two pressures: resolving (intervening) potential or effective crises on the international stage, and domestic concerns for their constituencies with a narrowed attention to keeping up their leadership. In this case, it is likely that leaders, advised by their supervisors, could choose a policy of more involvement in foreign policy in order to shift the attention of their electors from domestic concerns to noble foreign concerns (Houghton, 1998). History shows us that this policy does not always work and President George Bush probably lost the election to Bill Clinton in 1994 because of the domestic perception that he did not do enough for the well-being of American citizens. "It's the Economy, Stupid!" was the winning slogan with which Clinton gained votes during the electoral campaign. The thoughts and emotions elicited by the terrorism phenomenon seem instead to have favoured the second President George W. Bush's mandate in 2004.

Which leaders' interpretations prevail in the formulation of foreign policy depends on the nature of the decision unit and who is ultimately responsible for making decisions. The worldviews of leaders are shaped in large part by the generation that they happened to be born into, specifically, and by what critical political events they and their collaborators have faced during their lifetimes (Quaglino, 1999). Yet, we have also observed leaders who appear to have undergone substantial changes in their perspectives. Consider former Egyptian President Anwar el-Sadat and his journey to Jerusalem; or former Israeli Prime Minister Yitzhak Rabin and his pursuit of the Oslo accords; or ex-President Richard Nixon and his decision to open U.S. relations with China. Arguments abound as to whether these leaders themselves changed or whether they were merely responding to changes in the international scene, their own domestic arenas, or perceived opportunities to attain goals that might previously have been foreclosed to others.

Another critical issue is how leaders assess the intentions and attitudes of their foreign counterparts. Leaders tend to extrapolate from their own perspectives in problem solving when they have had little or no contact with their counterparts on the other side. But even with contact, a decision unit led by a crusading leader, for example, will see what that leader wants to see (Beck, 1999). When leaders make incorrect assessments, the consequences can be serious. Nikita Khrushchev's attempted deployment of Soviet missiles to Cuba in 1962 is one example of how strategies can backfire if there is confusion as to what the other side's leadership is doing (Janis, 1982). Kim Jong Il could soon understand that the role of brinkmanship he has been playing for a long time in international negotiations could backfire, especially if his most important concern, the perception that the United States is preparing an imminent military attack on his country as justification to go ahead with building up nuclear weapons, is revealed to be not a real one. Will this shift in dealing with North Korea be handled with care by the main actors? Do actors know how to really communicate this probable shift to both direct interested actors and to the world?

2.8 International Crisis

An international crisis in a broad and accepted sense is defined as a time when the values and principles of an international subject are under threat and one should react quickly to avoid a deterioration of such elements (Oppenheim, 1984). It is understandable that leaders will be taking decisions in a short period of time and they will try to avoid all the bureaucratic and political steps that could, in a certain way, undermine their authority through the length of time employed. The leader will trust individuals or groups that she believes are the top figures to help to maintain the government in power. It is vital to know that the way these individuals or groups perceive and interpret crisis will define a state's reactions. Past experiences, cognitions, belief systems, assumptions, emotions (i.e., fear, rage, sadness, disgust, hatred, sorrow, surprise, to name but few), interests, and expectations about the past and the future of these decision makers will determine and affect strategy and actions taken by them. Aggressive political behaviours perpetrated in the name of a just cause may, however, "produce" loss of credibility, active contribution to the spread of hatred against oneself and the referring "world," and serious concerns about the use of potentially harming political doctrines and powers for the same principles and values they would like to protect.

2.9 Can Crisis Be Managed?

For a moment, imagine yourself in a car driving along at a normal speed, down a familiar road. Due to some unexpected circumstance, whether it be internal (you suddenly feel desperately ill and momentarily slam your foot on the brake) or external (you drive over an ice patch and the car begins to skid), suddenly the car goes out of control. This situation could certainly be called a crisis: the timespan in which to respond to the circumstances is limited, the threat to your life is evident (the situation has come as a complete surprise), and choices regarding your situation must be made (i.e., if you do not react, you may become seriously harmed). However, as we all know, with careful and rational manoeuvring (sometimes even without doing anything at all), it could be possible to regain control of the car. This skilful manoeuvring may be called *crisis management*. With this we intend to argue that crises can be managed effectively. But first, we must answer the question: What constitutes management? In our opinion, the most comprehensive definition of (international) crisis management should include in it both the process and the outcome. The process involves controlling risks enough to decrease misperception on the part of the adversary so as not to lead to an escalation; but at the same time, ensuring that the risk tactics remain effective for gaining desirable concessions from the adversary while maintaining one's own vital position intact. The outcome is naturally one in which the crisis is resolved satisfactorily such that the initial interests of states are secured and protected.

2.10 Crisis Management

The main aim of crisis management, in accordance with the previously given example, is to try to keep the situation under control. The manner in which international crises could be managed includes a series of steps (Janis, 1982; Janis & Mann, 1977):

- Identifying the crisis
- Obtaining information
- Evaluating possible solutions
- Selecting solutions
- Implementing the chosen response
- Coping with the feedback

First, the crisis must be well defined. The more well defined the crisis, the more likely it is to have dominant features (from which it is easier to formulate a response). The crisis must next be narrowed. It could be useful that a decision maker face only one crisis at a time. It is highly plausible, for instance, that big powers that are involved in a difficult crisis situation do not want – even having enough tools to do it – to be militarily involved. Therefore, it is wise to delegate other personnel to prepare for problems that may arise during the crisis. It seems appropriate not to let any other problems compete for the attention, energy, and resources that are likely to be needed for the crisis. At this stage, it is also a good idea for the decision makers to be cognizant of time: to look beyond the crisis, to anticipate long-term problems, and also to see if there is any capacity to delay response (because an increase in time may help to de-escalate the crisis).

Also important during this phase is the awareness of audiences. For there is a tendency that the greater the number of audiences observing the decision-makers' actions and statements, the more restricted becomes the decision-makers' freedom of action and negotiation abilities, as well as the more the commitments are publicized, the firmer the commitment. Therefore, it seems logical that audiences ought to be restricted until their support is needed (or, as can be argued, until public announcement is desirable to add to the credibility of a commitment).

The second stage is that of obtaining information. It is disadvantageous for a decision-making unit to rely on one channel of information lest it create distortions. According to Janis (1982), it appears that President Kennedy's decision-making unit relied to a considerable extent upon the CIA's information (primarily given by Allen Dulles, head of the CIA) during the Bay of Pigs fiasco (a fiasco which can be called a quasi-crisis). We could say the same for the Iraqi crisis where apparently a decision-making unit relied to a considerable extent upon Secret Service information on weapons of mass destruction information in order to implement possible military actions. Moreover, if one does not want to look forward to finding information that can match his belief system, he could rely on simple techniques for evaluating the fidelity of information sources that might also prove helpful (i.e., a system of checks and balances).

2.11 Options and Strategies

The third phase deals with the evaluation of solutions. During crisis decision making there is a tendency for fewer numbers of alternatives to be considered. Janis (1982) states that this negative quality tends to appear also as a result of groupthink in decision-making processes. Therefore, decision makers ought to attempt to expand the range and differences among the alternatives. Moreover, it has been noticed that during a crisis, as stress increases, various costs of a preferred option tend to be neglected. Incidentally, this could also be listed as another symptom of groupthink.

When judging an option, one ought not to restrict oneself to economic, political, technical, or material costs lest important psychological and social costs be ignored (cost-benefit analysis). A decision-making unit also must take into consideration costs which may create intense feelings of rage, hatred, frustration, and bitterness from opponents, especially because these could prove to be incredibly difficult to root out. In fact, tangible and concrete questions such as money, resources, borders, territories, and the like are much more favourable for a successful conflict management.

On the contrary, dealing with intangible abstract questions, such as beliefs, ideas, principles, values, and ideologies is much more difficult. Intangible questions may only be afforded through negotiation and especially specialized mediators. However, do we really have this straight division between tangible and intangible questions? Also important in this category of evaluating solutions is the potentially dangerous implication of perceptions and misperceptions. Because crises increase a tendency toward rigidity of perception, a decision maker ought to try to avoid simplistic renditions of the problem (i.e., those put in terms of the adversary's capacity without reference to their attitudes or intentions). And finally, the decision maker ought to have the awareness of a certain action which, being irrevocable, may lead to fewer opportunities throughout the rest of the crisis.

The fourth stage centres on the decision makers' selection of a strategy, because there is no unique strategy that one could apply to all conflicts. There are two main points: one is that during a crisis actors' perceptions of their own alternatives appear to contract whereas the opponents' seem to grow. For example, in the early stages of World War I, the Germans repeatedly asserted that they had no choice but to take vigorous military measures against the threat to the East. On the other hand, the Germans credited Russia with complete freedom to take the actions necessary to prevent war (Holsti, 1965). The other point is the tendency of the actors to judge the strategy in zero-sum terms. In regard to the first point, it is necessary that the decision-making unit really recognize that their adversary is probably experiencing similar feelings of limited alternatives. Therefore, it seems advantageous to suggest that the unit give the opponent a range of choices (by their action, if possible), so as not to force the opponent into a corner. Secondly, in response to the tendency to perceive choices in zero-sum terms, the unit ought to search for outcomes to the problem that would amount to mutual losses or mutual gains.

2.12 Implementation Strategy

The fifth step, or implementation stage, is most tricky; for in order to master the difficulties associated with this phase, the decision-making unit should put itself into the adversary's shoes (so to speak), so as to completely understand and attempt to predict their responses. Conscious steps must be taken to ensure that the opponent reads the intended messages correctly. This most likely involves the attempt to make all communications explicit and consistent. For it must be remembered that perceiving the opponent correctly is different from ensuring that the opponent perceives the unit's moves correctly (Jervis, 1976). Moreover, with respect to threats that are made, the unit ought to first ask the question: are our threats necessary and if so are they credible? It seems logical to state that the credibility of threats increases when there is consistency regarding both verbal statements and actions, and between threat and capability. It is also a good idea to communicate the threats to the opponent consistently and redundantly.

Secondly, the opponent's ability to counteract statements or actions must be considered. Overwhelming the adversary increases their feeling of helplessness which may provoke an attack as a response. For example, during the Sinai campaign and the Six Day War, Egypt applied harsh coercive pressure against Israel (in the summer of 1956 and again in late May 1967) in the form of raids, blockade of the straits (and in 1967 blockade of the roads and straits), concentration of forces in Sinai, threatening speeches, and finally a military pact with Jordan (Janis, 1982). It is easily understandable that with all these "adversities" and with past fear, by October 1956 and again in late May 1967, the Israeli decision-making unit believed that countercoercion was the only way to ensure survival (Jervis, 1976).

The same applies to the actual North Korean crisis: the United States has been trying to negotiate for a long time with this nation labelled as rogue state. Around the world specialists in different disciplines have delineated a precise picture of North Korea's leader, Kim Jong Il. He and his regime often are indicated as a paranoiac regime (obviously he is identified with the regime ... or the contrary?). Now, how the United States publicly deals with this regime seems not to be taking into account the psychological diagnosis made by those experts. The question arises spontaneously: Why?

The final phase has to do with coping with feedback. In this crucial stage, there is one very important basic reminder: Do not humiliate the opponent. For if the unit does humiliate its opponent, the more likely are increased costs of any solution to the crisis and increased rigidity on the part of the opponent. It is better to learn from past errors not to treat an adversary in a humiliating way. It seems, according to this author, that if decision makers follow these guidelines during a crisis, the feeling of being out of control could diminish substantially, as the process can become more rational. Furthermore, if the process becomes rational, it may be concluded that a crisis could be thus managed.

2.13 How is it then that so Many Crises Have not Been Well Managed?

A crisis by definition limits rationality: the timespan in which to react appears limited, a threat to values is perceived, and the situation perhaps has come as a complete surprise. These factors may combine to create constant feelings of anxiety, which could undermine policy makers' attempts to be rational. As we have explained above, a person experiencing intense stress tends to suffer increased cognitive rigidity, and erosion of general cognitive abilities, including erosion of creativity and the ability to cope with complexity because cognitive distortions and dysfunctional beliefs, together with erosion of more complex mental abilities (discussed in the next chapters) replace adaptive skills, diplomatic negotiation tools, problem-solving abilities, and thus compromise achievements (Ellis, 1992; Beck, 1999).

It could be suggested that the following limits on rationality may occur during a high crisis situation: limits on the individual's capacity to receive, process, and assimilate information about the situation; misperceptions; emotional arousal; inability to generate the entire set of alternatives; fragmentary and confused knowledge about the consequences of each option; inability to order preferences for all possible consequences; and disadaptive behaviours able to provoke negative counterreactions (Oppenheim, 1984). It is interesting to add Holsti's (1971) following list of possibly accompanying limits: the ability to establish logical links between present action and future goals; to search effectively for relevant policy options; to create appropriate responses to unexpected events; to communicate complex ideas; to deal effectively with abstractions, to perceive not only blacks and whites, but also to distinguish them from the many subtle shades of grey that fall between; to distinguish valid analogies from false ones, and sense from nonsense; and perhaps most important of all, to enter into the frame of reference of others.

In addition to problems of high stress, there is the seemingly high possibility of groupthink entering into the policy-making process, mainly because it is in a crisis that the small group (which is so typical of crisis decision making in most countries) is best insulated from outside pressures, and also because the existence of stress may generate a feeling among decision makers of the need for affiliation, thus inviting the policy makers to provide mutual reassurance and support for each other (Kelman & Fisher, 2003). However, the main danger of groupthink seems to arise when the members of the unit exert great self-confidence and firmly believe that the policy they adopt is almost bound to succeed.

This problem can be seen in action with reference to the Bay of Pigs fiasco, the escalation of the Vietnam War (under President Johnson), and the invasion of Iraq in 2003 when the overconfidence of the units' plans and underestimation of the capabilities and resourcefulness of the counterpart, as well as the inability to foresee the strength of enemy hatred (probably increased because of these invasions) played a large role in the process of policy making. In brief, leaders and their restricted list of close advisors were unable to consider the impact of their country's actions on the thinking, belief, and goals of autochthon groups.

However, it also seems evident that in situations when leading nations are locked in a direct confrontation with a counterpart they consider potentially armed and dangerous, there is a tendency to adapt very cautious attitudes and behaviours. This can be seen especially in the Cuban Missile Crisis of 1962 as President Kennedy deliberately tried to give his Soviet counterpart more time to react, and chose a course of action that would be less aggressive, but still effective (McLean & McMillan, 2003).

2.14 The Role Cognition Plays in the Outbreak and Conduct of War

At the November 28, 1950 meeting of the National Security Council, Secretary of State Acheson articulated the administration's view that,

> The Soviet Union is behind every one of the Chinese Communist and North Korean moves.... We are in competition with the Soviets all around the globe.... Korea is the world matter, not merely a regional matter. If we are to lose sight of the fact and allow Russia to trap us on the Asian mainland, we will risk sinking into a bottomless pit.

A year after, in testimony describing Soviet intentions, before the Senate Committee on Appropriations, Acheson declared:

> The very fact of this aggression ...constitutes (s) undeniable truth that forces of international communism possess not only the willingness but also the intention, of attacking and invading any free nation within their reach at any time that they can get away with it. The real significance of the North Korean aggression lies in this evidence that, even at the resultant risk of starting a third world war, communism is willing to resort to armed aggression, whenever it believes it can win. (Jervis, 1976: 50)

These words by Acheson illustrate the perceived intentions of Russia as an aggressive force and the need to check that force. According to the cognitive approach (Beck, 1999) in these cases:

1. Individuals and groups perceive themselves as wronged or threatened in some way.
2. They perceive the other as the enemy.
3. Cognitively, they progress from distancing, to devaluing, to dehumanizing, to demonizing the counterpart.

With such a perception of the adversary, it is no wonder that the U.S. government felt the need to involve itself in a regional conflict in East Asia. Thus, the way one country in a conflict views its adversary and the nature of the opponent's moves, is extremely important. The cognitive processing of threat could be summed up as (Beck, 2004):

1. Image of enemy projected onto adversary.
2. Individuals see only the image.
3. They react to the image.
4. If the image changes, the reaction changes.

The final common pathway consists of consequential steps worth to bring a nation to war through a serious escalation of the conflict (Beck, 1999, 2004):

1. Perceived wrong/threats
2. Categorical dysfunctional beliefs and cognitive distortions in cognitive processes
3. Recall grievances
4. Mobilising for action/fight/flight
5. Pre-emptive strike/counterattack

The individual psychology of the actors involved is an important and integral part and group dynamics plays a major influential role in a decision-making process. The basic principles of the cognitive model we use for this work are summarised (Beck, 2003, 2004) thus.

1. Group psychology has its roots in individual psychology.
2. The nature of the threats and responses to them are the same in group as in individual conflicts.
3. The aggressors/perpetrators see themselves as the victims.
4. In both conventional and asymmetrical warfare, the biases produce cognitive distortions and dysfunctional beliefs that impede peacemaking and peace-keeping.
5. Each side idealises itself and devalues the opponent.
6. Successful negotiation and mediation involve understanding biases and distortions.

2.15 Perceptions and Misperceptions

The category is itself a broad topic including belief systems, attitudes, automatic thoughts, assumptions, images, cognitive distortions, dysfunctional beliefs (irrational ideas), emotions, and behaviours. As Jervis (1976: 31) said, "Perceptions are one of the immediate causes of behaviours. The roots of many important disputes about policies lie in differing perceptions." It is generally recognized that an individual's behaviour is in large part shaped by the manner in which he perceives, processes, and evaluates his physical and social environment. Similarly, it is recognized that in order to experience and cope with the complex confusing reality of the environment, individuals tend to rely on simplified structured beliefs about the nature of the world (Jonsson, 2002). Perceptions are filtered through the lens of beliefs drawing cognitive maps of different parts of one's social and physical environment (Holsti, 1976).

A cognitive map is generally explained as a mental representation of some area of one's environment. It might be a representation of the layout, of the interior of one's house, one's neighbourhood, or even one's country or the world (Eysenck, 1990). It is sometimes useful to speak of cognitive maps because people can use their mental representations of their environment in ways similar to their use of maps. Thus, for example, in a well-known environment, people can plan their routes in advance, take short-cuts, and in general move around in a sensible and economical way. Holsti (1976) defines a cognitive map as a certain way of representing a person's assertions about her beliefs with respect to some limited domain, such as a given policy problem. It is widely accepted that everyone may form his or her own cognitive map, or images that could be generally distorted by simplifying assumptions and preconceptions (Colman, 2003).

2.16 Misperceptions and Self-Fulfilling Prophecy

It seems that if a state must often go to extremes because they use moderation and conciliation as guiding principles, it is likely to be perceived as a weak state. It also seems that if a major power is seen to be very powerful and very firm, any opponents will think twice before clashing with it. In fact, deterrence theory appears to have led to a nuclear arms race (Snyder, 2000). Sometimes this race is justified by having termed it defensive. For, the state may believe: what he (the adversary) can do to harm the state, he will do (or will do if he gets the chance). So to be safe, the state should buy as many weapons as it can afford (Jervis, 1978). But this can be called irrational (Ellis, 1992). On this subject, Jervis (1976: 65) quotes Lord Grey, the British foreign secretary:

> The increase of armaments, that is intended in each Nation to produce consciousness of strength, and a sense of security, does not produce these effects. On the contrary, it produces a consciousness of the strength of the other Nations and a sense of fear. Fear begets suspicion and distrust and evil imagining of all sorts, till each Government

feels it would be criminal and betrayal of its own country not to take every precaution, while every Government regards every precaution of every other Government as evidence of hostile intent.

It has been argued that psychological pressures account for this arms race or vicious circle. For once a state develops a hostile image as stated above, it will not realize how the adversary perceives the action. A peaceful state knows that it will use its arms only to protect itself, not to harm others. It further assumes that others are fully aware of this. John Foster Dulles, secretary of state of U.S. President Eisenhower's administration for six years, once said, "Khrushchev does not need to be convinced of our good intentions. He knows we are not aggressors and do not threaten the security of the Soviet Union." (Jervis, 1976: 68). Most important, the

... security dilemma can not only create conflicts and tensions but also provide the dynamics triggering war. If technology and strategy are such that each side believe that the state that strikes first will have a decisive advantage, even a state that is fully satisfied with the *status quo* may start a war out of fear that the alternative to doing so is not peace, but an attack by its adversary. (Jervis, 1976: 67).

Moreover, the perceptions and reactions of the adversary are still likely to deepen the misunderstanding and the conflict (Herrmann, 2003). In the case of the Korean War, Truman's administration believed that China's intervention was a sign that it was aggressive (Janis, 1982), and not that it was concerned about its security (very legitimately, if one looks at China's proximity). Had the administration believed the latter, it might possibly have increased the likelihood of effective negotiations in order to halt the war. It has even been argued that President Johnson continued the bombing of North Vietnam mainly because he believed that halting would have led North Vietnam to conclude that American resolve was weakening (Levy, 2003). Thus, it seems that many wars are begun and continued because of certain perceptions about the adversary.

Coming to our times, take for example North Korea's case (aware of the ongoing stressful negotiation process and Korea's attitude to cheat): Koreans are eager to resolve the nuclear weapons crisis, but only by concluding a step-by-step denuclearization agreement linked with progress toward the normalisation of ties with the United States. In 1994 President Bill Clinton's administration signed a deal with North Korea under which Pyongyang would have been rewarded with energy aid for freezing its nuclear programmes. President George W. Bush's administration has instead promoted the much tougher standard of "complete, verifiable and irreversible dismantlement," probably perceived by the counterpart as an aggressive process that North Korea still may find humiliating. Moreover, it seems that the famous U.S. State of the Union speech of 2002 (*The Economist*, 2nd February 2002) and the consequent invasion of Iraq one year later may have completely scared an already isolated regime. The definition of "an axis of Evil"– Iraq, North Korea, and Iran – which the U.S. president accused of arming themselves with weapons of mass destruction, could have definitely convinced North Korea of being the next target of an American intervention. And Iran maybe has been following the same path.

2.17 Misperception and Communications Failure

Communication failure holds an important place in the study of causes of war. National leaders could perceive one another through ideological lenses and with stereotypical images, with the result that their communication, whether formal or informal, may be biased by thinking errors and metarepresentative deficits. Several attempts have been made to identify and even to quantify the specific forms of misperception that interfere with communication. Among those that have attracted the most interest are a hostile image of the adversary, a victimized self-image (an actor regarding himself as a victim and the enemy as the victimizer), obsession with these polarized images, a moral self-image, a selective abstraction of critical events and signals, dichotomous thinking, absence of empathy for the opposing party's problem(s), military underestimation and overconfidence, and perception and misperception of the counterpart's might and capabilities (Beck, 1999; De Rivera, 1968; Herrmann, 2003; Holsti, 1976; Janis, 1982; Jervis, 1976, 1989; Jonsson, 2002; Rubin, 2002).

The distorted perception that results from these phenomena causes biased interpretations of messages and signals, and mutual misperception of intentions. For example, potentially threatening messages from an international subject may get absolute attention or could be more perceptually prominent than are cooperative or conciliatory statements. Listeners hear what they expect to hear, as in the theory of cognitive dissonance. The fixed image that nations have of some other nations is seen not only as a threat to the existence of personal and national identities often failing to match the reality, but these images are fueled with an ideology of hatred and are highly resistant to change even when evidence and experience could collide with already imagined scenarios. Just as communicators are driven by their own perceptions of both the subject matter and the receiver, there are domestic political circumstances that may shape (or misshape) messages (Levy, 2003). Communications failure and protracted negative emotions such as fear and rage, to name but two, may contribute to an escalation of tensions by multiplying the consequences of international crisis (Jones, 1997).

Technology has increased the efficiency of modern weapons. Consequentially the need for improved communication to help the world's leaders to better convey their intentions should be at the heart of a strategy for mutually slowing down misperceptions and tensions in the international arena. Technical tools seem to support these needs: direct telephone connections between different nations around the world, communications satellites that transmit information around the world in seconds, computers that communicate with each other over great distances, and so on. The difficulty, of course, is that as technical supports are more sophisticated and we would say directive as never before in the history of communication, risks of reciprocal negative influence among world leaders have become higher and more likely.

Furthermore, international political communication tends to mask political aggressive messages through public statements. It is not uncommon, for example, for the president of the United States to deliver a message to an adversary abroad, such as Kim Jong Il of North Korea, in a State of the Union speech and in a combative tone designed for domestic purposes that may risk distorting the message in Pyongyang. Although because of technology international political communication has become modernised, the strategic aspects have become more egocentric and ambiguous, bringing with them an inner danger of complicated political confusion and deterioration of working relationships.

This is particularly true in regard to the language of escalation. Usually, the earlier, equally critical, phases of the escalation process are largely verbal and symbolic (Houghton, 1998). Later, in final stages, does the escalation of international events involve active logistic framing such as deciding military actions, making plans, deploying troops, and looking for possible coalitions. Unfortunately, the verbal structure strategically conceived for domestic political audiences as well as for international communication, may make de-escalation all but impossible.

The thinking of leaders may show kinds of cognitive distortions and dysfunctional beliefs that can heavily influence present and future more peaceful interactions among them (we examine in detail those thinking errors in the next chapter). Offences, threats, manipulation of images, propaganda, public humiliation of the enemy, rejection of proposed compromises, and domestic mobilisation: political negatively reframed positioning could be the foreseen result of this way of thinking. These attitudes as well as tons of other episodes, all with the common denominator of communicating intractability of the conflict to the adversary, precede actual preparation for combat (Jones, 1997; Snyder & Diesing, 1977). It is as if they head straight at each other like two drivers playing "chicken,"[4] each determined to force the other off the road by sheer resolve of purpose. But unlike the two drivers, neither can remove its steering

---

[4] According to a tidy explanation of the *Oxford Dictionary of Psychology* (Colman, 2003: 125–126), a game of chicken is "a two person strategic game, generally considered to be the prototype of a dangerous game. In its canonical interpretation, two motorists speed towards each other. Each has the option of swerving to avoid a head-on collision or driving straight ahead. If both swerve, the outcome is a draw with second-best payoffs to each; if both drive straight ahead, they risk annihilation and each receives the worst (fourth-best) payoff; but if one chickens out by swerving while the other exploit the co-player's caution by driving straight on, then the swerver loses face and earns the third-best payoff, and the "exploiter" wins a prestige victory and earns the best payoff. The game provides a strategic model of brinkmanship. This game became popular after the release in 1955 of Nicholas Ray's film *Rebel Without a Cause* starring James Dean, in which teenagers played a slightly different version of the game involving driving cars over a cliff and jumping out at the last moment."

wheel and throw it onto the highway to signal its inability to change course. The two parts collide in combat because they are unable or stubbornly unwilling to heed an enlightening last-minute communications-led display.

2.18 Evolving Circumstances

When new and straightforward data are found within a theory, it could happen that nothing is compatible with old findings. It changes the paradigm in some rather regular and well-defined way: an amendment can be made, no fundamental revision is necessary; and a revolutionary change is needed, leading to a paradigm shift. The human information process shares the same qualities. It seems there is a reluctance to change, even to the point of discrediting discrepant information. For example, Holsti (1967) showed that John Foster Dulles readily accepted any information about the Soviet Union that conformed to his schemata or image, but needed overwhelming evidence before he would take any information seriously that contradicted his view.

Jervis (1976: 144) gave an example of Hermann Göring, head of German aviation during World War I: When he was told that an Allied fighter plane had been shot down over Aachen, thus proving that the allies had produced a long-range fighter that could protect bombers over Germany, he told the pilot who had commanded the German planes in the engagement: "I'm an experienced fighter pilot myself, I know what is possible. But I know what isn't, too. ... I officially assert that American fighter planes did not reach Aachen. ... I herewith give you an official order that they weren't there." When a statesman and his entourage have developed a certain image of another country they may maintain that view in the face of large amounts of discrepant information. General expectations and rules may guide their interpretations of other nations' foreign policy intentions and thus influencing the images of others that he will come to hold.

Categorisation or grouping seems to be a basic property of human perception, such that when new stimuli are perceived, the first thing people try to do is categorise the stimuli as another instance of some familiar group. The dominance of the categorical rules can distort the specific features of a situation. For example, the biased beliefs of the depressive or paranoid person produce biased interpretations of reality. Such biased beliefs and thinking occur both in psychopathology and in interpersonal animosity and intergroup conflict (Beck, 1999). Overly cognitive distortions and dysfunctional beliefs about strangers or foreigners can lead to erroneous appraisal of friendly or unfriendly subjects. Human beings may be predisposed to react to unfamiliar or different people in unknown ways depending upon the categorical beliefs they hold regarding strangers composed of a mixture of evolutionary and cultural heritage and peculiar learning history (Beck, 2002).

It could also be that incoming data may have an impact on categorisation insofar as influencing information if it has been saved under the categories through which lens it is later seen as relevant. For example, in June of 1950, a cable from the U.S. ambassador (to South Korea) sent home a report of heavy North Korean arms build-up along the 38th parallel and warned about their superiority. This information could have been perceived with alarm, for it might have suggested a forthcoming attack, which actually did come a few weeks later. But the person in the State Department who received the message interpreted it as part of a plea to boost military aid to South Korea and filed it with other appeals (De Rivera, 1968).

When the North Koreans did in fact attack, the U.S. government looked for information about the adversary's army and found very little because the report had not been filed there. Apparently, the secretary for Far Eastern affairs, who received the cable, "Was not aware that there were two conflicting possible ways of interpreting the event" (De Rivera, 1968). The secretary quite possibly interpreted the data according to a preconceived notion, for the ambassador had been in Washington shortly before to request tanks and other equipment for the South Korean army.

Category and past schemata-based processing are cognitively efficient because once incoming information is perceived broadly as another case point of some pre-existing schemata, a more accurate analysis of a new stimulus could unconsciously be avoided and values associated with the schemata may be held in new situations that recall past experiences.

Cognitive efficiency operates in order to master information processing in ignoring details of some particular stimulus that are present in the information environment if the stimulus tends to be affiliated with some familiar group. To make category-based inferences about the particular stimulus even when the detailed information is not actually present in the information environment reveals efficiency and saving of time avoiding additional information search (Lau, 2003). The need for cognitive economy helped to explain the tendency toward cognitive consistency. It also pointed to the use of cognitive heuristics or short-cuts, which could potentially pollute both elites' decision-making process and the mass public's awareness and preferences as a whole (Kelman & Fisher, 2003).

In politics too, discrepant information or assimilating it into pre-existing beliefs will perpetuate inaccurate images and maintain unsatisfactory policies, but these processes are necessary if decision makers are to act at all (Jervis, 1976). Also, once the image has shifted from the onset of major discrepant information, the adversary's actions will seem very different than they had before. For example, the beginning of the Cold War with Russia completely changed the Americans' view of that state, but also changed the views of this state during World War II from what had previously prevailed (Kissinger, 1994). Moreover, Kenneth Boulding (1956) posited a theory of national images underlying the importance of the symbolic image of a country or state.

He argued that the images which really count in international systems are those that a nation has of itself and of those other bodies in the system that constitute its international environment. In his conception, the perceived hostility or friendliness and the perceived strength or weakness of a unit were the central features of a subject's image of that unit. These two core dimensions of both self-image and images of others were thought to shape strategic decisions and thus provide a parsimonious focus for the study of an actor's beliefs (Boulding, 1956). It can be argued that this image may be developed to the point where

> It has become seriously pathological in its extreme forms.... The national symbol becomes the object of the kind of totem-worship. ... In cartoons, lions, eagles, bears, loving ... fighting. By these symbols the web of conflicts is visualised ... as a simple tug-of-war between large opposing elements. This symbolic image is one of the major causes of international warfare and is the principal threat to survival of our present world. (Beck, 1999: 40–54).

2.19 Problem Identification

This may seem more directly associated with the topic concerned with the outbreak and conduct of war, but it is necessary to realise that, albeit indirectly perhaps, images, and ideology inside a belief system are extremely relevant to the topic. This can be seen in the close link between these first two stages, for this stage involves perception/misperception and stereotyping in the definition of the situation and in the focus of attention. After World War II, Truman announced his policy of containment, which suddenly lay out commitments all over the world (that consequently depended on America's word being believed).

This Truman Doctrine[5] became the underlying reason for America's involvement in the Korean War, regarding the necessity for containing the expansion of "world communism" in order to protect the "free world." Moreover, the particular issue of the North Korean advancement raised geopolitical concerns for the United States. The fall of Formosa would have created grave strategic problems in Japan and in the Philippines because these countries had become essential for U.S. survival as a Pacific power (i.e., U.S. military bases were located on the islands). Clearly at the beginning of the war, the aim was to prevent the pro-Communist North Korean government from taking over the South.

At first, aid was given, but then, day by day, as "little emergency decision after another was made to cope" the United States sent in troops (De Rivera, 1968). After the collapse of the South Korean military, MacArthur, in command of United Nations' forces, was called in to fight. After four months of tactical successes, the policy was switched from "containment" to "roll back" (Jervis, 1976). At this point in the war (November, 1950), the Truman administration

[5] Truman's doctrine was thus the starting point for the strategy of containment of communism developed by successive U.S. presidents during the Cold War.

was clearly convinced that the Soviet Union was behind every one of the Chinese Communist and North Korean moves. Therefore, the perceived central enemy became the Soviet Union.

Could Truman's advisory group, in deciding the conduct and strategy of the Korean War, have become influenced by groupthink? For, after the initial successes in the war, the group began to hold the illusion of invulnerability. At this point, seemingly ignoring all dangerous risks, the group decided to allow General MacArthur to attempt to occupy North Korea. This decision was essentially opportunistic, with the group justifying their decision in terms of restoring peace and security in the name of the United Nations (Janis, 1982). Moreover, the group apparently tended to stereotype the military strength of the North Korea and the China. In fact, Janis (1982) noted that "Members spoke of North Korea, China and Russia as a homogeneous entity and accepted the concept that communism had decided that China should intervene to divert the United States from its anti-Communist role in Europe." De Rivera (1968) described the failure of President Truman's advisers to correct their stereotyped misconceptions which can be linked with the group members' likelihood for supporting each other in taking excessive risks. In addition, these two authors noted that the members' views of China's military capacity were based on ideological presuppositions, that Red China was a weak nation and depended on Russia for its strength. This stereotyping, it is argued, led to the unrealistic estimation of the enemy's strength and to incorrect problem estimation.

2.20 Information Processing

This stage includes the obtaining of information, production and evaluation of solutions involving search capacity, strategies for coping with discrepant information, and satisfying/maximising. Concerning search capacity, it has been argued that the source–message interaction and irrational consistency are very important (Herrmann, 2003). For instance, regarding the former in the aforementioned example of information gathering before the North Korean attack on the South, the interpretation of the message by the assistant secretary of Far Eastern affairs is of key concern. His downgrading of the ambassador's reports that the North Koreans were far superior militarily (to the South Koreans) depicts the idea of cognitive consistency because it was in the ambassador's interest to make exaggerated claims. Moreover, the ambassador had recently been in Washington requesting military equipment for the South Korean army. Therefore, in examining political communications, actors must inquire about possible conflicting perspectives and interests between the actor and the source (Oppenheim, 1984).

In addition, when cognitions are organised to produce irrational consistency choices (the theory that people who favour a policy normally believe that it is supported by many logically independent reasons) are easier because all considerations are seen as pointing to the same conclusion (Colman, 2003). Relating again to the Korean War, General MacArthur supported his claims such as these: "Minor concession to China would do no good, establishing a buffer zone in northern Korea would be seen in Asia as a defeat, sending US troops to the Yalu would not provoke Chinese intervention, and if China did enter, its troops could be destroyed from the air" (Jervis, 1976: 133–134). Therefore as we can see, the U.S. general's production of solutions to the problems in North Korea was affected by his tendency to use irrational consistency.

The basic point is that if an actor does not comprehend the other's beliefs about his own actions, he is not apt to be able to see what inferences others are drawing from his behaviour. In other words, this could be seen as a sort of genuine communication failure. This lack of communication may ultimately lead to deteriorated relationships, war, or the escalation of a war. It is evident that, if an actor does not understand his adversary's inference, the product and the evaluation of a solution to a given problem will be less than effective; if not extremely dangerous for the consequences it could bring to the fore.

2.21 Ends and Means

The last characteristic has to do with the link between ends and means and its impact on the strategy to be arrived at. On April 1980, President Jimmy Carter decided to use military force to rescue American hostages held in Iran. However, President Carter's advisory group failed to properly assess the risks or the huge difference between the means and the desired ends, and the mission was a flop. Steve Smith (1985) lists five factors which were not realistically assessed in detail that ultimately led to disaster.

1. Because of the concern for security, there was no overall written plan for the mission to study and review in the privacy of the members' offices, only oral briefing were used.
2. There was no independent review of the plan. Decision makers were told optimistic reviews by only the joint chief of staff.
3. There was no overall rehearsal of the mission (however, the rescue force did rehearse in separate units). Such rehearsals as were undertaken were by no means unqualified successes: one participant described the final dress rehearsal as "the sorriest display of professionalism I've ever seen" (Smith, 1985).
4. No one political leader questioned the helicopter force despite the fact that the group had been informed that it was the weakest element in the plan.
5. A number of issues which might have led to the failure of the mission, had it not been ruined in stage one, were not discussed, namely, the rescue force did not know exactly where the hostages were.

This example shows that the decision makers accepted very optimistic assessments of the likely successes of the plan and did not search for detail even those weaknesses acknowledged during the planning stages. President

Carter's advisers chose this plan over a diplomatic solution through a long and certainly stressful negotiation process which, in fact, could have been explored by parties without running the risk of losing face.

2.22 Concluding Remarks

Coping with and learning from negative feedback affects psychological factors leading to the outbreak and conduct of war. The theory of cognitive dissonance is especially relevant to this topic. In some cases, after a fiasco, a political leader may deflect his anger away from his advisors (who may be partly to blame for the fiasco) toward another group including the press and/or an opposing domestic group. For example, President Truman, after receiving the bad news on November 28, 1950 that MacArthur forces were being attacked and driven back by 260,000 Chinese troops, became furious. But instead of blaming his experts who misled him, or his advisors who failed to caution him, he directed his fury toward the Republican newspaper publishers and other Republican "vilifiers" (Janis, 1982). The morning of 28 November, at the end of a routine conference with his White House staff, President Truman excitedly cried out,

> Well, the liars have accomplished their purpose. The whole campaign lies we have been seeing in this country has brought about its result ... what has appeared in our press along with the defeat of our leaders in the Senate, has made the world believe that the American people are not behind our foreign policy and I don't think the Communists would ever have dared to do this thing in Korea if it hadn't been for that belief. (Janis, 1982: 65)

From this evidence, one may infer that Truman did not effectively learn from this negative feedback. Had he coped with it in a more rational manner, he may have seen his mistakes and may have tried to learn from them. But by not learning from one's mistakes, one may be inviting the reappearance of a similar problem, which would produce a new kind of vicious circle. Evidence for this assertion can be seen in opposite form in the process of decision making within the Cuban missile crisis. Immediately following the Bay of the Pigs fiasco, John F. Kennedy appointed a commission to find out exactly what had gone wrong. During the second Cuban crisis, it is quite evident that President Kennedy had learned from his previous mistakes, as the decision-making process appeared to be the antithesis of groupthink which was shown to be a major course of the first fiasco. Had he not learned, evidence suggests that an air strike would have been decided as the course of the first fiasco. This decision may have prompted very grave actions on the part of the Soviet. Therefore, even in the final stage of the decision-making process, groupthink may or may not play a large role.

In conclusion, according to the eminent authors cited all along in this chapter, it appears quite evident that psychological factors may play an important role in negotiations, conflict escalation, outbreak, and conduct of war. This role can be seen in every stage of the decision-making process regarding relations with an adversary. But it is also obvious that psychological factors are only part of the complete picture. Nevertheless, this interdisciplinary addition to International relations should not still be overlooked. Although many authors – such as Beck, De Rivera, Ellis, Janis, Jervis, Jones, Herrmann, Levy, Oppenheim, Sandole, Snyder, Tetlock, and Van den Assem, to name but a few – have pinpointed the errors in the thinking of national leaders, this knowledge up to now has not yet been put to real practical use by directly interested actors on the spot.

2.23 Practical Guide: Cognitive Processes and Emotions

Cognitive processes that are the modalities with which every individual structures knowledge of itself and of the world, are "impregnated" with emotions and meanings. Although the cognitive–emotional processes, being of psychobiological nature, appear equal for all human beings, the internal organization of their components appears strongly diversified among individuals. An awareness that appears essential to the negotiators is that which concerns the knowledge, development, and articulation of these cognitive processes. These cognitive processes could be grouped in the following categories (Gambini, 2006), that for the time being we just list.

a) Sensation and perception
b) Consciousness and attention
c) Memory
d) Learning
e) Thought
f) Language

All the cognitive processes, regardless of how psychobiologically determined from the start, are subject to distortions following the experience (or derived from missed exposure of experience activation). An example can immediately be comprehensible for that which concerns the distortions of the memory: an individual can forget all the experiences inconsistent with her opinion on a determined matter, and to keep continuing to remember and recall in her mind, also obsessively, the episodes that had to confirm her judgement (or prejudice). In such a way, it is as if the events that could be able to unconfirm a determined opinion would never happen, while also few observations present in the memory (but constantly repeated in mind) could unveil the effect of so many confirmations of an opinion. On the other hand, the emotional processes are innate factors that characterize all human beings from the cradle to the grave, and they are at the basis of the motivations for the action, especially for the social actions. The main emotions described and studied by a very large specialised literature can be summarised in the following way.

1. *Happiness*: Presence or harmony with a beloved person, in presence of general conditions of life considered acceptable; everything is all right.
2. *Sadness*: Loss or disharmony with a beloved person, even eventually because of general conditions of life considered unacceptable; desire of relational restoration and/or environmental restoration, and/or of comfort.
3. *Anger*: Competitor's presence; competitive desire, and/or to regulate the rank.
4. *Fear*: Presence of danger; desire of reassurance and/or of reduction of the danger.
5. *Disgust*: Presence of harmful entity (or of elements or behaviours considered consciously or unconsciously harmful, in a relationship however desired or considered necessary); necessity of identification and separation or modification of the possible harmful factor.

Many other emotions are present in humankind, and some of them require particular attention, because of their connection with the international negotiation processes. The most important so-called "secondary emotions" are (which for the time being we deliberately do not describe so as to not make the conversation heavier with too many concepts altogether).

9. Surprise
10. Guilt
11. Shame
12. Gratitude
13. Envy
14. Jealousy
15. Return game
16. Revenge
17. Safety/security

As previously summarised for the main emotions, every emotion (included the so-called secondary) seems to carry out a determinant psychobiological role, signalling precious information on the internal reality, on principal affective relationships, and on the external world. Knowledge of and familiarisation with the emotions appear therefore fundamental for the understanding of meaningful interactions among human beings. In addition, the correct and functional use of the emotions requires the previous acquisition of complex abilities, named metacognitive or metarepresentational, that allow us to recognize properly one's own and other people's emotions without misunderstandings, to express and to adequately decode them, and to modulate their expression (to avoid being overwhelmed by them, or to avoid a negative chain reaction arousal).

Training deliberately focused on the recognition, expression, and modulation of the emotions appears therefore essential in order to get effective management of one's own and other people's emotions in overcoming auto-destructive – and above all – heterodestructive habits that can derive from a deregulation of the emotional apparatus. Such disregulation, in the thought group processes summarised in this chapter, could be strengthened in "special groups," until they reach subversive or terrorist processes. The importance of the relations among knowledge, emotions, and the transfer to action therefore appears decisive.

3
Cognitive, Emotional, and Communicative Aspects in International Negotiation: Affective Neuroscience Contribution to the General Understanding of the Negotiation Process

3.1 Introduction

As previously remarked, we would like to recall that people who have to negotiate, even before they take a seat and prior to becoming fully aware of all the necessary steps of the real negotiation, often have a particular predisposition from which they have to judge a subsequent determination of facts, the nature of the conflict and, last but not least, the negotiators that are seated on the other side of the table. In such a context, the person's consciousness is not a *tabula rasa*. Negotiators bring to the negotiation table their own beliefs, perceptions, emotions, moods, and communication styles. Therefore, on many occasions, the cognitive processes result in implicit automatic thoughts "disturbed" by a series of cognitive distortions and dysfunctional beliefs (Beck, 1999, 2003; Ellis, 1992, 2002), especially when actors are in stressful situations and vital (or not so vital) interests are also at stake. Accordingly, it is easily understandable that decisions taken in this context might be based on wrong perceptions, negative emotions, and on a consequential emotional misattunement with the counterpart that provokes a chain reaction of failed verbal and nonverbal communication, coupled with behaviours able to drive the negotiation toward a serious impasse or a troubled path when instead a good result could have possibly ensued.

In such an "opaque" emotional situation we could observe, for example, political leaders and top negotiators, throughout the world, actively distorting the reality, as a result of bias, through a number of cognitive distortions[1] (e.g., overgeneralization, dichotomous thinking, selective abstraction, labeling, tunnel vision, and personalization, to name but a few), and because

[1] Thinking errors.

they hold so-called "dysfunctional beliefs"[2] that are often "transposed" into the specific realm of international negotiation as zero-sum beliefs ("I must always be in control by having indisputable arguments," or "Not listening to the counterpart and showing it to him, is a sign of power." "If I am wrong, as I must never be, others will disrespect and reject me," or, "He is a bad guy and if I make concessions he will be unfairly rewarded." "The first impression is always the best one for understanding people."). These may lead to the lack of acknowledgement of pieces of objective data during human information processing. As the negotiation proceeds in an attempt at problem solving, such cognitive distortions and dysfunctional beliefs can sabotage and limit important adaptive skills and the basic capacity to reach mutually beneficial compromises (Beck, 1999; Ellis, 1992).

This subjective predisposition could and often does have an impact on the manner in which negotiators assess not only the contents of the negotiation but also the actors participating in the negotiation. Moreover, it may lead to actors often making less positive and sustainable decisions based on wrong perceptions and negative emotions. As the negotiation proceeds in an attempt at problem solving, such cognitive distortions and dysfunctional beliefs can sabotage and limit important adaptive skills and the basic capacity to reach mutually benefiting compromises.

3.2 Perceived and Misperceived Reality

We open with Gallucci's words (2002, interview cited p. 10), which seem very interesting and worth being widely applied on the international scene to all the international actors (not just the United States): "One of the things that's very difficult, and I haven't quite figured it out yet, and this [Bush] administration is not helping me figure it out, is how to bring the American people along to believe that negotiations can be an honourable way to deal with the national security issue."

Has the Iraq war in 2003 prevented Saddam Hussein from attacking the world with lethal weapons or rather has it shown that it was really unlikely that he had the intention (and real means) to paralyse the world with nuclear weapons, or to sponsor the new international terrorism? Has the preventive war been successful in avoiding this "virtual" massive attack against the western world, or was Saddam just looking for the best way to save face mainly before his peoples and the Arab world? Shock and awe (Iraq or the world as a whole?) was the name in code of the military operation launched on Iraq in 2003. Did we really need that operation at that time or would it have been worth trying all possibilities offered by international negotiated diplomatic processes? May we say with certainty that invading Iraq has been a good decision for

[2] They are characterized by absolutistic and dogmatic evaluation of events.

safeguarding the Middle East's delicate political balance and improving the security of the western world? Or, maybe, has such an invasion and the consequent occupation of Iraq, spread the seed of hatred and resentment, poisoning relationships with Arab countries and the western world alike? Has this war really helped America's cause in the world?

To give interpretations and set up hypotheses, after the events have occurred, has the merit of explaining the reason for the event from each perspective adopted. If we change perspectives we often have different interpretations of the event. We risk being stuck in an epistemological endless conversation. The international environment is complex and its actors may often simplify automatically all the flood of information for reducing the complexity, ambiguity, and uncertainty of this environment. Decision makers may base their decisions on a simplified image of the reality, and actions are taken accordingly. Policies that appear to match a certain situation may be seen as inadequate from another perspective (Tetlock, 1996).

Researchers and scholars have underlined the importance of examining foreign policy decision-makers' belief systems for a better understanding of how leaders prepare prompt responses on the fundamental questions of international politics (Jervis, 1976; Jonsson, 2002; Tetlock, 1996; Van den Assem, 2000). Political leaders may hold an internally coherent vision of the world, but their decisions are predisposed toward a normal simplification of the information that brings with it the inherent risk of bias, and thus unbalanced decisions (Jervis, 1976; Van den Assem, 2000). The personal assimilation of new information to a belief system occurs much more easily than accommodation of a belief system to new information (Robins & Hayes, 1995). The realm of international negotiation is prone to unforeseen and ambiguous situations. To negotiate means also to tolerate a certain degree of ambiguity and the capacity to manage a series of potential (or perceived) conflicts that could be resolved without harming the negotiation working relationship (Pruitt, 2002). Information processing can become more easily biased if there is a high degree of ambiguity in the perceived message. The more ambiguous the information is, the greater will be the receiver's commitment to the established view. In a situation of ambiguity actors' perceptions and bias are far more egocentric (Aquilar, 1994).

3.3 Negotiators are Human Beings

A basic fact about negotiation, easily forgotten in human transactions, is that you are dealing not with abstract representatives of the "other side," but with human beings. They have different backgrounds, beliefs, deeply held values, viewpoints, emotions, and they are unpredictable (Oppenheim, 1984). The conflict script exists in the minds of the persons who are involved in it because each individual interprets her surroundings differently, and it is the "movie in the mind" that allows people to function within their environments (Damasio, 2003). People's active creation of their reality may be driven by their belief system. Then, the representation of the conflict and the adoption of negotiation techniques and tactics may be influenced by the negotiators' core belief system. Beliefs are so deeply engrained into negotiators' minds (without their being even aware of them) that they are likely to hinder effective negotiation. A few kinds of dysfunctional beliefs that we have noticed in our research and ongoing empirical investigations on negotiation simulations (see also Ellis, 2002; Gardner, 2000) that may be held by negotiators of different nationalities are:

1. "Emotion is a weakness."
2. "The world is a rotten place."
3. "Might makes right."
4. "A gain for me is a loss for you, and vice versa."
5. "I'd better get you before you get me."
6. "People are untrustworthy."
7. "We can't satisfy our respective needs at the same time."
8. "Winning is the only thing that really matters."
9. "I'll teach him or her a deserved lesson."
10. "People will hurt me."
11. "People will never change."

The more embedded the nucleus of the belief system is, the higher the potential impact it will have on communication, interpersonal relationships, the decision-making process, and accordingly on taken decisions. Often, messages that could be a meaningful contribution for improving relationships and negotiated outcomes may be interpreted differently by different actors; or a situation may be overvalued or undervalued without any objectivity. Kissinger's (1979: 522) reflection on United States–Soviet Union beliefs and thinking offers food for thought:

> The superpowers often behave like two heavily armed blind men feeling their way around in a room, each believing himself in mortal peril from the other whom he assumes to have perfect vision. Each side should know that frequently uncertainty, compromise, and incoherence are the essence of policy-making. Yet each tends to ascribe to the other a consistency, foresight, and coherence that its own experience belies.

Research, studies, and clinical assessments have identified the influence of particular cognitive distortions and dysfunctional beliefs in human information processing in the examination of subjective appraisal of present and future events and the consequentiality of taken decisions (Beck, 1988, 1995; Dattilio, 1998; Ellis, 1994, 1995). As matter of fact, belief systems resist changes, because cognitive distortions and dysfunctional beliefs protect them from changes.

3.4 Interpersonal Relationships

A negotiation is certainly about issues, but it is also about feelings and personal relationships. Trust, credibility, positive emotions, or alternatively, anger, hostility, and distrust, are intrinsically linked to the negotiation outcome.

In fact, the relationship that is established, for better or for worse, surrounds and profoundly affects the outcome of ongoing and future negotiations (Pruitt, 2002). One must constantly work at managing relationships during the negotiation. It is possible to be hard-nosed and tough, and still establish a good relationship with high levels of credibility (Fisher, Ury, & Patton, 1991). The key is to separate the conflict elements, which are political/business-driven, from personal elements, that relate to you and the other party as people. Therefore, it is always important to look ahead and focus not only on the interactive-cooperative exploration of the current negotiation, but also on your future interactions. It would be of the utmost importance to bear in mind that all the actors in the negotiation process play an active role in shaping relationships. Believing that working relationships improve without collective and individual efforts is really dangerous for the negotiation process.

3.5 Emotions and Negotiation

Emotion plays a primary role in the human communication process. It summarises a complex array of information that is processed at an unconscious level and provides us with a tacit, rapid, and sophisticated appraisal of what events and interpersonal interactions mean to us as biological organisms, and what things mean to us in terms of the actions in which we are prepared to engage (Frijda, 1987, 2004; Liotti, 1994; Safran, 1998). In Panksepp's estimation (2003), affective/emotional processes provide intrinsic values – organic "pressures" and "drives" – for the guidance of behaviour. People may be communicating emotions to other people without being fully aware that they are doing so.

Empirical evidence (Ekman, 1985, 1999; Ekman & Rosenberg, 2005) shows how different emotions are linked to different expressive-motor behaviours, and how they may be spread through nonverbal communication cues without awareness, playing an important role in interpersonal communication. Thus, for example, a feeling of hostility evoked by a counterpart during the negotiation process may be based upon multiple cues that are unconsciously perceived, such as tone of voice, gestures, quality of eye contact, and posture. Ekman's work has demonstrated that different persons from different countries and continents will exhibit the same facial expressions in situations that evoke anger, fear, sadness, disgust, surprise, or joy (Ekman, 2003). This research has also demonstrated that in nonverbal communication, most of us are quite incompetent at decoding emotional expression, especially when that expression is of a mixed emotion (such as being sad and angry at same time) or, when people are in conflict, they are likely to decode each other's emotional expression inaccurately.

However, it is also true that if one tends to be focused on the counterpart's emotional world, she will completely lose the sense of relatedness that binds together all of the actors of the negotiation process. Instead, the more open we are to our own emotions, the more skilled we will be in "reading" feelings of our counterpart. Empathy for ourselves and for others, a crucial skill for negotiators and mediators, plays a basic role in international negotiation and helps to prevent dysfunctional interpersonal-cognitive cycles that usually bind negotiators in a stereotypical negative interpretation of one's counterpart's actions, answering them with hostility, thus provoking even more hostile reactions thus confirming internal schemes and self-fulfilling prophecy.

3.6 Human Communication Process

Human beings are different and different are their own perceptions of the world surrounding them and of events linked and provoked by the external world and often by the interaction between the latter and the subject/actor. It is easily understandable that for our work we attach importance to human perceptions and the ways in which cognitive processes operate to produce responses. Cognitive processes (which may involve language, symbols, or imagery) include perceiving, recognizing, remembering, imagining, conceptualising, judging, reasoning, and processing information for planning, problem solving, and other applications (Borgo, della Giusta, & Sibilia, 2001).

Internal cognitive operations can transform symbols of the external world, because the interplay between genetics and environment determines individual cognitive development and capabilities (Guidano & Liotti, 1983). The mind detects, selects, recognizes, and verbally represents features of a particular stimulus. Among the many specific topics investigated by cognitive psychologists are language acquisition, visual and auditory perception, information storage and retrieval, altered states of consciousness, cognitive restructuring (how the mind mediates between conflicting, or dissonant, information), and individual styles of thought and perception (Eysenck, 1990; Eysenck & Keane, 2005; Reed, 1989). The challenge of studying human cognition is evident when one considers the work of the mind in processing the simultaneous and sometimes conflicting information presented in daily life, through both internal and external stimuli. Although this attention to multiple stimuli is a common phenomenon, complex cognitive processing is clearly required to accomplish it (Robins & Hayes, 1995).

Human communication comes to the fore as the medium to connect people during the negotiation process. It consists of the verbal and nonverbal expressions through which we intentionally or unintentionally communicate emotional states. Human communication has the same importance for the negotiation process that blood pressure has for the human body. It is important because it is a process that involves a shared code, or codes, or verbal and nonverbal symbols. In fact, misunderstanding is a huge problem in human communication, because the meanings of symbols are in the people that use them, not in the symbols themselves (Safran, 2002). What one says, the other may misinterpret. Where the parties speak different languages the chance for misinterpretation is compounded (Fisher, Ury, & Patton, 1991).

This interpersonal process clearly shows how perceptions are shaped upon actions and how unfortunately world leaders and negotiators often do not pay enough attention to their own words, attitudes, behaviours, and actions that can provoke the counterpart's reaction. When we say something to the other side it does not mean that they have interpreted the message as we would like them to do. It just means that our words have been processed according to their own culture, belief systems, personal representation schemas, and emotional states. Leaders should be aware of this gap between their intended messages and the counterpart's interpretation. As brilliantly remarked by Jervis more than 20 years ago (1985: 30), "Because statesmen believe that they understand the other side's view of the world, they usually assume that their messages have been received and interpreted as intended. If the other ignores a signal, statesmen often conclude that it has been rejected when in fact it may not have been received."

Communication is an interactive dynamic. Communication between human beings appears as a nonlinear process, a domain of the temporality: the sense of things we tell each other is highly influenced by the contingency of the communication, positions, expectations, change of position, and reciprocal adaptation of interlocutors. The sender and receiver should be aware that the value of a gesture or of a word is between what the sender had the intention to say and what the receiver has really understood (Gensini, 2004).

Take the example of North Korea (aware of the ongoing stressful negotiation process). Koreans are eager to resolve the nuclear weapons crisis (according to their words), but only by concluding a step-by-step denuclearization agreement linked with progress towards the normalisation of ties with the United States. According to a first article in *The Financial Times*,[3] an interview with Kim Yong-Nam, number two to Kim Jong-il, the latter expressed the fear of being attacked by Americans. In his words: "The only reason we are developing nuclear weapons is to deter an American pre-emptive attack. After all, we have been singled out as the target for such an attack and we are the justification for the development of a new generation of US nuclear weapons. We don't want to suffer the fate of Iraq." In the same article Gen Ri Chan-Bok, spokesman for the Korean People's Army, said: "We don't mind the possession of nuclear weapons by Russia and China, because they're not a threat to us. Although, Japan is not friendly, I don't know whether Japan is developing nuclear weapons or not, but in any case, our nuclear deterrent is not against Japan or anyone else, just against the United States."

A more recent article in *The Financial Times*[4] follows the same line: North Korea's foreign ministry said its decision to conduct a nuclear test was prompted by Washington. "The US's daily increasing threat of a nuclear war and its vicious sanctions and pressure, have caused a grave situation on the Korean peninsula ... and the Korean nation stands at the crossroads of life and death,"

---

[3] S. Harrison, Inside North Korea: leaders open to ending nuclear crisis, 4 May, 2004, p.3. See also: A. Fifield; N. Korea and US begin to close gulf over nuclear arms; p. 3, 30/31 July 2005; and J. Gawronski; *Corea del Nord*: "Come possiamo fidarci degli USA?" La Stampa, p. 8, 27 July 2005.

[4] Fifield, A.; Khalaf, R.; Fidler, S.; US says NK weapons test would threaten peace (4 October, 2006, p 1).

saying it needed to "bolster its war deterrent for self-defence." In the *Wall Street Journal*[5] it was declared by North Korean leaders that "The threat of nuclear war and sanctions from the US force it to undertake a test. Our goal is that of settling hostile relations between North Korea and the US."

As matter of fact tensions with North Korea have worsened since September 2005 when the United States imposed financial sanctions that have curbed North Korea's ability to trade and earn foreign exchange. According to the *International Herald Tribune*[6] the U.S. Treasury Department has persuaded 24 banks in China, Mongolia, Singapore, Vietnam, and other countries to shut down North Korean accounts. In August 2005, Australia and Japan ordered their financial institutions to block transactions by companies suspected of having links to North Korea's weapons programs.

Moreover, leaders' answers made on the spot as a sort of ultimatum could not really work with this kind of isolated regime. On the other hand, Taro Aso, Japan's foreign minister said (in the same newspaper): "A nuclear test is a threat to peace. We would never be able to forgive such a move." The United States' answer was more open and "seductive": the United States said it would work with its partners to bring North Korea back into six-party talks, in which Pyongyang has refused to participate for 11 months. The European Union's statement was adamant: "Such a test is always bad news." The North Korean official press agency, KCNA, carried a statement that said: "US extreme threat of a nuclear war and sanctions and pressure compel the North Korean nation to conduct a nuclear test, an essential process for bolstering nuclear deterrent." It added that North Korea would "never use nuclear weapons first but strictly prohibit any threat of nuclear weapons and nuclear transfer." However, it seems that there is a strong doubt whether North Korea has enough technology to miniaturize its nuclear weapons for delivery on long-range missiles.

Leaders and negotiators should pay attention to the impact of their words and actions on the beliefs and thinking of their counterparts. Understanding the counterpart is the foundation to any successful negotiation. As stated by Gallucci (2002): "...*It is important* to understand what the other guy's perceived interests are. If you can, it's nice to just aggregate those and know what their bureaucratic situation is, and any arguments they may be having between the energy people and the military and all that. But understand your own interests, understand their perceived interests." If the communication is good, each side understanding the other, then the outcome is likely to be good. But if one side cannot understand the other, the negotiation will not only fail, but will also perhaps leave things worse than they were at the beginning (Fisher, Kopelman, & Schneider, 1994). Moreover, helping the other side understand your thinking may reduce their fears, settle perceptions, and implement cooperative attitudes (Fisher, Ury, & Patton, 1991).

---

[5] Ramstad, E.; Moffett, S.; Fairclough, G.; North Korea plans nuclear-bomb test (4 October, 2006, p.11).

[6] Sang-Hun, C.; North Korea planning nuclear weapons test (4 October, 2006, p. 1/7).

To grasp the subtleties of intentional communication is fundamental to the process. Many times we perceive an intention to communicate when instead a counterpart did not make attempts to communicate. Or, on the contrary, we do not perceive any communication when the counterpart instead made an attempt to communicate. These two situations may easily be described as communication failure. Due to a limited capacity to process large amounts of information, we run the risk of making less than optimal decisions, and here communication strategies can be evoked that facilitate more effective decision making. However, selectivity, hidden agendas, interpersonal conflict, the use of stereotypes, and universal decisions are all factors that impede effective decision making (Burgoon, Hunsaker, & Dawson, 1994).

Moreover, helping the other side to understand your thinking may reduce their negative emotions, favour a positive impact on perceptions, and increase the possibility of better cooperative attitudes. In short, when a leader or a negotiator assumes the fact that "When I use a word, it means just what I choose it to mean, neither more nor less," he ignores the role of the other people involved in the human communication process.

3.7 The Cognitive Model

The cognitive model hypothesizes that people's emotions and behaviors are influenced by their perception of events (J.S. Beck, 1995). The way people perceive the external world and their resulting propositional thoughts about those perceptions are of high interest for this model (Panksepp, 2003). It is not the situation in and of itself that determines what people feel, but rather the way in which they construe a situation (Beck, 1976; Ellis 1962). The way an individual feels and behaves is influenced by the way he structures his experiences. Individuals are viewed as "architects" of their experiences, influencing the data they create and collect. Rather than being passive, individuals may inadvertently and even unknowingly behave in ways that elicited the very reactions in others that they could take as evidence to confirm their views of themselves and the world (Meichenbaum, 1995). Negotiators may distort reality as a result of automatic thoughts based on a number of cognitive distortions and because they hold so-called dysfunctional beliefs. The cognitive model emphasises the influence of cognition on mood and behaviour (also if it recognizes the influence of emotions on cognition), and interventions primarily aim to change people's cognitive processes.

3.8 Analysis of Beck's Cognitive Model (1976, 1988, 1999, 2002)

Beck's cognitive model has been expanded to focus on cognitive variables that shape an individual's reactions to life events, in order to provide a better understanding of cognitive mediation in interpersonal relationships (see also

Dattilio, 1998). Beginning in childhood, individuals develop certain beliefs about themselves, other people, and their worlds, used to perceive, code, and recall information (see also Robins & Hayes, 1995). According to a tidy explanation of J.S. Beck (1995), people's most central or core beliefs[7] are understandings that are so fundamental and deep that they often do not articulate them, even to themselves, regarding them as absolute truths, their reality. Beliefs about relationship interactions are learned early in life and are not fully articulated in an individual's mind, but exist as a vague concept of what "should be" (Dattilio, 1998). In a specific situation, one's underlying beliefs influence one's perception, which is expressed by situation-specific automatic thoughts. These thoughts, in turn, influence one's emotions. Ideas and beliefs play an important role in the negotiation process, as they may contribute to shape the entire process and determine the final outcome choice.

Automatic thoughts are defined as stream of consciousness ideas, beliefs, or images that individuals have from moment to moment, often elicited by specific situations (see also Dattilio, 1998; "My counterpart is late, she doesn't care about the negotiation," or "She does not respect me!" or "She does not want to eat with me tonight because wants to keep me distant!"). The word "automatic" indicates the spontaneous quality of these thoughts which are not the result of reasoning, but seem to spring up automatically, rapidly, and very briefly (see also J.S. Beck, 1995). These automatic thoughts, which reflect the individual's appraisal of a situation, rather than the actual objective situation, lead directly to the person's emotional and behavioural responses (see also Robins & Hayes, 1995). If the appraisals are distorted, person's responses will be disadaptive.

Cognitive distortions are the links between beliefs and automatic thoughts. When new information or memories are cognitively processed, the information is often biased to fit a relevant belief (see also J.S. Beck, 1995; Robins & Hayes, 1995). The result of this biased appraisal may then become accessible to consciousness in the form of distorted automatic thoughts or images. Aaron T. Beck has described a number of specific types of cognitive distortions that tend to be present in the thoughts of individuals. Although these types of cognitive distortions can be conceptually separated, any given thought may reflect more than one type of distortion. According to Beck, with the conceptual help of J.S. Beck (1995) and Dattilio (1998), we can summarise a nonexhaustive list of cognitive distortions[8] that could affect negotiators, as follows.

1. *Dichotomous thinking* (called also "all or nothing" or "polarized thinking"). We can exemplify this cognitive distortion with the aphorism: "Who is not with me is against me." Defiance, not cooperation, is often the response.

---

[7] These core beliefs are referred to as schemas by other authors, but A.T. Beck differentiated the two.

[8] We have detected, in our ongoing research, many of these cognitive distortions in negotiators, from the European Union, belonging to different European cultures.

Experiences are classified as complete successes or total failures. You view a situation in only two categories instead of a continuum. For example, "If I won't be able to bring home a great negotiated outcome (for me) I will be a failure." The counterpart (and our) behaviours are appraised through the lens of this distortion as: right/wrong; correct/incorrect; victim/guilty; good/evil, and so on.

2. *Overgeneralization*. In overgeneralizing, a single contingent experience is taken as the basis of a general theory. An isolated incident or two is allowed to serve as a representation of general explication that goes far beyond the current situation, whether or not they are truly related. For example, a negotiator has been deceived (or he thinks of being deceived) by the counterpart and concludes, "All negotiators are liars."
3. *Catastrophising*. In catastrophising, the future is anticipated negatively without substantial evidence and without considering other, more likely outcomes. A minimal factor is depicted as a sign of an already anticipated negative event. For example, "Because I am unable to master all the issues the negotiation will be a disaster," or "I am so nervous that I won't be able to perform at all," or if the negotiation experiences the beginning of a "physiological" impasse, a negotiator may think, "I knew it; the negotiation will be a complete failure."
4. *Arbitrary inference*. This is one of the most important mechanisms for repeated human information processing mistakes. A conclusion is drawn from an event, in the absence of supporting substantiating evidence. People may transform experiences so that an in-the-moment disappointment becomes a dominant memory. For example, a negotiator waiting for the counterpart who demanded a pause for a telephone call concludes: "My counterpart is willing to disregard our last achievements," or "He will refuse the reached compromise." Or, "He is a powerless coward."
5. *Selective abstraction*. Some aspects of a typically negative situation are attended to or remembered, at the expense of other, more positive aspects and of the whole picture. Information is perceived out of context; certain details are noticed or highlighted, and other important information is ignored. For example, a negotiator may be focused on an impasse over a small detail without noticing smooth negotiation on the main issues. Or perhaps, she could be concentrated on an isolated "weird" (for her) behaviour of the counterpart, but fail to notice his positive and lasting cooperative actions. A counterpart's frustrated answer may be, "You are blind to my constructive attitudes." This distortion may inhibit far-reaching compromises and long-term cooperative behaviours.
6. *Labelling*. Behaviours such as mistakes made in the past are generalized as traits to define oneself or the counterpart. One puts a fixed global label on oneself or others without considering that the evidence might more reasonably lead to a less disastrous conclusion. For example, subsequent to making a few errors in a written text a negotiator says, "I am really stupid," or if it is the contrary, "He is really stupid," as opposed to recognizing the

errors as situational behaviour (perhaps influenced by fatigue). Similarly a negotiator who observes the counterpart taking more time (according to his belief of taking time) to reflect on a particular subject of a negotiated agreement, concludes, "This person is really a provocateur."

7. *Personalization*. You believe others are behaving negatively because of you, without considering more plausible explanations for their behaviour. For example, "The counterpart went outside the room because I said something wrong," or if the counterpart is lost in her thoughts he reaches the conclusion, "I am sure she has something against me," or "She is organising a dirty manoeuvre to take advantage of me."
8. *Tunnel vision*. People only see the negative or positive aspects of the situation when they are distressed (what fits their attitude or state of mind). For example, "The counterpart refused one of my compromising proposals. She was critical and insensitive and she is not a good negotiator" (ignoring that 90% of the negotiation has been smooth).

3.9 Analysis of Ellis' Cognitive Model: Rational-Emotive, and Behavioural Approach (1992, 1994, 2004; Ellis & Crawford, 2000)

Historically, the views of Albert Ellis are important because he was one of the first psychologists and psychotherapists to propose a systematic, explicitly cognitive approach to psychotherapy. According to Ellis, when people create rigid demands out of their more flexible preferences, they tend to concomitantly create cognitive, emotional, and behavioural intrapsychic and interpersonal disturbances. Rational, emotive, and behavioural therapy (REBT) holds that unrealistic and illogical self-talk about unfortunate life events, and not these events in their own right, "created" or "caused" emotional disturbance. People often hold dysfunctional beliefs, defined by Ellis as ways of thinking of human beings characterized by absolutistic and dogmatic evaluation, that often determine emotional suffering and disadaptive behaviors in individuals.[9] Words that have a high frequency in human thinking such as "must," "absolutely," "always," and "all," all show their dogmatic character. Catastrophisation, awfulisation, damnation, tyranny of musts, and low frustration tolerance are the five categories or basic nucleus of dysfunctional beliefs.

Human beings frequently stay rigidly with their grandiose demands, and thereby create several ideas, emotions, and behaviours that sabotage their understanding and acceptance of their disagreements with each other, and

[9] Research at the Albert Ellis' Institute has demonstrated that these dysfunctional beliefs have been detected in human beings belonging to different cultures. Our ongoing research, concerning negotiators from the European Union, belonging to different European cultures, seems to be confirming these results.

thus block working through agreements of at least "peacefully agreeing to disagree." According to Ellis, people often sabotage relationships within the negotiation process because people think they have to put across their own view, must get others to agree, and have got to fulfil their personal goals, insisting on a win/lose game. Often, these people see counterparts' reasoning with which they may not agree as "wrong" (often they also paranoically tend to attribute to them the deliberate intent to do wrong) and their views as clearly "right." This way of thinking is based on either/or instead of and/also thinking and tends to see important issues in black and white. They define a rigid and fixed role for themselves and their counterparts. Instead, roles may change according to the interpersonal process that binds people together.

3.10 Cognitive Interpersonal Cycles

People face the world with preconceptions about the reality without which they would never manage the chaos. Particularly, they will develop previsions on the interpersonal relationship course on the basis of expectations and intentions and will be looking for signals showing them the coincidence between desires and the state of the things (Dimaggio & Semerari, 2003). The human being during his development builds up interpersonal schemata on the basis of repeated interactions – and his innate dispositions – with the reference persons (Guidano & Liotti, 1983). These representations of the interactions help to describe to the subject the self-image, the image of the other, and the relationship that bound them together (Semerari, 2000).

Safran (1984; Safran & Segal, 1990), inspired by Bowlby and Stern's work, has formulated a fundamental concept: the cognitive interpersonal cycle. The individual continuous constructive processes of the reality bring to typical behaviours and communications that elicit foreseen answers in others. The subject has expectations on the relationship formation and with this charge will enter in relation with others waiting for those certain foreseen familiar answers. His previsions will provoke automatic or unconscious behaviours that are in line with his desires. The interaction, even if unconsciously, will be influenced by just those desires, expectations, and behaviours. These interpersonal dysfunctional cycles even if dissociated from the conscious experience will come out in nonverbal behaviour and will provoke answers in the counterpart (Dimaggio & Semerari, 2003; Safran 2002; Safran & Segal, 2000). These answers reinforce the beliefs (also unconscious) that are behind the cause of dissociating those aspects. For example, if the subject feels that he is unjustly the victim of something may dissociate the emotion of rage. But the rage will come out in his expressions and behaviours, maybe in eliciting an unforeseen rage in the others, which in itself will reinforce the belief of being subject to unmotivated attacks.

We know that human beings are predisposed to react automatically in following established paths, to the affects expressed by the others through facial and posture expressions (Argyle, 1994; Ekman, 2003; Frijda, 1986; 2004; Russell

& Fernàndez-Dols, 2002). Then, dissociated affects and thoughts, even if they are unconscious, are communicated throughout emotional expressive behaviour. This elicits in others automatic answers. For example, an expression of rage that appeared on the face or on the body (of which the subject would be conscious or unconscious), provokes an automatic answer of rage or fear (to an expression of fear we react with fear: is there a threat in the environment? Or we may offer protection). In brief, the answer that the counterpart gives to the first expression (rage against rage, for instance) confirms the underlying assumptions of the behaviour of the subject in promoting in him automatic, unconscious answers that reinforce the dysfunctional cycle (Dimaggio & Semerari, 2003; Safran, 2002).

Safran's studies and research on cognitive-interpersonal cycles help to bridge the gap between cognitive theory and accounts that emphasize environmental determinants of emotional problems (Safran 1998, 2002; Safran & Muran, 2000; Safran & Segal, 1990; Robins & Hayes, 1995). For example, one actor at the negotiation table anticipates others will not take into proper consideration his concerns and hence will not respect him. A dysfunctional cognitive-interpersonal cycle has been automatically started giving negative feelings to the actor who thus behaves in a tenacious dependent fashion that ultimately alienates people and confirms his expectations. Another negotiator anticipates that others will be critical of her and thus acts in an excessively self-justifying fashion that irritates people and ultimately elicits the type of criticism that she expects. When a counterpart acts in a fashion that is consistent with the actor's dysfunctional cognitive-interpersonal schema, he perpetuates an existing dysfunctional cycle. For example, the counterpart who responds to the actor's hostility with counterhostility may confirm his belief that the world is a hostile place that should be met with hostility. Conversely, if the counterpart is able to refrain from participating in the actor's cognitive-interpersonal cycle, the actor could encounter an important experiential challenge to his dysfunctional beliefs. In this view, emotional disturbances may indeed result in large part from situational determinants. But these cannot be separated from the role that the individual's cognitive processes may play, not only in interpreting the situations but also in generating many of them (Safran, 1998, 2002).

3.11 Metacommunication Process and Working Relationship

During periods of stress to which the negotiation working relationship is submitted, it is of utmost importance to focus on the process of metacommunication, that is, communicating about the communication that is taking place. In this way one should make efforts to raise awareness among parties on the importance of collaborative exploration, here and now, on what is going on in the interpersonal process between parties in a mindful way. As brilliantly remarked by Safran and Muran (2000) this could be described as "mindfulness in action." Our reasoning in this section has been largely influenced by Jeremy Safran's thoughtful insights (Safran,1984, 1998; Safran & Muran, 2000; Safran & Segal, 1990).

The contextual technique of metacommunicating consists in not blaming and not addressing responsibilities to the counterpart for short-cuts or breakdowns (that could come up during the negotiation process) that could put a strain on working relationships. This implemented collaboration in looking forward together to detecting clear and present problems, as well as potential negativity in a working relationship, could be useful in analysing interactions that may cause a breakdown or dangerous stalemate. In effect, to give a sense, a meaning, to the negotiation relationship and achieve a mutually satisfying outcome we should refrain from assuming that our interpretations of the negotiation process represent the reality. Instead, we should keep in mind and share with the counterpart that our/their interpretations are just representations of the reality; therefore potentially wrong and at least probabilistic. This mental tool requires the ability to recognise one's own and others' emotions appropriately and thus assess interactive sequences, being able to assume (and remember) someone else's point of view in the relational context. In periods of stalemate, parties through a communication tool can direct their efforts toward a cooperative and exploratory path in order to bring to light inner and hidden dynamics (to parties as individuals and to the relationship as a whole).

The practical techniques should be based and reasoned on the contextual environment because techniques are not embedded in an abstract strategy: they acquire meanings from the same contextual situation in which they are employed. The negotiation process should be afforded a step-by-step genuine interested discovery attitude with the aim of being committed to the relational implications of communication. This is in order to refrain from sending "me" as opposite to "you" messages and being concentrated on building up, through this mutual cooperative behaviour, a sense of "we."

It is useful to understand that every negotiation is different from previous ones and human bounds (from superficial bounds to deeper ones) that could be construed are different according to different negotiations and actors on the spot. Tensions and problems that can arise should be addressed now and here (even if it seems that they have similarities with past experiences). All perceptions should be remarked as personal perceptions in the communication process in order to understand with a high degree of trustworthiness what is going on here and now is a joint effort of collaboration that should ensue. Remarking on the personal and subjective nature of one's observation will help to establish a common playing ground without giving the impression to the counterpart of being "Ms/Mr I know everything" and even worse, that of patronising her.

Our own contribution (positive or negative) to the interaction should be recognised and shared with the counterpart. In conveying feedback about behaviour or actions or interpersonal style it is important to raise to the counterpart the effect it has on us. For example, it will be important to talk about how we feel about it in the present time, because tomorrow morning when we start a new negotiation round emotions and feelings could be different from yesterday (also because maybe in the meantime the negotiator has been changed).

In this process, it is important to pay attention to specific and concrete elements rather than general or abstract elements that could bring strain into the relationship. A concrete attitude and a respect for the observational and subjective positions could help to establish a common discovery process in order to facilitate a breakthrough in the human change process. A next step is that of being aware of the sense of relatedness with the counterpart, which quality reflects an ongoing interplay between interpersonal and intrapersonal dimensions. A strategic tension between more or less relatedness between parties may signal implementation of attunement of consciousness and help to master one's own and others' mental states in order to face complex situations fairly. The working relationship should be, however, strictly monitored with discretion in order to understand if our interventions are really eliciting the desired responses in the counterpart. It could be that despite all our good intentions and specific training, the counterpart perceives our intervention as manipulative, patronising, and critical or accusatory. The attention should be focused on the way the counterpart builds up relationships and her personal schemas.

The negotiation process is constantly changing and we can work with it provided we fully acknowledge and accept what the situation/context is. Even the situation of feeling trapped or wedged is a situation that requires our active interventions: once we have accepted it we can shift our energies from fighting to exploring and cooperating. In accepting the situation as it is in this precise moment (not yesterday or tomorrow) we can be freed up from "conflicting ghosts" and related negative emotions and then deploy our energy to take all various possibilities that the contextual environment produces in that precise moment.

It could happen, however, that even if a negotiator is skilled at metacommunicating, his efforts correspond to deterioration of the working relationship because metacommunication may be unconsciously motivated by negative emotions; in this case a trained negotiator should be able to operate a shift on the intrapersonal level: formulating interventions in a nonaccusatory way is to master the negotiation process, but we should keep in mind that unconscious affective communication could influence the whole communication. Undoubtedly, emotions and feelings behind negotiators' words inevitably mediate their impact on the counterpart. A growing awareness of one's own contribution may shift the feeling behind the words, so that an emotion of frustration may be substituted by a reflection of his growing empathy for the counterparts' needs and problems. It is important for the negotiator to approach each manifestation of a potential impasse with a "beginner's mind" (Safran & Muran, 2000). Last but not least, negotiators should never forget that they can lose hope in the possibility of moving forward. It is important to know that periods of hopelessness and demoralization are part of the process of working through stalemates.

The process of becoming aware of one's own experience should be communicated to the counterpart. Being aware of inner mental states demands the identification, expression, and modulation of emotions and feelings, and responses that the counterpart evokes in the negotiator. The identification of feelings as well as that of mental states (related thoughts, memories, etc.) could be really useful for a smooth negotiation process. This could bring to the awareness of action tendencies, because most of the time it is easier to identify the actions one feels like taking than what one feels and consequentially the impact that the counterpart has on one. Also it is very important to identify specific behaviours and communications that may evoke or contribute to negotiators' feelings in a way that helps them to better articulate their feelings. Intrapersonal and interpersonal worlds should be investigated with tailored psychotherapeutic techniques in order to have a more coherent and comprehensive picture of the negotiation process.

3.12 Neuroscience and International Negotiation

The modern study of neuroscience has been shifting its focus on the brain function to complex functions such as cognition, emotion, and behaviour (before the focus was primarily on simple motor behaviours such as walking and breathing). Neuroscience is helping us to explore the biological bases of consciousness and mental processes, by which we perceive, learn, remember, and act (Damasio, 1999, Panksepp, 1998). Neuroscience research into decision-making processes has both complemented and updated traditional views of decision making derived from such fields as psychology and economics (Damasio, 1994). As a result of this research, it became increasingly clear that individuals do not express a stable set of preferences for given choices, but that these preferences are often constructed, not merely revealed, when presented with a choice problem (Erzenzinger, 2002).

These findings have demonstrated that what we perceive as rational thought is a result also of tacit knowledge (mental states) that we cannot explain in a rational way (Guidano & Liotti, 1983). Although emotional influence has been analysed by scholars, in different areas of the political environment and the negotiation process, there has been little or no direct discussion of the applicability of these new findings to the field of the international negotiation (and that of international relations as a whole), as for instance in analysing emotional competence in order to "detect" and "reorganise" the breakdown of the relationship in an international negotiation context. According to all the material now available in the areas of psychology and neuroscience, we can give new input as to how these scientifically observed insights in the human decision-making processes can be used for the achievement of a more strategic emotional competence of leaders (and actors in general) in the realm of the negotiation process.

3.13 The Influence of Emotion in the Decision-Making Process

Damasio (1994, 1999, 2003), one of the world's leading neuroscientists, has been demonstrating the role of emotion and feeling in the decision-making process. Neurological research has highlighted the fact that the region of the human brain primarily responsible for rational judgment and decision making cannot function properly without input from regions responsible for emotion (Damasio, 1994). Much of the time this input and its influence shapes our decisions and judgement in radical ways even if a subject is not conscious of this process. This provides an interesting neurobiological underpinning of psychological research. As we have already seen, the tendency to use reasoning short-cuts, so-called heuristics, is normal in human beings because this reasoning may favour a useful decision-making process when a choice is necessary but nevertheless there is a lack of time and a lack of information. However, in the absence of an objective examination of a stressful context, heuristics could produce cognitive bias in leading people toward dangerous paths. For example, narcissistic personalities use the self-enhancement heuristics in an excessive way; paranoids are focused on the hypothesis that others are threatening them (and they try to look for proof to confirm this hypothesis). They do not believe in different explanations and exclude data that could confirm the opposite explanation.

In addition to these psychological reasonings other neuroscience elements describe the human modalities of choice. The human being makes decisions by interrupting at a certain point the undertaken cost-benefit analysis of all the possible and likely options and "pushes" his mind to adopt one of the foreseen futures. Damasio through his research and studies, set up a theoretical framework in which to define how such interaction may be produced. A lifetime of experience has resulted in the "marking" of input to the prefrontal cortex with positive or negative emotions, a process that has been learned over time by the association of emotional input from the body (somatic input) with predicted future outcomes of certain scenarios (Erzenzinger, 2002). The somatic marker (Damasio, 1994) is a decisive factor that allows humans to make such a selection: there is a device in our brain that undertakes a preselection of the action options in associating the representations of future scenarios of these options to positive or negative body states. Desires are subject to this device: if we imagine a state of negotiation, related to a satisfying sensation of the body, we will work in a way to make it real.

The somatic markers are emotional learned reactions to "demark" foreseeable incoming scenarios; the not "marked" scenarios are kept out of the decision-making process. In practice, somatic markers are often automatic and beneath our conscious awareness, and their function is that of immediately linking images of future outcomes with either negative or positive sensations and thus helping human beings to increase the accuracy and efficiency of the decision-making process. In the absence of those markers individuals would be endlessly exploring all possible solutions and likely consequences to a given contextual situation when faced by a choice, losing the ability to weigh one alternative as superior to another. Relying on an affective impression can be far more efficient than continually checking all of the pros and cons or retrieving many relevant examples from memory in their entirety (Damasio, 1994).

Utilization of affective influences on decision-making in the area of evaluative judgements has much to do with *framing*, or presenting options in such a way that bias is created toward a particular choice (Erzenzinger, 2002). For example, an important negotiation described as having a 65% chance of success has more appeal than the same negotiation described as having a 35% chance of failure. The rapid and immediate affective association produced by the mind of the actor may constitute the neural basis for framing pervasive and persistent effects, even if it is usually described in terms of individual risk aversion. For instance, in negotiation contexts the process is highly affected by uncertainty over some of the main points of the agenda; moreover, ambiguity as well can also influence judgement and consequential decisions. Regardless of how logical or statistical we would like to think our assessments of risk are, affective associations "define" risk assessment (Erzenzinger, 2002). In the end, it has been proved that affective associations play an important role in the decision-making process and that this role could influence decisions in conscious and unconscious ways.

3.14 Human Consciousness

The origin of the term refers to awareness of our own mental processes (or the product of such processes). Edelman (1989), Damasio (1994, 1999), and Maturana (1990) have been demonstrating in their research the intersubjective nature of self-knowledge, emotional knowledge, and consciousness functions. From these works we may consider the consciousness not as a complex, compound, and changeable process, which is in a continuum interexchange process with the unconscious mind (Liotti, 2001). Moreover, different studies on metacognitive monitoring, on mind's theory, on working memory, and on metarepresentation to name but a few, have demonstrated the composite nature of consciousness. And from those titles we can understand scientists and authors when they refer to consciousness operations precisely defined and investigated through scientific empirical procedures.

This new vision of the consciousness demonstrates that classic competition between conscious and unconscious is outdated. Therefore, consciousness is studied by cognitive psychology in its multiple *modus operandi*. Transformation of unconscious mental activities in conscious activities is important because they may nurture and facilitate the communication process (through the language) and hence enrich the intersubjective dimension. Emotions are certainly the main mental processes that should reach the quality of consciousness in order to be regulated (Liotti, 2005b). Damasio (1999) and Panksepp (1998) recently have been empirically demonstrating that emotions are a phenomenon of a continuum that ranges from the radically unconscious level of physiology up to the self-regulatory level allowed by consciousness.

3.15 Motivational Processes

Liotti, an eminent Italian psychiatrist and cognitive psychotherapist, has been empirically working on specific causes of emotional disorders paying attention to the interdependence of consciousness, as an intrinsic intersubjective process, and the modulation of emotions that are generated from this interdependence. Liotti's contribution to the development of a cognitive psychotherapy, within the cognitive-evolutionary perspective, has as its solid secure base, attachment theory (Bowlby, 1969, 1988). According to Liotti, for understanding the meaning and value of emotions in their intrinsic intersubjectivity it is useful to understand the physiology of interpersonal motivational systems.[10] Human beings have since their birth a series of innate dispositions or trends that are the result of a long story of the evolution of primates and they differ deeply from the classical methodology to conceive instincts (Liotti, 1994). Following Liotti's theoretical framework (2001, 2005b):

1. They can be thought of as behavioural regulation systems (Bowlby, 1969; Gilbert, 1989; Liotti, 1994).
2. They are susceptible to continuous modification by learning and cognitive processes (Bowlby, 1969).
3. They concern not only bodily needs and reproduction, but also basic forms of social interaction (attachment, caregiving, competition for social rank, co-operation, affiliation to the group, creation of relatively stable sexual couples (Gilbert, 1989; Liotti, 1994). Therefore, they allow us to study in a particularly efficient way the relationships between acquired knowledge of the self-with-the-other and innate communication bases.
4. They do not need consciousness to operate because they evolved before the appearance of human consciousness and because they still subsist nowadays (in very similar form to human ones) in animal species without consciousness of the self. Therefore, they configure the innate foundation of an unconscious mental activity very close to neurophysiology (Panksepp, 1998).
5. The results of mental operations guided by innate dispositions may begin consciously in the human being, and conscious choices may influence the modalities with which the innate dispositions are applied (Bowlby, 1969, Liotti, 1994).
6. The innate dispositions to the social relation, in particular, begin consciously in the form of emotional experiences (Bowlby, 1969).

3.16 Interpersonal Motivational Systems

We have seen that different motivational systems take shape in human beings, depending on both their innate fundament and the concrete and variable interactions of the individual with the environment. Comparing social behaviour's observation of various animal species and of the human being suggests that social behaviour is regulated by five control systems, the basis of

[10] They are human beings' neuropsychological regulatory systems, deeper understanding of which will shed additional light on interpersonal dynamics in the negotiation process.

which is innate and results from evolution (Gilbert, 1989; Liotti, 1994, 2001). Every control system of social behaviour (that we can consider as a social motivational system) has a defined objective; it regards a fundamental aspect of the relation and it becomes active in precise circumstances of communication between individuals interacting within a social group (Liotti, 2005a,b).

Activation rules of motivational systems do not require language or consciousness, but they can be conventionally and intuitively expressed in terms of consciousness and language in order to illustrate synthetically the specific functions of any system that in human beings can be considered as an interpersonal motivational system (IMS).[11] Each one of these systems mediates the production of specific nonverbal signals with high emotional meaning answering to the specific nonverbal signals made by a conspecific because social behavioural systems of two acting individuals are in an intrinsic structural coupling (Liotti, 2001). Then, in order to study, in psychology and psychopathology, the meaning and the value of the emotions in the intersubjectivity dimension it is useful to know IMS physiology (Gilbert, 1989; Liotti, 2001, 2005b). Every motivational system expresses itself through specific sequences of emotions, which appear in functions of the various and changing environmental contingencies, favourable or not to the reaching of the goal or aim in which the system itself operates (Gilbert, 1989; Liotti, 2001, 2005b; Panksepp, 1998).

We believe Giovanni Liotti's conceptual framework could find interesting application in a deeper psychological investigation of the negotiation process. It is relatively simple, but at the same time, it is particularly comprehensive and explanatory of the whole complexity and dynamics of interpersonal relationships.

3.17 Affective Neuroscience

In recent years, a relatively neglected aspect of decision making and judgement has secured greater interest among scholars and researchers: the affective neuroscience of our mental life. Liotti's work has also been supported by other research on neurobiology and emotion and Jaak Panksepp (1998, 2001, 2003), a neuropsychologist and neurobiologist, is among a handful of active investigators who are working on the neurobiological nature of emotional processes. His empirical and theoretical work during the past decade has directly touched most of the known brain systems that elaborate the basic emotions.

Panksepp argues that emotional systems in humans, as well as in other animals, are necessarily combinations of innate and learned tendencies; there are no routine and credible ways to really separate the influences of nature and nurture in the control of behaviour. His present research is devoted

[11] The rules and the functions of the five principal Interpersonal Motivational Social Systems (attachment, caregiving, competition for rank, sexuality, and peer cooperation) are explained in detail at the end of this chapter in the Practical Guide section.

to the analysis of the neuroanatomical and neurochemical mechanisms of emotional behaviours in the emerging field of affective neuroscience with a focus on understanding how separation responses, social bonding, social play, fear, and anticipatory processes are organized in the brain. In our opinion, together with Damasio and Liotti, he is leading the field in understanding the neurobiology of emotions. This research is extremely important in defining patterns for becoming accustomed to physiological effects of emotions that for definition are triggered quickly and do not last a long time (without our being aware of such process). This finding will improve sharply the understanding and development of emotional competence.

3.18 Concluding Remarks

The insights of affective neuroscience and psychological researchers over the past two decades have provided a new understanding of the role that emotional associations play in decision making and judgement. Although the theories of Damasio, Panksepp, Liotti, and cognitive psychologists and psychotherapists may differ in some of their details, they share the overriding assertion that emotional influences play an important role in the decision-making process. However, it is important to remember that despite these generalisations on decision-making processes and their help for further investigations in the realm of international negotiation, negotiation strategies must be tailored for specific cases to fit both the situation and the participants.

3.19 Practical Guide: Interpersonal Motivational Systems and their Application in the Negotiation Context

Although it could appear relatively simple to learn the existence of automatic thoughts, cognitive distortions, dysfunctional ideas, beliefs, pathogenic beliefs, and negative interpersonal cycles, it appears, instead, particularly difficult to identify them inside oneself, and to radically modify "bad habits" of thought and of relation. It is necessary a discrete training because, in reality, there is no isomorphism between words and convictions. In other words, a person for instance, may "believe" she does not have cognitive distortions simply because she does not recognize their presence inside herself (even if she could "agree" on the fact that they, in the absolute, represent an obstacle and a problem).

This difference among the "real" characteristics of the people and the awareness of their own processes represents the main motivation for the necessity of having specific training provided for specially prepared exercises. This training should be wide and should be necessarily carried out in a group so far that from the interactive experience it is possible to identify one's own mistakes and one's own unawareness.

In this sector, the conceptualization of interpersonal motivational systems, mentioned in this chapter appears particularly remarkable and it is necessary to deepen for the important implications that could derive in the negotiation processes, referring us to the most complete actual redefinition available in the literature (Liotti, 2001, 2005b). Interpersonal motivational systems are a complex of innate psychobiological rules, largely modifiable by experience, that push human beings to interact among themselves, and they derive from the ethological-evolutionist research applied to psychotherapy (Bowlby, 1969; Eibl-Eiblesfeldt, 1984; Gilbert, 1989; Liotti, 1992, 2001; Aquilar, 2006a,b). For the scientific and clinical tests proving the utility of this model, we refer to the above-mentioned references. What is important to note here, is that it is as if inside each of us there were continually present innate thrusts/pushes toward social interactions that have a well-defined structure. The following are the interpersonal motivational systems.

1. *Attachment System*: Desire for proximity, contact, closeness with request (implicit or explicit) for help toward who appears stronger or wiser. This system is active from birth, toward one's mother (or who replaces her), that becomes one's "attachment figure," and it takes its name from the fact that the attachment behaviours implicate "to grab/cling on." This system appears hierarchically superior to the others, and its regulation or deregulation strongly influences all the other systems. The implicit rule could be summarised as (Liotti, 1994, 2001, 2005b): "If you have difficulties, approach who appears to you stronger and wiser, and ask for help."
2. *Caregiving System*: This is the mutual one of attachment; it is the desire to give or to offer proximity, contact, closeness, help to whom appears weaker, a younger child in need, especially if it is a biological descendant (children, nephews) or to the figures easily assimilated to them (students, "spiritual children,"); the implicit rule could be summarised thus: "If someone asks you for help, give it to him; and give it to him with particular attention if it is a young child of your descent, or of your group."
3. *Procreative Sexuality System*: This is the system that deals in order to favour the generation of new "human pets," and it expresses the desire to select, to see, and to maintain contacts with a suitable and adequate partner of the other sex for recreational exchanges (i.e., to game-pleasure), relational exchanges (i.e., specifically tied up to "that" person, considered as preferred in that period), and procreative exchanges (i.e., tied not only to the conception and bringing up of children, but also to any construction of common elements: a home, a book, or a working activity; Aquilar, 2006a).
4. *Competition System*: This is the desire to fight for access to limited resources, in order to define rank in the group and/or in society, the desire for certain rules in order to put "the right person to the right place," with the purpose of receiving an advantage for oneself and for the whole group of affiliation or of reference as well.
5. *Peer Cooperation*: This is the desire to put aside, temporarily, differences of rank in order to unite efforts among more persons and then together to reach a common objective/goal (which would have been unattainable if one were alone).

It is clear how the presence of these interpersonal motivational systems could represent a useful code of interpretation of human social behaviours, and how in applying this conceptualisation to human behaviours, it is possible to decode some apparently incomprehensible modalities, especially compared to the interaction between competition and peer cooperation which is a determinant in the conflicts between people and nations, and in the search for negotiated solutions to the problems.

It is possible to analyse any behavioural sequence of human interaction in the light of the activation (or deactivation) of one or more of the interpersonal motivational systems, and in this way it is possible to understand (and also to a certain extent to foresee) the powerful emotions that are "hooked" both to the obstacles that the activation of the systems may find, and to the positive fulfilment of the objectives of each of them.

We provide an example that will facilitate a better, however initial, understanding of things mentioned above. We can examine an important behavioural and emotional momentum, using an emotive-motivational analysis grid, starting from a recognized emotion.

A negotiator recognizes internally a powerful emotion of rage and tends to connect it with an aggressive or disdainful attitude of the adversary negotiator. The sequence object of investigation can be inserted in a grid such as that shown in Table 3.1.

The hypothetical negotiator of the above-mentioned example does not succeed in conceiving alternatives to the idea that has come to his mind, that is, to propose a temporary break, and he has immediately conceived the situation as a shift/move from the peer cooperation to the competition attitude. Probably, he did not consider carefully that the threat of abandonment/giving up belongs to the interpersonal motivational system of the attachment, and that it may have aroused in him these reactions of "abandoning" the game. Such reactions could be tied up to the childlike attachment or to the romantic adult

TABLE 3.1. The sequence object of investigation

Emotions	Environment	Situation	Thoughts	Actions	Systems	Alternative
Surprise/anger [subjective intensity of the emotion (1–10)]: Surprise: 4 Anger: 8	Comforting hotel, uncomfortable armchairs, annoying lights, late afternoon	The adversary negotiator is accusing me of disloyalty and is threatening to abandon the table.	You want to abandon the negotiation table to have much more at stake. Now I will show you who I am!	I propose a break to think about it before interrupting the negotiation.	An abrupt shift from the cooperative system to the agonistic-competitive	???

attachment, of exaggerated rage, and of "ancient" protestation that prevent him from having access to alternatives or to negotiate possible solutions.

He is highly confused by the rage, and have been accustomed "to control" his emotions (but without understanding them deeply), he tries to save the negotiation by taking time and asking for a timeout. A more careful analysis of the motivational systems could increase the negotiated creativeness, especially if the negotiator of the above-mentioned example had been able to decode the real emotions of the interlocutor, not only and just his intentions.

4
Emotional Competence in International Negotiation and Mediation Practice

4.1 Introduction

Cognition and emotion have a great deal in common and yet they serve complementary roles; both make use of information from the environment to guide action, and both are processes that may operate unconsciously (Planalp & Fitness, 1999). Essentially, cognition and emotion provide information about the environment, and about the self in interaction with the environment (Aquilar, 2000; Safran & Segal, 1990). Thinking is understood to be an embodied process: we know things not just through our heads, but also through our actions, and our bodily felt experience (Damasio, 1994). Thinking, feeling, and acting are interdependent aspects of the same process (Safran 2002).

Unfortunately, the belief that emotion is a weakness still gives rise to the common attitude that people at the negotiation table must keep a "poker face." On the contrary, we think that emotions are a compass that the negotiator has at his disposal for being able to manouevre in the complex labyrinth of the interpersonal relational world. Emotions typically arise because of the evaluations of events in relation to a person's individual concer ns and expectations and emotional negative arousal could cause conflicts to escalate and negotiations to break down.

We can better understand how to solve conflicts if we first of all understand our emotions, what we feel, because if one does not have the possibility of feeling what's going on in his body, he has no possibility of being concerned with others. The emotional process may be considered as a predisposition to action: the emotion if recognized brings with it the awareness of being a protagonist of our own actions (Safran & Muran, 2000). For example, a negative emotional reaction could be provoked if one of the actors participating in the negotiation process is angry, but he pretends (most of all with himself) that he is not angry at all. Similarly, the negotiator that adopts a strategy of hiding emotions may contribute to a deterioration of the relationship during the negotiation process, provoking an ambigons interaction with the counterpart.

Cognitive psychology and psychotherapy-focused techniques could help find several tools for a better understanding of psychological interdependent dynamics within the realm of international negotiation and for a far more cooperative way to try to resolve common shared problems. Certainly, we cannot eliminate the entire spectrum of arbitrary conclusions or stereotypical interpretations, but we could work at the modification of dysfunctional attitudes and thoughts helping to improve cognitive processes. Negotiators could be trained to improve their awareness of the psychological intrapersonal and interpersonal dynamics, so as to acquire the ability to recognize both their cognitive distortions and dysfunctional beliefs and those of the counterpart. They should be ready for the interaction and for answering positively to changes that could appear during the negotiation process: it is essential to be awake and not to sleep during the negotiation process.

Awareness and mastery of the story of the negotiation process as a whole are really important. The negotiator will then learn how to recognise and modulate emotions which have been generated and acquire meaning because of the interpersonal process that binds negotiators together. Being conscious of emotions offers flexibility of responses based on the particular history of one's interactions with the environment (Damasio, 1994).

4.2 Emotional Experience

There is an interdependent influence between emotional experience and social experience. In this book emotion is meant as being from a social functional perspective, as a management tool in conflicting situations in order to better coordinate interactions between actors trying to resolve interpersonal relationship problems, especially in the negotiation context. Emotions are evolutionary processes found and regulated or organised by cognitive and metacognitive processes and affect the way we think and behave in a variety of personal and social contexts (Aquilar, 2000, 2006a; Liotti, 1994).

Recent studies have investigated the social functions of emotions, arguing that emotions enable individuals to respond adaptively to the problems and opportunities that define human social living in regulating interpersonal relational problems (Aquilar, 2000, 2006b; Damasio, 1994; Haselton & Ketelaar, 2005; Liotti, 2001, 2007; Morris & Keltner, 2000; Panksepp, 1998; Saarni, 1988, 1999; Safran & Segal, 1990). Damasio (1994, 2003), Liotti (1994, 2001, 2005b), and Panksepp (1998, 2001, 2003) have demonstrated that we cannot escape from emotional experience. Emotions have been shown to provide the very first evaluation of events (Frijda, 1986, 2004; Zajonc, 1980) in terms of how they affect humans' well-being. In other words, emotions are information that signals, in the moment of voluntary choice, in which tendency direction to act within the relationship (i.e., automatically on course) in oneself and the other one (Frijda, 1987; Liotti, 1994, 2001). The best method is trying to work with emotions, integrating these experiences with the already structured general awareness and knowledge owned by human beings.

4.3 Emotional Communication

Emotional competence could be satisfied in mastering emotional communication in conflict interaction, because emotions typically arise in the evaluations of events in relation to a person's individual concerns and expectations (Greenberg, 2002; Safran, 2002). Very often in an international negotiation context negative emotions arise from interpretation of the counterpart's actions rather than from an objective appraisal of their actions. Then in this case the conflict may be created either from a lack of knowledge, or wrong assessment of the actions of the other side (that usually is another nation with different traditions, culture, history, etc.; Kremenyuk, 2002b).

There is general agreement among researchers and clinicians that people may be communicating emotions to other people without being fully aware that they are doing so. Empirical evidence (Argyle, 1994; Ekman, 2003; Ekman & Rosenberg, 2005; Russell & Fernàndez-Dols, 2002) shows how different emotions are linked to different expressive-motor behaviour, and how they may be spread through nonverbal communication cues without awareness, playing an important role in interpersonal communication. Even if people are consciously listening to your verbal communication, they will subconsciously react to your body signals. Thus, for example, a feeling of hostility evoked by the counterpart during the negotiation process may be based upon multiple cues that are unconsciously perceived, such as tone of voice, gestures, quality of eye contact, and posture.

We do not communicate with all people in the same way. The nature and quality of the relationship represents the framework within which to modulate our communication. As accurately observed by Saarni (1999), from an emotional competence perspective, self-efficacy would be satisfied if one were aware of his way of communicating his feelings to others and contemporary if one were aware that the emotional communication is a mutual process in which actors on the stage influence each other according to the nature of the relationship. Our emotional communication style has a high degree of expectedness depending upon the quality of the relationship and the consistencies appear to be related to our goals in relational transactions (Saarni, 1997).

In order to accomplish some social goals people try to master, modulate, disguise, or hide their feelings for different reasons. Many manoeuvres aim at being socially and professionally accepted: how to be accepted, how to persuade others, how to communicate, how to protect oneself, how to save face, how to project oneself favourably, how to restore interpersonal balance when someone loses face, how to face a stalemate or a breakdown in the negotiation process, and so forth (Saarni, 1988, 1999).

But even deeper, emotional control or lack of it is influenced by culture (Argyle, 1994; Ekman, 1993, 2003; Morris & Keltner, 2000). There are some cultures that are more expressive and others that teach people to hide their emotions. In addition, conflict may result from using your cultural display rules appropriately according to your habitual environment, but having them offend someone from a different culture (Argyle, 1994). In these cases, emotional expression could provoke conflicts instead of resolving them. Moreover, we have cases where a conflict may get worse because of the inability to encode emotional expression. For example, we want to communicate sadness and think we are communicating sadness, but our encoding skills make us seem disgusted instead.

On the other hand, we have cases where the conflict could escalate because a negotiator does not have the right ability to decode emotional expression. For example, you may think you are accurately reading the nonverbal cues of your counterpart in the negotiation process, but actually, you are unable to see them or accurately interpret them, especially if she is experiencing different emotions at the same time. Accordingly, your emotions and actions will follow your interpretations of the situation.

4.4 Addressing Emotion in a Negotiation Context

Over the past two and more decades it has been surprising how relatively little attention has been paid by theoreticians, researchers, and practitioners to psychological elements and in particular to emotions in the international relations field and especially in the international negotiation field. In a famous (Raiffa, 1982) list of characteristics[1] a good negotiator should possess in order to be effective in the international arena, is number 13 (out of 34), "self control, especially of emotions and their visibility" (p. 120). In fact, it seems recommended to negotiators not to display emotions at the negotiation table. However, we see, for example, in this list, number 29, the "skill in communicating by signs, gestures, and silence (non-verbal language)" (p. 121). Taken together the prescriptive maxims regarding the role of emotion in negotiation derived from this approach are often contradictory and confusing (see also Thompson et al., 2001).

Parts of recent studies on negotiation practice have dealt with emotion (Adler, Rosen, & Silverstein, 1998; Bazerman, Curhan, Moore, & Valley, 2000; Bosman, Sonnemans, & Zeelenberg, 2001; Forgas, 1998; Galluccio, 2003, 2004, 2005b; Isen, 1987, 2004; Jones & Bodtker, 2001; Morris & Keltner, 2000; Van Kleef, De Dreu, & Manstead, 2002, 2004; Thompson et al., 2001). But to be sincere, some of these authors have been focusing on and discussing selected important emotions such as anger, fear, and happiness (see especially Adler, Rosen, & Silverstein, 1998; Bosman, Sonnemans, & Zeelenberg, 2001; Van Kleef, De Dreu, & Manstead, 2002, 2004). Also Forgas (1998) and Isen (1987, 2004) have been giving importance to positive affects as well.

The core of this work has been focusing on the impact of such emotions on conflict escalation and later on in the negotiation process. In practice, it has

[1] Raiffa (1982: 122) defined this list "thought-provoking and valuable."

been extrapolated, thanks to very useful, serious, and admirable work, from a series of negative and positive emotions in laboratory experiments that have left the reader with "cognition of cause," with an emotion of dissatisfaction at the end of the lecture. Moreover, this literature usually after having shared with lectors the correct perception of the importance of rage, fear, embarrassment, and contempt (see also Morris & Keltner, 2000) in the negotiation process, and warmly having recommended paying attention to them, fails to really address causes and implemented awareness of the interdependence among cognition, emotion, and behaviours, and most of all, fails to advise on sustainable training opportunities to "really and deeply" face and master these emotional states.

However, we have seen in the previous chapter that recent and very interesting studies and research refer to the observation that when people interact, each person tends in nature to synchronise her behaviour in accordance with the behavioural and emotional states of the other person because of inner interpersonal motivational systems. Thompson et al. (2001) have interestingly remarked especially for the negotiation context that when people interact, each person seems to synchronise his behaviour in accordance with the behavioural and emotional states of the other person.

Social relations are favoured by this natural biological process called *entrainment* (Kelly, 1988). In time, people develop an interpersonal rhythm that reflects a shared emotional and behavioural state. A negotiator who is deliberately focused on repressing emotions may interfere with this process and prevent negotiators from developing a naturally synchronized pattern of interacting. Specifically, the negotiator who deliberately adopts the poker-face strategy may contribute to a more "stilted and awkward interaction" (Thompson et al., 2001).

Other studies and research support the intuition that negative emotion may have a detrimental impact on negotiation (Adler, Rosen, & Silverstein, 1998; Bosman, Sonnemans, & Zeelenberg, 2001; Van Kleef, De Dreu, & Manstead, 2002, 2004). However, negotiators who show blatant negative emotion (e.g., anger, rage, indignation, impatience) can be extremely effective at the bargaining table (Morris & Keltner, 2000; Thompson et al., 2001). This could be due to the fact that an emotional outburst within the negotiation process convinces the counterpart that the opposite negotiator could be willing to take great risks that would hurt both parties if they do not get what they want. Instead, negotiators in positive moods seem to plan to use more cooperative strategies, to engage in more information exchange, to propose more alternatives, and are less likely to engage in contentious tactics.

Regarding positive emotions and information processing, Forgas (1998) and Isen (1987, 2004) have elaborated a theoretical perspective based on empirical data in which it has been remarked that effective negotiation requires creative information processing and it is positive, rather than negative emotions, that instigate such cognitive processing. However, it could be true that positive moods could induce more heuristic, as opposed to thoughtful, information processing but sometimes it would not be the same as cognitive bias.

Instead, studies that emphasize domain-specific influences of emotion quickly lead to the realization that not all negative emotions have the same effects on decision making (Aquilar, 2000; Fessler, Pillsworth, & Flamson, 2004; Haselton & Ketelaar, 2005; Liotti, 1994, 2001; Panksepp, 1998). For example, Fessler and colleagues (2004) proposed that although anger and disgust are similar in valence (both negative) they will have distinct effects on behaviour. Anger is a response to experiencing a transgression and attempting to deter it through action against the source. Disgust, in contrast, is a response to a potential contaminant and it motivates distancing from the source. It follows that these two negative emotions should have very different effects on risk taking: anger should increase it and disgust should decrease it (Fessler, Pillsworth, & Flamson, 2004; Haselton & Ketelaar, 2005).

Liotti's interpersonal motivational systems theoretical model helps us to see how an emotion of anger could be different in valence depending upon a particular activated system. Better knowledge of interpersonal motivational system activation and related emotion eliciting could be of great importance for better understanding emotion-eliciting in the realm of international negotiation. Moreover, it teaches us that even negative emotions if correctly identified, recognised, and modulated could help to manage delicate situations: negative emotions are important as well and one should not be afraid of them. To summarise, the rich variety of functions precludes any easy generalisation about emotion's role in negotiations. Those who would "eliminate" emotions in negotiation wrongly focus only on the negative aspects, missing the critical nature of emotion; after all, emotions are what give sense to principles, values, and goals that negotiators bring to the table (see also Jones & Bodtker, 2001).

4.5 Emotional Communication in Action During International Negotiation

When engaged in a conflict people interpret the sequences of communication in personal ways. In international negotiation, as in other interpersonal contexts, each party parses or "punctuates" the conflict situation differently (Jonsson, 2002). That is, each party sees its own negative behaviour as a defensive reaction to the unprovoked negative behaviour of the other side, and simultaneously perceives the other party as an aggressor (Beck, 2004; Ellis, 2002; Kissinger, 1979). Negative conflict spirals could be the cause of war and continuing conflict between nations, but at the root of all conflicts there are emotions that could guide the behaviours of actors in certain directions instead of others (Aquilar, 1994; Beck, 1999; Deutsch, 2002; Ellis, 1992; Marcus, 2003). Consequentially, we could say that emotions are inherent to all negotiation and mediation contexts. Hence the identification, expression, and modulation of emotions could be of high importance to the negotiators and mediators.

The insight offered in this book about emotion and negotiation practice transcends the strict difference between negative and positive emotions and a certain discrimination against negative emotions. Emotion is a management tool in conflicting situations serving social function's improvement. Then too, negative emotions (i.e., fear, anger, sadness, disgust) if correctly identified, expressed, and modulated may help to bring peace into the negotiating room that can also last outside the room. Negative emotions are important because they signal that something in someone has been touched. If we feel anger, for example, it could be because we may have perceived a violation of something to which we attach a certain importance, or because we perceive that the counterpart's words or behaviour are disrespectful. Moreover, someone can show anger, but in fact he is afraid of losing face and is feeling shame and sadness as well. Fear could be a manifestation of an inner insecurity about the ability to carry on a positive negotiation outcome or it could be an incorrect monitoring of the negotiating situation (actors, environment, etc.), or it could be simply a lack of self-efficacy (see also O'Connor & Arnold, 2003).

When one's self-perception of one's own abilities to perform positively and achieve a good result is scarce, a feeling of being inadequate can "envelop" the actor[2] (Bandura, 1995). The same examples are valid for the counterpart's emotional state interpretations; and once again the ability to be "connected" with the counterpart could help us to find the right path in this subtle web of intrapersonal and interpersonal dimensions of the negotiation process.

Emotional experience is fundamentally moral (Saarni, 1999). Values affect how we experience emotions and our emotions reveal what we value (Manstead, 1991). Our beliefs of right and wrong, good and bad, appropriate and inappropriate, determine our emotional response to the events (Beck, 1999). Impasses or delicate difficult situations in international negotiation processes are simply due to the fascinating and complicated mix of interdependence of negotiating issues and of interpersonal dimension of the negotiation relational context. The negotiator/mediator can better appreciate the possibilities of resolution and how those possibilities need to be framed to the parties to increase the potential for acceptance by understanding his own emotions and the emotional response of the counterpart/disputant as an indication of the importance attached to issues and options (Jones & Bodtker, 2001).

Most significantly, emotional competence, the capacity to articulate and manage the emotion-related abilities an individual needs to deal with relational problems raised in a variable and challenging social environment (Saarni, 1997), can serve as a compass for negotiators and mediators to find an orientation into the ideology and morality of the counterparts. For example, in insisting strongly to walk on a demanding path for concessions at the wrong moment, when our

---

[2] Incomprehensibly, this feeling has not been mentioned in different studies on emotion and negotiation. We think that the emotion of inadequacy felt by an actor is one of the most dangerous ones for the negotiation context and it should be attentively handled with care and emotional competence.

counterpart is facing and experiencing delicate emotions, not only do we show an emotional incompetence, but we risk actively participating in the negotiation breakdown. Awareness of emotional communication should be one of the core features of training programs for negotiators and mediators because any particular negotiating transaction can prepare a script for the emotional communication and the consequent counterpart's responses to it.

4.6 Emotional Competence

The experience of emotion always takes place in an intersubjective context, such as a psychological field made by the experience of interpersonal and interacting worlds of at least two people (Stolorow & Atwood, 1992). Emotional experience and social experience are reciprocally influential. Thus, our relationships and emotions reciprocally influence each other's (Aquilar, 2006a,b; Liotti, 1994, 2001; Saarni, 1993). Saarni eloquently situates emotional competence in its wider social, cultural, and moral context; consistently focussing on emotions in social contexts and with regard to the individual's self-efficacy[3] and moral sense: without a sense of what is the right thing to do relative to our subculture, we lose direction. Fortunately, culture provides us with a way, namely, values. They are an indispensable part of what gives meaning to emotional experience, and they drive what become the goals of motivated behaviour. The common thread provided by culture allows us to find consensual meaning with others in emotional experience.

Drawing on the latest research and an abundance of case material Saarni (1999) explores the range of skills that lead to emotional competence:

Skill 1: Awareness of one's own emotions

Skill 2: The ability to discern and understand other's emotions

Skill 3: The ability to use vocabulary of emotion and expression

Skill 4: The capacity for empathic involvement

Skill 5: The ability to differentiate internal subjective emotional experience from external emotional expression

Skill 6: The capacity for adaptive coping with aversive emotions and distressing circumstances

Skill 7: Awareness of emotional communication within relationships

Skill 8: The capacity for emotional self-efficacy

[3] Self-efficacy is the psychological concept that refers to a sense of accomplishment and considers how people can respond emotionally and strategically apply their knowledge about emotions and their emotional expressiveness to negotiate their way through interpersonal exchanges (Saarni, 1999; see also Bandura, 1995).

In terms of emotional competence, empathic responsiveness is one of the most significant components for promoting social bonds among people and fostering prosocial behaviour. Empathy is critical in the process of distancing from personal egocentric preconceived plans; caring about the person or group in pain (about negotiation and violent conflict) involves a willingness to detach from one's own program, agenda, or policy (Beck, 1999).

However, we think that Saarni's theory of emotional competence does not take into due account the physiological aspects of emotion; rather, it focuses on the nurturing of the above-mentioned skills. Our understanding of these aspects is best integrated by Liotti's theory and research on interpersonal motivational systems and metarepresentation function monitoring (see Chapter 6).

4.7 Concluding Remarks

It goes without saying that our coverage of cognition and emotion in international negotiation has been selective and understandably not exhaustive. Additionally, our aim has been that of providing an overview of a cognitive-motivational model for negotiator and mediator training. It will be interesting to see how better understanding of the interworkings of cognitive psychology and cognitive psychotherapy can equip the international negotiator with tools to reach a more balanced outcome notwithstanding the varying perceptions and metarepresentations pre-existing in those seated at negotiating tables.

The ideas and theories developed by the above-mentioned eminent psychologists, psychotherapists, and neuroscientists have demonstrated their empirical efficacy within the areas of cognitive psychology and psychotherapy and neuroscience. We believe that the cognitive-motivational model we set up could be applied with some benefit to the realm of international negotiation. This cognitive-motivational model could help to find several tools to open the door to a deeper understanding of psychological interdependent dynamics within the realm of international negotiation and for a far more cooperative way to try to resolve common shared problems.

Many factors influence personal decision making and it seems that satisfaction with personal decisions improves if people are aware of more of these factors before they make the decision. The problem of controversies, prejudice, conflicts, and misunderstandings seems not only to be the inability to understand other people, but also the habit of considering only one side of things. If more people could at least consider the possibility of seeing things differently, communication between people would probably improve considerably, both on the level of intimate relationships and on the more global level in conflicts and wars. If we cannot agree with each other, at least we can respect each other's different perspectives and agree to disagree. It would be of utmost importance bearing in mind that all the actors in the negotiation process are interpersonally linked and play an active role in shaping relationships. Believing the negotiation working relationships improve without individual effort is mere wishful thinking. Believing that relationships can exclusively deteriorate because of the counterpart is a demonstration of emotional incompetence.

Emotional competence provides the social ability to understand and manage people (ourselves and our counterparts) in order to try to display intrapersonal and interpersonal intelligence in human relationships in developing rapport with the counterpart. It could be a powerful tool to boost the development, preservation, and enhancement of relationships of understanding, empathy, and trust within the negotiation process. Emotional competence can be used as a compass at the negotiator's disposal for being able to work through the complex labyrinth of the intrapersonal and interpersonal relational world.

4.8 Practical Guide: The Metarepresentational Functions and their Application to the International Negotiation

The metarepresentational functions introduced in this chapter, as well as the interpersonal motivational systems delineated in the previous chapter, may develop a determinant role in widening the understanding and relational abilities of individuals, in helping to reduce the risks of negotiation failure due to the psychological characteristics of the implicated subjects, rather than to "unsolvable" political or economic problems.

In Table 4.1 we reiterate the emotive-motivational analysis grid of the example introduced in the previous chapter.

Remember that the column of alternatives appeared dramatically empty. It was probably due to a metacognitive deficit of the negotiator's representation taken into our example. The represented negotiator having been, however, good enough to fulfil the emotions column, had probably neglected the fact that he was dealing with a sequence that also concerned the interpersonal

TABLE 4.1. Restoration of the emotive-motivational analysis grid

Emotions	Environment	Situation	Thoughts	Actions	Systems	Alternative
Surprise/anger [subjective intensity of the emotion (1–10)]: Surprise: 4 Anger: 8	Comforting hotel, uncomfortable armchairs, annoying lights, late afternoon	The adversary negotiator is accusing me of disloyalty and is threatening to abandon the table.	You want to abandon the negotiation table to have much more at stake. Now I will show you who I am!	I propose a break to think about it before interrupting the negotiation.	An abrupt shift from the cooperative system to the agonistic-competitive	???

TABLE 4.2. A first grid of metacognitive analysis (the questions)

Identification	Decentring	Differentiation	Integration	Mastery
Quality of my rage: does it come from competition or from threat of abandonment?	How would the sequence appear if it were seen by an observer *super partes*? Which other elements couldhave influenced the manoeuvre of the interlocutor?	How different is this situation from analogous situations that happened in the past?	Which other aspects of the interlocutor's personality may I consider in order to formulate a counterproposal?	How could I find a way not to show my excessive surprise and excessive anger? How could I do to neutralize the threatening manoeuvre? How could I provoke positive emotions in the interlocutor that may improve the dialogue? Do I use caregiving? Do I use competition? Or rather do I bring the discussion back to peer cooperation from which we started and for which we are here?
Which emotion/s has my interlocutor been feeling?	Which of my behaviours or my proposals could have aroused negative emotions?	How much is my interlocutor able to differentiate the negotiation situation from his or her possibly destructive habits? How much is he or she is obeying orders independent of his or her will?		

motivational system of attachment, and he had not distinguished between the anger belonging to the attachment system and that belonging to the agonistic-competitive system (this difference appears meaningful to the reader when he or she receives further information on the different emotional forms compared to the activated systems, and which for now we skip for brevity).

We imagine now that the negotiator of the example is trained in such a way as to analyse the sequence also using the metarepresentational functions. A first grid of metacognitive analysis (the questions) could be derived as shown in Table 4.2.

Moreover, it would be hypothetically possible to give more training to the negotiator in the example in such a way for him to be able to compile a second grid of metacognitive analysis (the answers), that would allow a greater mastery of the negotiating behaviour, and that could help the negotiator in the creative creation of behavioural alternatives.

What has been brought to your attention here represents only an example of what is possible in allowing the development of emotional competence through cognitive, emotional, motivational, and metacognitive methods that could be concretely developed in a training program.

It is unavoidable, in an inexperienced cognitive area-trained reader, that there may be a certain sense of discouragement and incomplete understanding of the information we have been giving up to now. This is not due to a cognitive or a metacognitive deficit of the reader, but rather to a precise manoeuvre of teaching operationally by showing rather than describing. Through small and incomplete examples we have been trying to imagine a possible training project by showing excerpts of the material, aware that we have not furnished all the necessary information for understanding the sense of the proposed techniques.

In doing that we have been trying to propose a situation analogous to that of the negotiation: the negotiator often misses precise information on the "real" objectives of the interlocutor. However much the negotiation apparently has rules, objectives, and precise modalities, in reality it is never this way. And as every surprise in the negotiation context cannot be directly managed by the negotiator (who has to consult her government before taking any decision), the direct relational aspect beforehand asks for a notable ability of improvisation (apart from a remarkable interpersonal creativity). Also these last two abilities, improvisation and interpersonal creativity, could be improved by well-structured training. This volume tries to represent one practical guide even in this field: to lead the reader to directly undertake tasks and assignments that he is studying, and finding himself in the "uncertain" situations that the negotiators are used to facing. Such uncertainty (requiring cognitive, behavioural, and metacognitive abilities to be tolerated and well managed) is also proposed in the fragmentary modality of the transfer of information presented in this book.

5 Addressing Cognition and Emotion in Negotiation and Co-Mediation Practice: A Research Project

5.1 Introduction

This chapter provides a small picture of the European Commission (EC) of the European Union (EU) negotiation and co-mediation thinking and initiative in the specific field represented by European Union external relations. We focus our attention on the EC and African, Caribbean, and Pacific countries' (ACP) relationship and the related daily negotiating and co-mediation processes. Our aim is primarily to try to understand a little bit more European civil servant and diplomat thinking in its evolution, in order to provide a benchmark for future comparison and discussion. This is just the first step of the research. We used the tool of interviews with distinguished EC civil servants (international officials).

5.2 Improving a Working Relationship

Effective negotiators on both sides of the table should have a dual role as partisan advocate and as co-mediator.[1] In our view a good negotiator should mediate his own disputes (see also Fisher, Kopelman, & Schneider, 1994). A negotiator who is concentrated only on his own interests is a bad negotiator. The work of each negotiator, in order to produce a mutually satisfying final agreement, should be that of involving the counterpart in a joint problem-solving resolution aimed at reconciling opposite needs and interests. The ability to negotiate effectively ensures the creation and maintenance of a relationship with the counterpart.

[1] The term co-mediator is used for specific reasons. During the negotiation process the interactive process between parties and the context of internal and external negotiations does not allow two negotiators to use the tools, strategy, and techniques that a mediator could instead unfold.

A working relationship between the representatives of negotiating parties is indispensable in co-mediation. Without some level of interpersonal trust, representatives are unlikely to be able to co-operate tacitly or explicitly to manage their disputes (Watkins & Rosegrant, 2001). Personal relationships may create a higher degree of confidence and openness between negotiators, which facilitates communication between actors. This communication will help to manage uncertainty and ambiguity throughout the mastery of normal related emotions such as anxiety, fear, surprise, and frustration that may accompany, for a consistent part of the time, the negotiation process. Needless to say, communication does not bring results per se in the negotiation process, but nonetheless it helps a common search for a negotiated solution and in this case the process aimed at achieving a positive final agreement is undoubtedly facilitated.

International organisations such as the European Union, the United Nations, and the World Trade Organisation to name but a few, with a different degree of institutionalization in their integration process, play a fundamental role of utmost importance in serving as a "communication medium" to connect different national institutions through individuals that compose them. Managing positive working relationships helps to produce powerful antibodies in order to face conflictual situations and assess delicate situations in which a presence of distrust or the absence of positive emotions between parties may provoke unsustainable and harmful psychological dynamics. The realm of international negotiation is prone to unforeseen uncertain and ambiguous situations; to negotiate means also to tolerate a certain degree of ambiguity and uncertainty. The capacity to manage a series of potential (or perceived) conflicts in being concentrated on the problem and not the person that is in front of her is a major resource the negotiator has with which to preserve the working relationship.

As the former U.S. Secretary of State, James Baker, noted (in Watkins & Rosegrant, 2001):

> If honesty and trust is developed, even the most contentious talks could be brought to a successful conclusion. The negotiators feel free to set aside their formal negotiating positions and reveal their informal thinking – the assumptions, strategies, and even fear – that underlie their approach. ... But if the relationship soured – if it became infected with distrust and discord – then it mattered little how far apart the parties actually were. The perception of mistrust overwhelmed any objective reality.

However, it is indisputable that the interaction between human beings always involves the building of perceptions about others, which can influence the outcome of this interaction. In a negotiation process, depending on the degree of complexity of the negotiation, individual traits can be decisive in building favourable or unfavourable perceptions to the positive development of a relationship of trust between the involved parties. Relationship building is a main responsibility international actors are called upon to care about.

Negotiators face two kinds of pressures when they negotiate: external pressure represented by the counterpart and the internal pressure represented by their constituencies. A senior negotiator at the EC admitted: "Often when a negotiator talks he is referring to an invisible audience that is behind his shoulders. He talks to you, but it is likely talking to his constituency." A good negotiator should be aware of this dissociation and be able to detect delicate issues that if not adequately assessed could bring the negotiation process down a dangerous path. A seasoned negotiator during our research project eloquently said:

When a negotiation takes place apparently the EU representative (in this context) talks to the counterpart and we could name it *visible negotiation*. In reality, when the EU talks to, for example, an African or a Brazilian's counterpart and vice versa, talks are directed to people that are behind the negotiators (our partners and stakeholders; or our counterparts' partners and stakeholders). Rigidity could be a sign that we have a problem back home, on our behind. It is strategically important to understand that negotiators can tell many things just to make happy people *behind* them.

And another one added an interesting internal analysis of the negotiation process:

This is a problem that concerns not only the EU external negotiation processes but also the internal negotiation process. For example, during a particular negotiation on fishery an EU Member State from the South was really rigid in its positions because it needed a good result to show to people behind it in his country (trade unions, NGOs, environmental lobbies, etc.). This country had nothing against Mr. Fishler, the EU Commissioner for Agriculture and Fishery at that time, rather it had to take into account homeland groups' opinions and it was afraid of their reactions.

Moreover, an open and thoughtful contribution to this subject came from a senior adviser who said:

Negotiators and their elites should be aware that when there is a breakdown due to an excessive rigidity, it is better to come back to the negotiating table searching for a mutual satisfying compromise. At the same time, a part of the whole negotiation strategy could be enriched with new tactical talks all along the negotiation process with groups situated *behind their shoulders* aiming at persuading and making them *swallowing a pill* of a negotiated compromise. The art of negotiators is to work on different negotiating tables: domestic and external. The negotiator has never a whole mandate but in this way the mandate can be also amended without particular shocks.

Even more,

Rigidity can be harmful if it is on both sides. If one is less rigid than the other, he can try to move on; otherwise there is a breakdown. It creates resentment from the other side and reduces rooms for manoeuvres. To accept to negotiate means to reach a compromise within the negotiation process. Negotiators do not have the possibility of obtaining everything they are asking for, but accept the acceptable. Later, the negotiated result has to be presented to your partners and stakeholders that have been watching at you during all the negotiation process. Here we find another ability of the good negotiator: showing and maximizing what he has obtained in hiding and minimising what he has lost.

5.3 Social Change

Deutsch (2002:318) stated that

> Although there has been significant progress in the study of conflict, the progress does not yet begin to match the social need for understanding conflict. We live in a period of history when the pervasiveness and intensity of competitive conflict over natural resources are likely to increase markedly. And currently ethnic and national conflicts pose great danger to peace in many areas of the world. We also live in a period when hydrogen bombs and other weapons of mass destruction can destroy civilized life. The social need for better ways of managing conflict is urgent. In relation to this need, it is my view that too few of us are working on the scientific issues likely to provide the knowledge that will lead to more constructive conflict resolution of the many intensive conflicts which await us all.

Nowadays, new scholars and researchers in the negotiation realm have been paying more attention to and improving methods regarding the definite importance of psychological dynamics of the negotiation field. The field has been assuming a due dignity in the explanation of a part of the negotiation process and it could represent a powerful tool in the hands of negotiators not to win at any price, but rather to understand in a more emotionally competent manner the whole process of international negotiations. At the end of the day, we think that not all the negotiations dynamics and characteristics have been discovered yet. A great part of their inner potentials are still underestimated and uncovered. It is a task of researchers and academics in general to help negotiators to unfold these underlying qualities to improve a decision-making process sharply. All the information and new awareness of psychological dynamics – we hope – could potentially make mindful negotiators present and conscious actors, now and here, in the negotiation process.

One of the results of our project seems to have been that the mastery of the language of emotions among interviewed negotiators should be better monitored. It is interesting to know that the subjects talked a lot about emotions and in theory everything was fine. Instead, when we went a little bit deeper into details a major part of them became normally embarrassed. This normal discrepancy could probably be due (but it should be assessed through new research in the field) to a sharp reduction of their metarepresentative abilities (i.e., a knowledge or belief about one's own mental states that regulates the mental activity of the subject and that will play a major part in shaping behaviours).

Western education has overemphasised analytical skills to the detriment of practical and multiple intelligence, creativity, real problem-solving skills, and social and emotional competence skills. A remedy to this static and rigid situation could be represented by an evaluation of the real importance of nonanalytical skills. This could be obtained by organising specific and emotional competence-focused training programs in order to expand our knowledge base, our intrapersonal and interpersonal awareness skills, creativity, and emotional and social competence. We think it is essential for the organisations to develop ability tests in order to hire their personnel, that take into account the fact that there may be no single rigidly correct solution to complex real-life problems. (See also Salovey et al., 2004.)

In the end, with a serious and focused negotiation training program we could help free negotiators from mental traps and habits by giving them the possibility of thinking about their mental states (thoughts, emotions, and images) and developing their nonanalytical skills as well, in a way to give their part of an active contribution to transform the negotiation arena into a more liveable environment as a catalyst for further social behavioural changes.

5.4 The EU Negotiation Process

Our research project provides a picture of the European Commission negotiation and co-mediation thinking and initiative in the specific field represented by EU external relations. We have focussed our attention on the EC and African, Caribbean, and Pacific countries' relationships and the related daily negotiation and co-mediation processes. The 78 ACP countries and the European Union have been negotiating a special relationship and partnership for a long time. In 2000 they signed the Cotonou Partnership Agreement. The agreement represents the achievement of a comprehensive and thorough negotiation process between the ACP and EU over a number of years. Most important is that Cotonou has been just a first step because the implementation of the EU–ACP relationship and partnership is an ongoing and constant exercise which a variety of actors from both fields are aimed at strengthening. Our aim is primarily to try to understand better the European civil servants' and diplomats' thinking in its evolution, in order to provide a benchmark for future comparison and discussion. We used the tool of interviews with distinguished EC civil servants. Thus, opinions expressed are liberally quoted and lightly interpreted.

The European Union is certainly characterised by a huge and soft negotiation process based on a daily ongoing communication process nurtured by an exchange of information between main actors favouring a mutual learning attitude in order to reach satisfying compromises. We can say that the EU can help to spread this important negotiation mentality even among nonmember countries and international organisations to improve at the same time its capacity of communication toward external actors. Communication will help to bring international actors closer and could represent a catalyst for social changes because negotiating actors must refer to their hierarchy and a mutual learning attitude could spread the seed of a better understanding between international actors at the highest political level.

All human interactions, of which a negotiation working relationship is a part, may crumble under the impact of uncontrolled arousal of negative emotions (e.g., rage, fear, disgust, hate, to name but a few). When people feel hurt or threatened they may often misinterpret the counterpart's behaviour. Distortions of each other's motives and attitudes may lead negotiators to feel trapped, injured, and depreciated. These perceptions (or rather, misperceptions) may fill them with negative emotions, which if not adequately mastered may impel them to retaliate or to withdraw into hostile behaviours (Beck, 1999). Mutual empathic understanding and compassion will be a major ally in softening positions and overcoming hostility, which most often comes more from an interpretation of our counterpart's actions than from a real action undertaken by him, and implementing a co-operative attitude among the main actors. Communication can help us to improve our knowledge of the other side and to reassess the interpretation of actions accordingly.

Unfortunately, as we have seen, the dominant perspective in research papers about negotiation published in the last few years focusses its attention on the decision processes, devaluing the traits and skills of the negotiator as a determining factor in the outcome (Bazerman, Baron, & Shonk, 2000). The main objective of our research project has been that of identifying and analysing the importance attributed to some personality traits in generating a climate of confidence and establishing a negotiation working relationship. We also wanted to evaluate the impact of some specific personal characteristics (assertiveness, aggressiveness, empathy, to name but few) of our sample for the variables to be studied.

5.5 Research Aim

The research aim has been that of pointing out, through investigation of direct experiences between actors on the spot, the existence of some human personality traits and the way in which they may or may not affect the result of a negotiation. This approach is used to single out those traits a competent negotiator should improve in order to guarantee a smooth negotiation process and the achievement of a mutually satisfying negotiated outcome. It is enlightening how our research project has clearly shown a general awareness among EC civil servants (officials) that communication is of utmost importance in playing a pivotal role and helping actors to negotiate and co-mediate their own disputes. This level of importance is not just for exchanging written and oral technical information, but especially for facilitating the growth of an open attitude to know the counterpart better in understanding her needs and constraints: in short, in facilitating a mutual learning attitude. Moreover, this attitude should be kept from the birth of the negotiation process until the negotiated outcome has been reached and during the implementation stage as well. Further analysis will be useful to try to set up a special selection process in which to choose the right negotiator for the right place at the right time.

5.6 Research Methodology

International diplomacy is, of course, a constantly evolving practice, with as many variations as there are countries and diplomats involved. But there is also a rising EU culture of diplomacy, meaning an evolving set of norms and practices that are widely understood and followed across the European Union. European civil servants, while playing a large role in influencing and shaping this culture, also reflect it. We used interviews and questionnaires. Thus, interviews with EC's civil servants may provide a small window into new international negotiation thinking, in addition to revealing the thinking of the EC in an important and growing slice of the Common Foreign and Security Policy (CFSP) pie.

Interviewees were guaranteed anonymity, thus quotes in the text are given without identification. To select interviewees, we followed up our experience and knowledge of the EU institutions and advice given by scholars and practitioners of the European diplomatic environment. We interviewed 120 civil servants who are among the best- informed practitioners about the EU–ACP negotiation process. These interviews ended with a compilation of a questionnaire on psychological characteristics of a personality trait considered useful or dangerous for them within the realm of the EU–ACP international negotiations. After this first phase, in order to cover a greater range of understanding, we carefully selected 80 civil servants (from the 120) – key participants to the negotiation tables – from different EC Directorates General (DG DEV, AIDCO, ECHO, RELEX, TRADE, EC delegations)[2] dealing with the EU–ACP negotiation process (in practice all the top management involved in negotiations with ACP countries). To them we submitted a series of 19 open questions on personality traits (personal characteristics) that are safe to come out in international negotiations. We examined some cognitive, emotional, and behavioural characteristics and the way in which they could affect the negotiation process and working relationships between parties, and the consequent negotiated result, allowing or not a mutually satisfying outcome. We had frank and in-depth interviews with each of the 80 selected subjects. Each interview lasted not less than two hours. Most of the interviews were taped and transcribed. Officials were interviewed between May 2002 and November 2005.

Then, we did a univariate descriptive data analysis and a multidimensional data analysis. Concerning the latter, we underline that although the methods we have applied come from multidimensional data analysis, single techniques

---

[2] DG DEV: Directorate General for Development and Relations with African, Caribbean and Pacific States.

AIDCO: EuropeanAid Cooperation Office

ECHO: Humanitarian Aid Department

RELEX: Directorate General for External Relations

distinguish them. We have used principal components analysis for data, let's say, generally, and cluster analysis and we have used correspondence analysis (applied to lexical tables) for the analysis of open-answer questions. The analysis focussed on identifying the range, as well as the most frequent opinions, within each thematic question. Potential difficulties for collaboration between the EC and ACP were also identified throughout the interview process. We analysed and tried to interpret objectively with valuable tools coming from statistics, sociology, politics, and psychology fields.

5.7 Descriptive Analysis

5.7.1 Overview

The survey involved 120 negotiators from 15 EU countries[3] and was conducted in two steps: at the beginning a half-structured interview was done, with 19 open questions asking the interviewees their own opinion (based solely on their experience) about some personality traits/characteristics that could promote a sustainable negotiation process with mutually satisfying final outcomes or that could thwart it. Successively a table with a list of 17 personal characteristics was given to them asking them to fill it in. For each of these characteristics the interviewee had to express her or his opinion using a scale of five values, between "very useful" and "very dangerous" with an important central value represented by a "neutral" answer in order to try to avoid excessive polarisation of answers. Some social-economic-demographic (SED) variables were pointed out, such as sex, age, nationality, and kind of experience. In order to reach the fixed aims, in addition to classical descriptive techniques, we also used some factorial, classification, and textual techniques, typical of multivariate data analysis.

5.7.2 Sample of Social-Economic-Demographic Variables

From SED variables analysis the sample results were distributed as shown in Figure 5.1: 75% men and 25% women all with a certain degree of previous experience in negotiation in different fields and especially in the ACP countries field. Moreover, 42% of the sample is represented by commissioners, commissioners' political cabinet members, general directors, directors, heads of units, task managers, and desk officers that have had negotiation experiences with ACP countries and specifically with their leading figures (presidents, heads of government, and ministers). Nonetheless, the remaining part is composed of distinguished officials that have been representing an important *trait d'union* between the European Commission and the ACP institutions. They

[3] Austria, Belgium, Denmark, Finland, France, Germany, Greece, Ireland, Italy, Luxembourg, The Netherlands, Portugal, Spain, Sweden, United Kingdom.

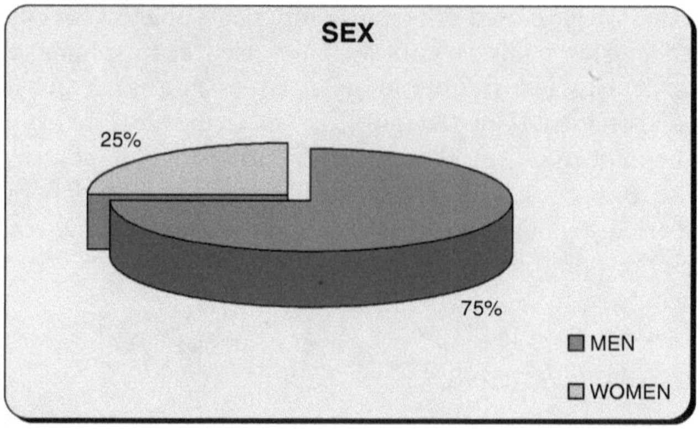

FIGURE 5.1. Sex percentage.

have been helping negotiations working relationships building, spreading the awareness of developing a huge sense of empathy, respect, and understanding through a good communication tool in the prenegotiation stages and playing the valuable role of shadow advisor in shaping relationships and mediating the emotional exchange between parties in delicate moments.

All these actors are negotiators and – sometimes unknowingly – able co-mediators of their own negotiation processes. These figures are important because they represent the channel through which the dialogue between EU and the ACP has never been really interrupted, even in difficult and tense periods. They have been helping each other (EU–ACP) to continually revise their perceptions, through a correct communication process in facilitating a mutual learning process and most of all in avoiding, or watering down, the polarisation of judgements that could cause the occurrence of negative emotions such as rage, frustration, fear, disgust, and hate with the consequential adoption of dangerous rigid positions.

Concerning nationality, we found a prevalence of Italian, Spanish, German, and Belgian nationalities, but also other EU nationalities are present as shown in Figure 5.2. Various personal psychological characteristics are shown in Figure 5.3.

Analysing the results, it could be possible to classify the examined characteristics as

- Characteristics considered negative that are able to drive the negotiation process toward an extremely dangerous path with a consequential unsatisfying final outcome, or even worse, toward a negotiation breakdown with a painful stalemate (especially for ACP countries).
- Characteristics considered extremely useful that can set the negotiation process on a good track with a consequential satisfying and mutually acceptable outcome.
- Characteristics for which a lot of neutral answers have been counted, even if the majority has given a positive or negative opinion. As we have previously said, we introduced this neutral answer into our questionnaire because we

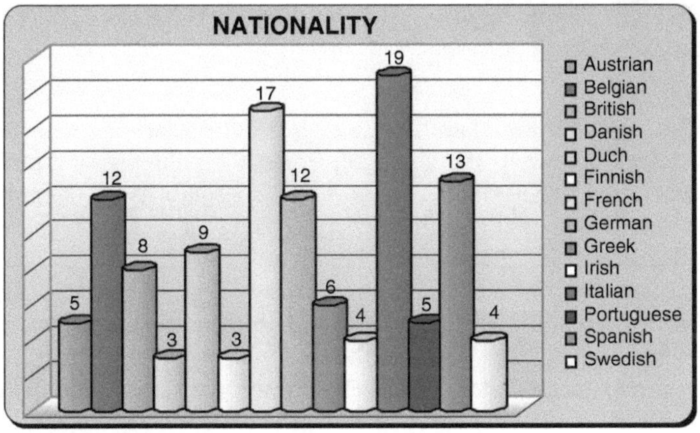

FIGURE 5.2. Nationality sample.

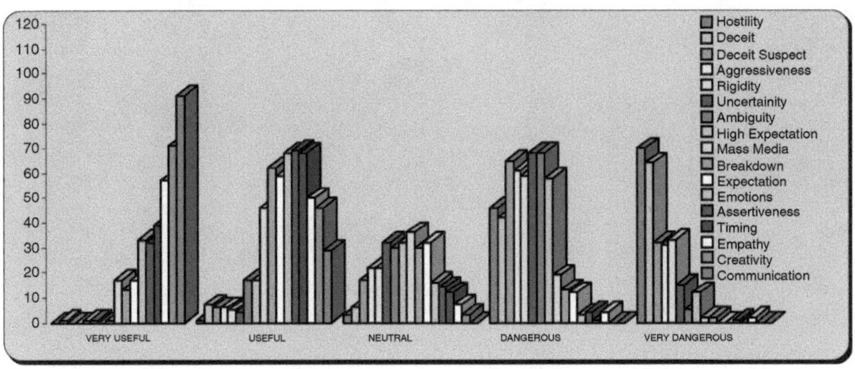

FIGURE 5.3. Psychological personal characteristics in international negotiation.

wanted to try to avoid the polarization of extreme answers. It was useful to see, for example, that a lot of those interviewed were pleased to have this option because it was like a grey colour between white and black answer options. It is also extremely interesting to know that a substantial percentage of those interviewed, sometimes choosing the neutral option, showed a tendency to mark the paper on which the questionnaire was written, in ambiguous handwriting (not in the opposite cell, but on the right of the cell, or on the left of the cell, or even stranger between lines (neutral and dangerous – neutral and useful). When the ambiguity reached the latter point the author of the research asked for a better clarification of the mark and the cell was properly filled in according to this genuine and interested request for clarification for the sake of the final result of the research.

5.8 Answer Percentage on Researched Personal Characteristics

In Table 5.1, a dangerous or useful rate is shown in shades of grey: completely negative factors belong to the dark grey zone; the lighter grey zone includes those characteristics considered dangerous by the majority of the people; and the cross-hatched zone indicates those characteristics for which a high percentage of neutral answers has been found. It includes both those characteristics considered negative but for which nonetheless a high percentage of neutral answers have been found (cross-hatch) and those characteristics considered positive by the biggest part, but nonetheless for which a lot of neutral answers have been found (cross-hatch). Furthermore the pale grey zone includes the

TABLE 5.1. Answer percentage of different characteristics.

VERY DANGEROUS	Hostility	58%
	Deceit	53%
DANGEROUS	Rigidity	49%
	Aggressiveness	51%
	Deceit Suspect	54%
NEUTRAL	High Expectation	27%
	Ambiguity	25%
	Uncertainty	27%
	Breakdown	25%
	Mass Media	30%
	Expectation	27%
USEFUL	Emotions	56%
	Assertiveness	57%
	Timing	56%
VERY USEFUL	Creativity	59%
	Empathy	47%
	Communication	76%

useful characteristics. Finally, the black zone shows very useful characteristics. The highest percentage of answers for each characteristic is also indicated.

5.9 Negative Characteristics

5.9.1 Deceit

Only one person considered Deceit very useful, 5% considered it useful, and 4% gave a neutral opinion. Then, there are those characteristics considered by the majority of the sample as negative, because they are dangerous during a negotiation process, such as: Deceit Suspect, Aggressiveness, and Rigidity. Fifty-three percent of the sample considered Deceit Suspect to be a dangerous characteristic and hence detrimental for the negotiation, 35% said that it is very dangerous, 6% considered it useful, and only 1% defined it very useful; the last 5% of the sample gave a neutral opinion. A senior negotiator admitted that lying is a part of the negotiation game:

A good negotiator is inscrutable because he may have a poker face attitude. It is important to know that the EU officials are no so much sensitive to this kind of pressures, because they follow their mandate and are in a position of strength. If the counterpart is nice they can also try to find a compromise. Otherwise, they answer rigidity with rigidity.

EC officials have a material *Best Alternative to a Negotiated Agreement* (BATNA) with them. But morally talking, it is better if they strive for helping the negotiation process with ACP.

Another top negotiator instead said an interesting thing:

In a multilateral/multicultural context it is quite difficult to detect signals of deceit. I often have had experience of people not saying lies but not saying the truth as well. This is easier detected not in the body language signs, but rather in the language used paying attention on what do they say in their expositions and compare it with future and past conversations with the same subjects. Looking at the body language could be unproductive because it depends on so many cues and upon cultures and nationalities that we can easily be misguided.

5.9.2 Rigidity

About the other two characteristics, Rigidity and Aggressiveness, half of the sample considered them dangerous. Even in this case, among the rest of the sample, only a few people gave a positive opinion. In fact most of those interviewed (26% for Aggressiveness and 28% for Rigidity) considered them very dangerous. The negativity of these personal characteristics has been found also in the first step of the research during the interviews, when the question was asked, "Personal characteristics between negotiating actors that could potentially foster negative emotions and create barriers between the persons that must negotiate;" followed by this question: "According to your own experience, what were the causes for failed or troubled negotiations when a good result could have possibly come out?"

Many people, talking about their personal experience, mentioned exactly such characteristics as Rigidity, Aggressiveness, Hostility, and Arrogance but also Deceit Suspect and hence lack of confidence to indicate causes for failed or troubled negotiations. About Rigidity, it came out in the interviews that there was agreement that it was an element that could easily bring failure to the negotiation process, but is sometimes necessary, for instance on those points that it is not at all possible to give up. The important thing is represented by mixing it with the right amount of credibility.

"Rigidity is one of the fundamental elements that could lead to a breakdown because it is an attitude capable to drive people on the path of negative emotions with a consequent loss of empathy" said a top negotiator. He continued:

> People with fixed and rigid thoughts (schemas) tend to impose their positions as the best solution ever. Such rigid attitude favours misperceptions and misinterpretations during the negotiation process with predictable negative consequences. On the other hand, it could also be an element of a planned strategy used to provoke a voluntary breakdown in order to restart later on different and more favourable negotiating basis.

It is also true that

> Rigidity goes against the essence of the negotiation process that is per se a taking and giving exercise. Everybody has a bottom line to a certain extent, it is the matter on how quickly you jump down to your bottom line and stay with it and nothing can be done; or if you negotiate skilfully sometimes a bit below your bottom line and counterparts can take it a little bit above your bottom line for their applied strategy. But one has to be flexible otherwise he should not start negotiations. Even your bottom line can usually be a little bit negotiated within certain limitations.

It was detected that rigid strategies could bring negative effects to the negotiation process because the negative aspect of excessive rigidity is represented by a not-listening attitude. The communication channel begins to be flooded and this can bring about a painful stalemate where there is no longer any negotiation. Rigidity introduces a weakness in the negotiation process by harming the working negotiators' relationship. "It is a negative element because it puts a tolerance capacity under strain. It could provoke distrust and rage with a consequent loss of self-control."

We also detected from our sample that "Rigidity may be linked to the necessity of saving face (especially for the ACP countries). A good countertactic could be that of working on the counterpart rigidity (together with her) in searching a solution that allows her to save face." The overall sample showed us that "Rigidity is counterproductive because the negotiation process is an interaction. Metaphorically talking it is a dance and dancers need to be flexible in order to have a good performance."

A substantial number of senior and junior negotiators said that "There are a lot of negotiators that have a flexible mandate but they have rigid personalities [one interviewee called them constipated negotiators] and make from a flexible mandate a rigid one." In practice, according to the interviewee sample we can draw a nonexhaustive list of negative scenarios that could be produced by this human characteristic. As matter of fact, rigidity:

- Introduces a weakness in the negotiation process
- Favours misperceptions and misinterpretations
- Drives people to the path of negative emotions
- Brings about a painful stalemate
- Provokes loss of empathy
- Is harmful if it is applied to both sides
- Reduces rooms for manoeuvres
- Puts a tolerance capacity under strain
- Creates resentments from the other side
- Generates loss of self-control

In the negotiation process it is fundamental to distinguish what is important and what is not so that you can be less rigid on what is not important to you. As Reinhold Niebuhr said: "You strive to change the things you can change, to accept (but not like) those that you cannot change, and to have the wisdom to know the difference."

5.9.3 Aggressiveness

Regarding the element of Aggressiveness, we had different opinions worthy of mention here. Someone said that "It can have an important role and that it can be useful if properly used at the right time. For example, it can be useful in order to clarify and explain one's own position, to show determination." On the other hand someone said that "Using Aggressiveness depends also on different cultures. For example, in Africa it is a sign of weakness."

Few of the interviewed senior negotiators thought that verbal aggressiveness can play a strategic role. According to them in fact,

> There is a stage into the negotiation process where aggressiveness is tactically utilised. For example, when one wants to scare the other part and use drastic language and arguments. If aggressiveness is a part of a wide strategy it could have a positive impact, while if it is a trait of a negotiator personality could have a negative impact on the negotiation process.

A very expert negotiator said: "Aggressiveness should be an iron hand in a velvet glove. The counterpart should know that there are points on which we cannot give in." In short, aggressiveness could be useful in appropriate ways and at the right time.

On the other hand, another expert negotiator firmly believes that "Aggressiveness with ACP countries could easily lead to a breakdown." One of his colleagues said, "It is one personal characteristic that in this special relationship the EU has with ACP could be very damaging to negotiations (given that our partners already feel in a weak position)." He then added: "Sometimes putting a position strongly and clearly can be perceived as aggressiveness and I think that when you step over boundaries that is the point when you do have a breakdown." Moreover, "We are dealing with a group that is already feeling under defensive, feeling in a weak position, I think any use of aggressiveness in that case leads automatically to a breakdown or to a working relationship's deterioration."

Interestingly, this negotiator was not the only one that had this opinion. Another experienced senior negotiator said: "Aggressiveness is a negative element also if it comes from the other field" (the counterpart). He gave an interesting example,

> There was a negotiation meeting in a small room with three African ministers and an EC director. The EC senior official believed in good faith (because he received information that went in this direction) that there was a consensus on a certain item into the agenda and was keen to go ahead. Instead, it was not the case and unexpectedly one of the counterparts reacted with excessive aggressiveness and the EC official counterreacted by leaving the room. After a few minutes Ministry's collaborators understanding the situation apologised with the EC official and so did the Minister and everything was resolved.

It clearly demonstrated a case of co-mediation of parties involved in the negotiating process in repairing an emotional negative outburst based on real misperception due to the lack of information.

Listening to the whole sample of interviews, it seems that, according to their experience, "A good counter strategy to combating aggressiveness is the use of the same characteristic but modulating responses insofar avoiding chain reactions." In fact, "The aggressive negotiator is a loser even if he apparently gets a favourable deal because he will risk losing the working negotiating relationship. It is better to be firm, assertive with a kind behaviour." "I have never seen a case where aggressiveness has paid on a long-term period" affirmed a leading figure in the interview process.

5.9.4 Uncertainty

Then some factors came out for which it has been found – even if the majority considered them dangerous – a rate of neutral answers much higher than very dangerous negative answers. Uncertainty was considered by 56% of the sample dangerous, but 27% considered it neutral, and 13% considered it very dangerous. These data are interesting because they show how the same factors that for somebody represent a risk, for somebody else do not represent a risk and, on the other hand, they can even be useful. Thanks to negotiators' data analysis answers there appeared to be a clear negativity of the Uncertainty characteristic, even if it is appraised by interviewees as a natural element of the negotiation process that makes the process itself interesting and stimulating. The negativity of this factor depends on the problem that actors are going to face: the more the problem is touchable and concrete, the more quickly the uncertainty will lead to failure; the more general it is, the less probability there is that the uncertainty will provoke a negotiation breakdown. However, according to a senior negotiator,

Uncertainty is an important *physiological* element of the negotiation process and it is not an element that can provoke a breakdown. Uncertainty is usually part of the negotiation process because you do not know what the counterpart wants to achieve or can accept. It is a part of the game. Without uncertainty we would not have the necessity to negotiate. It is a factor which contributes to all our negotiations with ACP and it is necessary in the negotiation process.

Moreover, another actor said:

Usually we try to reduce uncertainty during the negotiation process as best as we can. We try to define clear and assertive positions and commitments. Anyway, a certain degree of uncertainty could be useful in order to allow negotiators to achieve a positive negotiated result. If negotiators say everything since the beginning of the negotiating process we risk to loose interest in the latter and there is a risk instead to producing dysfunctional mechanisms all along the negotiation process.

However, "If uncertainty is already big at the pre-negotiation stage, it is better not to start the official negotiations." We can easily see this uncertainty within the Council of the European Union reduced by the strategic role played by the Committee of Permanent Representatives (COREPER), which is in charge of establishing time ripeness in order to feel if an item can be submitted to the Ministers.

5.9.5 *Ambiguity*

Concerning Ambiguity, all the negativity of this element came out above because during a negotiation there should be transparency and clarity. On the other hand, a not small part of the sample said that Ambiguity could be useful at the beginning of a negotiation process, in order not to show directly what we want, but at a later stage, credibility, reliance, and clearness must prevail. "Ambiguity is not capable of provoking a breakdown as an isolated characteristic. It can cause a negotiation process to lengthen and can confuse actors. Consequentially, this confusion will certainly contribute to misinterpretations and misperceptions."

Moreover, a senior negotiator admitted that "It could be harmful if it is used outside a negotiation strategy because it does mean that people are not mastering the negotiation process. A major risk could be the huge difficulties that it will create in the application and implementation of negotiated outcomes." Another senior negotiator said, "Ambiguity does not necessarily lead to a breakdown because it makes it easy to use the person's own arguments against her. It will lead to a breakdown only if this is what that person is aiming at." Figure 5.4 illustrates the sample of personal characteristics defined as negative by those interviewed.

5.10 Positive Characteristics

We then took into account those characteristics that in the interviewed opinions could be able to influence positively the negotiation process such as communication, creativity, and empathy. Communication is the factor that reached

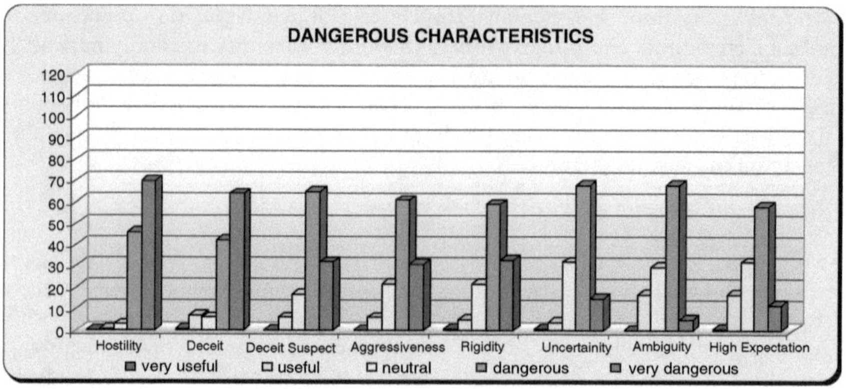

FIGURE 5.4. Negative personal characteristics.

the higher number of positive opinions; in fact 76% of the people considered it very useful, 24% useful, and nobody gave a negative opinion. About creativity and empathy, respectively 59% and 47% of the sample defined them very useful, most considered them useful, and almost nobody gave a negative opinion. Secondly, there are characteristics that are considered positive, therefore the biggest part of the sample thought they were useful. In 57% of the sample's opinions the characteristics of emotions and assertiveness could bring the negotiation to a good end, as well as the characteristic of timing, the right time to intervene in the negotiation process with proposals and good sense, and even the timing of deciding to provoke a breakdown or to retake a seat at the negotiating table after a breakdown has been produced (57% considered it useful).

5.10.1 Communication

According to the interviewees good communication is a fundamental ability to establish a link with the counterpart and create a positive environment. In accordance with some interviewees' personal experiences, "Often parties are not able to look face to face to each other and all these behaviours create barriers and nurture misperceptions and miscommunication increasing the gap between peoples." In fact,

It is also important that the physical space to communicate should be right. Well-organised rooms are needed in order to facilitate the dialogue and foster working relationships between parties as well as the creativity of subjects and that depends primarily on the ability to integrate pieces of disparate data in new ways in order to produce unusual, high quality solutions to problems.

In line with this statement a negotiator said,

The role of human communication is important. Unhopefully, rooms for negotiations are no so well organized. For example, there are rooms at the Council of Ministers' building that are too large in which negotiators are far away from each other. They cannot really look at each other, shake their hands or touch regularly, or make the table tour because the latter is so long. This represents a physical barrier that creates a distance between persons. If you want to whisper something in the ear of a negotiator you cannot do that. For that reason we must find way of communication outside these rooms: corridors, elevators, restrooms, with mobile phones, etc.

"Communication ability is a part of the negotiators' skills that should be applied since the pre-negotiation stages," said a negotiator. And one of his colleagues added, "When there are difficult negotiations a good strategy is that of looking for contacts outside the rigid framework of the negotiation. In this way we try to soften and round off too extreme positions." Another stated that "To confirm the same good communicators/negotiators for different negotiations may consolidate relationships based on trust and reciprocal respect between parties. Such negotiations could be smoother than others." Moreover, "A good communication pattern is a gain in the context of ACP countries' negotiations."

5.10.2 Empathy and Emotions

Empathy is also a fundamental element that can help overcome differences between the parties in "Obtaining reliance and mutual respect, understanding mutual limits and coming to mutually satisfying compromises." A part of the sample defined it as "One of the fundamental elements that builds up the credibility of a negotiator," because "It plays a fundamental role within the EU–ACP negotiation process, which is more a process-oriented negotiation: if we have a meeting without a final result it is still okay because at least we met." However, "Exaggerated empathy can turn into paternalism and become an obstacle towards treating the other as an equal partner."

"Empathy is a useful tool within the EU–ACP negotiation process because we need to understand their problems in order to achieve sustainable negotiated outcomes," said an experienced negotiator. Moreover, "We should always help them to save face." A top negotiator added, "Normally the richest countries feel empathy toward the poorest countries, but this determine[s] a lack of balance. The other side could feel manipulated by this feeling and could disagree with such a paternalistic attitude. This shows that empathy should be a two ways feeling to really yield smoother negotiation processes." Moreover, his colleague added an important reflection,

> Empathy plays an important role in a relation with ACP countries in managing the emotional exchange and mastering the cultural differences. Empathy should be used not to show our awareness of their weaknesses but rather a willingness to understand. It is good to remind that ACP countries' leaders have been educated, for the most part of them, in Europe and in [the] U.S. and insofar perhaps they understand our cultures better than we understand theirs.
>
> ACP countries are in a situation of extreme difficulty when they negotiate. We should understand that, sometimes, negotiators are rigid because they have a mandate

that is not so well defined and even more, is not flexible. ACP negotiators do not have a total room for manoeuvre because they have to refer to 78 countries in absence of a real co-ordination between them.

"Empathy works when there is a sincere attitude behind it. In this case, it is also an important element to build up trust, but only if used carefully," admitted a top and experienced negotiator. He continued, "Probably it is not the main factor but it can sometimes play a fundamental role in this kind on negotiation processes." A senior negotiator talked about his own personal experience in a Cape Town negotiation session (South Africa).

It was in 1997/1998, the discussion was focussed on all kind of trade related aspects and specifically on intellectual property issues which were quite a controversial issue to handle with the South Africans in order to set up a Trade agreement with them. They saw the issue as a tool to defending the EU Market, so they did not really want to go ahead on it and a dangerous stalemate was in the air.

This negotiator at that time worked at DG Development and was sitting at the negotiating table representing the EC side with DG TRADE negotiators next to him, DG Agriculture negotiators on the other side, DG Industry negotiators on his shoulders. "While I was making big efforts to watering down the Commission requests I could feel that the commission's colleagues were uneasy and they were passing notes between them and to me as they had the impression that I was going in a way too far." Meanwhile, "I noticed the South Africans were not impressed at all and were as stubborn as on previous occasions; they did not have any intentions to buy this opportunity for coming to a compromise."

He was very nervous and excited and in his words, "I had this folder in my hand so while trying to get a paper I deeply cut my thumb with all the blood exuding like a little fountain from my finger." Then, there was a big break and, "After this accident, we went back to the negotiating table and after a while they finally accepted the proposal that was even worse from the previous one." Probably they felt he cared and was serious and sincere about the issue, so they perhaps believed that those taxes were also a big concession from the EC side and they signed an intermediary agreement. As stated by this negotiator, "It was a great success! And I did not care about my finger anymore."

From the experience of the people interviewed it is clear that feelings play a fundamental role in the negotiation process. A negotiator, as all human beings, experiences feelings. Through them it is possible to understand the counterpart's intentions, values, principles, behaviours, even through a simple movement or sight. Feelings also help us to understand and handle delicate situations when, for example, there are conflicts among people of the same group (in the counterpart's side or even in our group's side). In this way we can help to avoid the negative influence of these kinds of conflicts on the whole process, because "A division inside a group has a negative effect on the whole negotiation process no matter to which group the division belongs," as a top negotiator stated.

A negotiator defined empathy as "a powerful tool. ACP countries love to negotiate with EU actors, because they are different from the World Bank (WB) negotiators that often use diktats, are tough, hard, and impersonal." To the ACP countries, "The WB negotiators are very aggressive, they dislike them." Instead, "Africans love to laugh, to make jokes and looking for affinities with their partners. It is enough to explain [to] them that they cannot overcome certain limits and the negotiation will be smooth and challenging." Moreover, his colleagues stated that

> Body language and nonverbal communication tool are really important to Africans, because they are used to this kind of communication that makes them feel comfortable. They can tell you a lot of things just with a glance. They can understand if someone is a representative negotiator just with a glance. The glance, the way they look at persons and things, is really important in their cultures.

In short, "Empathy is a fundamental characteristic in order to build up a negotiating relationship. It can help understanding the other person's attitude and ideas in helping her to open up more." It does not mean to give in on every issue, it just means *to* understand and respect the counterpart's positions and at the end of the day if there still are conflicting positions deciding to agree to disagree.

5.10.3 Expectation and Breakdown

Both parties should go to the negotiating table with rational expectations; but is it certain that rational expectations exist and are given equal meaning by all the parties involved in the negotiation process? Some advised that, "It is better to start with clarity on the general aim of the negotiation process. This because we have experienced that very often the two or more parties had not well defined possible options." Moreover, "Intellectual honesty and organised exposé of arguments and items carried on with clarity – trying to avoid ambiguous messages – will help a lot." His colleague admitted with a certain security coming from previous experience that "It is really comfortable to make a nice declaration, but that declaration could be perceived in different ways creating expectations by different actors and insofar could create ambiguity and uncertainty making things even more difficult for negotiators."

Some negotiators believe that "Negotiations in the examined field should be more secretive in order to reduce expectations" because "High transparency leads to a paralysis of the negotiation process." Continuing their reasoning we understand that "Professional negotiators know that they cannot obtain everything they demand for. Hence, they are aware they should and can live with certain reached compromises." Instead, "The problem is represented by peoples behind them (i.e., partners, stakeholders, journalists, NGOs, trade unions, and other actors) that have high and unrealistic expectations and put pressure on State's institutions, international organisations, for instance, and consequentially on negotiators." The result could be negative because,

> If the negotiation is too much transparent it happens that once an acceptable mutual satisfying compromise has been reached, on which negotiators could give their assent, these latter start to feel the pressure from those external actors (especially NGOs) and in the end they could be pushed to refuse an already agreed compromised outcome.

Concerning the breakdown topic, a senior negotiator stated that "The right moment to provoke a strategic breakdown is when you see that the negotiation has reached a point where all the parties involved are hopeless to gain something from the negotiation. In this case, the breakdown period is a useful moment to prepare a compromise able to allow a restart of the negotiation on new negotiating bases." Even if

> It is better to bear in mind that a breakdown is a dangerous point; however, it could be useful for re-balancing objectives. For example, the negotiation has taken a path that could bring more problems than solutions; or simply people are too demanding no matter your big efforts to look for compromises; or the counterpart erects barriers and you see that the balance is on their side. In these cases, it is much better to provoke a breakdown to find a new balance of the negotiation process.

In sum, when you have the perception that your efforts have not yet been repaid a breakdown is useful. But perceptions are subjective and they are not the same for every negotiator. A senior negotiator gave this useful example, "When you go fishing there is a time you decide to stop it. When? At what time? Maybe, when you are hungry. In general, it depends on your perception of the timing, if your results have been matching your efforts. If it is not a good day and you believe it would not be better, then you go." It is a mental state and not an objective decision. It also depends on the capacities and abilities of the person who chairs the meeting that has a final responsibility in mediating between parties.

According to the above-mentioned reflections, we can say that it is not always possible to give an absolutely positive or negative opinion about analysed characteristics because even if it seems that some of them can represent an advantage for somebody, for somebody else they can be a risk. Last, but absolutely not the least, once again the neutral answers helped to avoid a polarization of interviewees on two extreme opposite sides. Opinions expressed throughout the research process point out that it is better to start negotiations with clarity on the general aim of the negotiation process because very often it was discovered by actors, while parts were experiencing a stalemate, that two or more parties had not defined enough possible options. Intellectual honesty as well as exposé of agenda items and arguments with clarity will help to avoid ambiguous messages.

It is useful to have a general and well-elaborated picture of the negotiations. In practice, a structure is needed in order to hope to influence the game. An

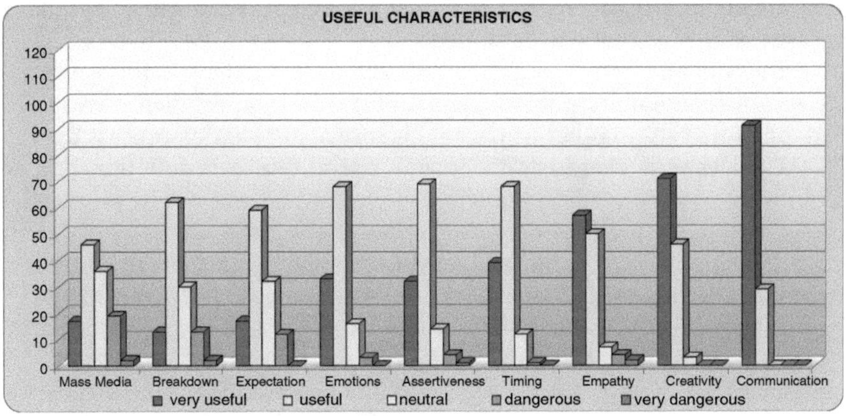

FIGURE 5.5. Positive personal characteristics.

accurate list of issues and problems (diagnosis) and an intelligent and defined negotiating framework (formula), capable of supporting the negotiation process, are very useful tools before going deeper into details and it is hoped could help negotiators to shift their minds from a high-expectations modality to a more normal set of expectations. Understanding the counterpart's constraints is also really important for lowering expectations in the negotiation process. Learning the counterpart's limits through an assessment of the strength and weakness of the counterpart (i.e., their mandate, psychological constraints, etc.) helps negotiators to put less pressure on the counterpart's shoulders. Figure 5.5 summarises the behavioural characteristics that during the interviews had been considered positive for the negotiation process.

5.11 Concluding Remarks

In an intense daily ongoing negotiation process such as the one between the EU and the ACP countries, negotiators get to know each other better every day. Meeting, talking, and sitting at the negotiating tables for months and years help the construction of a sustainable dialogue in order to listen to and understand often different positions and reach compromises on different needs and interests. Negotiators seem to agree on the importance of deploying verbal communication tools compared to nonverbal communication tools that could provoke major misunderstandings and misinterpretations. Vis-à-vis conversations, one should be careful with the detection of body language because often one could perceive the counterpart's emotions through his personal lens and easily be wrong and inaccurate in personal perceptions and assessment of the meaning of the real emotions manifested through the counterpart's nonverbal communication cues. Obviously, we can be wrong in our assessment; but who does not make mistakes in a negotiation process is someone that has never negotiated.

Negotiators and actors are forced to acknowledge the specific needs and interests of their counterparts if they want them to respect their own specific needs and interests. In other words, in this special negotiation process between EU–ACP although there is an ongoing give-and-take negotiation process, certain very specific needs and interests are respected and will be outvoted, if needed, within the long period as this would damage the very integrity of the countries involved. Negotiators can only be open to a smooth process of conceding and obtaining if they feel safe. And they will only feel that way if negotiators can put trust in the ability and willingness of their counterpart to take into account their core interests and values.

A general discursive remark that could be inferred from this first structured interview analysis is that usually ACP and EC actors are good partners in the negotiation process. However, the negotiation training of ACP actors is generally less sophisticated, particularly with respect to aggressive strategies and it should therefore be up to the EC to favour their training in order to have an enhanced cooperation and collaboration during the negotiation process on a more equal footing with sustainable benefits for both parties.

On the other hand, another aspect emerged from multivariate analysis: these characteristics are necessary, but not sufficient to guarantee a good result of the negotiation. What came out of the survey was that a possible positive win–win approach to the negotiation is to start from an efficient and secure communication base, from a good amount of creativity, empathy, and awareness and confidence with our own and the counterpart's feelings and emotions. Such an approach will allow us to understand our interlocutor and hence, to decide if we really want and need to use, at a certain stage of the negotiation process, a strategy and related techniques where characteristics such as ambiguity, deceit, and aggressiveness are contemplated.

Our analysis seems to show the development of the awareness between negotiators that the experience is important but not per se. It is a precious tool if the negotiator develops a series of structured and flexible mental models to be applied on different and large variety of situational and specific scenarios that she faces or is expected to face. Moreover, negotiators are not born with inner skills but they can learn them. What is important, but a little bit more difficult to learn, are the psychological skills of empathy, listening, understanding, and being present in the moment without being influenced by the past or fear of the future.

The focus is not just on tactics and strategies, which are important tools at the negotiators' disposal. Rather, the focus has been directed on the broader negotiation process and the role of the negotiator has been recognised as fundamental for this process. We will never have two negotiations that are the same. A negotiator is viewed not as a passive element of the negotiation process (already studied and planned by others), but rather as an architect of the structure and the process using breakthrough thinking. Moreover, we would add that a negotiator should be a creative architect always able to face new situations and able to define the situation through a broad set of elements in shaping the structure and the process actively according to the needs of the moment. Even more, to accompany the process in promising directions, the negotiators should not fall asleep during the negotiation process in order to seize worthy momentum to conduct mutually satisfying final agreements.

This conclusion already came out in the first descriptive analysis, where we found those characteristics that have a meaningful percentage of neutral answers. This evolved from a multivariate analysis in an even meaningful way. It is interesting to note that in the cluster analysis the wider class is the one with those individuals who have given a high score to positive characteristics, but they have also given a meaningful score to those characteristics that, in their individuality, may appear unfavourable in a negotiation process, but if assessed and used with a criterion they may be useful in order to assure a favourable position. From our research the empathic and communicative but not naïve approach seems to be the best suitable approach to this kind of negotiation. In sum, we can say that the negotiator should care about the counterparts even if he or she does not fall in love with her or him.

The above recommendations reflect our understanding of this particular negotiation process on using self-report methods best suited to survey- and questionnaire-based research. It is our hope that as more research is conducted we will learn more not only on how such characteristics may affect negotiation processes but also how to better assess emotion in negotiating contexts. Negotiators, all along our interview process have indeed taught us without noticing it, many things on international negotiation with different scenarios and a richness of human variety. But from some (we think) great negotiators humanly valuable, we have gotten gems of wisdom and the conviction that it is far more exciting and satisfying to enjoy the negotiation process day by day rather than thinking obsessively about the negotiated outcome that will (maybe) result from the process. Otherwise, a negotiator will lose the joy of travelling and the pleasure of sharing a common project with a counterpart.

5.12 Practical Guide: What Can the Negotiator Learn from the Research on Negotiation and from that on Hope?

In this chapter we have introduced research developed in interviewing numerous professional negotiators, and picking up their opinions on some fundamental questions. However, how much do the opinions expressed really represent the reality that they intend to describe? Which awareness is necessary so that one's own "narration" of the experience is indeed adequate to the processes that it tries to describe? How much is the meaning of the words used for defining some concepts different among the people? The risk is that we speak without understanding that everybody has been referring to a different network of meanings tied to each concept, even if the concepts have the same denomination.

For this, communication researchers have tried to give some operational definitions (and shared) of the concepts as the basis for the negotiation. That is, they have tried to define the meaning of words such as "hostility," "aggressiveness," and "rigidity" in a simple, articulated, and potentially shareable way, at least for convention.

The first implication, therefore, of the research introduced in this chapter as concrete examples, is that it is necessary to learn to look beyond oral/verbal appearances, aiming at identifying (where an operational definition of concepts that will be used has not been premised) the "network of meanings" that everyone subtends to a concept, and how much this can differ among individuals (but also among people, and among different languages).

The metarepresentational functions, therefore, that assume a fundamental role in this process are those of decentralization and of differentiation, that are clarified later.

The second implication is that some interpersonal motivational systems appear evident in the negotiation process: peer cooperation and competition. But others are slightly and subtly present in the process, only apparently developing a secondary function: that of the attachment, for instance, that is often activated by threats of abandonment.

The third implication, which derives directly from the present research, is that some factors of personality are considered "dangerous" by the negotiators interviewed. And the lesson of the history gives confirmation of it. Just the perceived "dangerousness" of some potential traits or characteristics of personality present in negotiators (or "structurally" present, if the governments, that have mistakenly selected them, believe that the "dangerous" traits or characteristics are instead tools that may potentially help the negotiation to go in the direction desired by them, with good or bad manners), necessitates a training process for negotiators that also keeps in mind the possibility that some governments intend to implicitly boycott the negotiation even if they apparently favour it and in which they are apparently participating.

For this reason, an approach such as the one we have been trying to introduce, based on psychobiological factors common to all human beings (from affective neuroscience to the interpersonal motivational systems, that have been evolutionarily put to use by humankind for global survival and for adaptation to the different conditions of life, included those that are adverse), can represent a global hope for the planet. Hope, the object of the study of philosophy and religions for centuries, has recently become the object of operational study for psychology and psychotherapy (Snyder, 2000): it is possible to measure hope, to develop it, to diminish it, and to restore it both individually and socially. This introduces a series of practical applications in the fields of emotions, meanings, and morality (Snyder & Feldman, 2000), tightly tied to international negotiation and mediation.

6
What Psychotherapy Has Done and Can Offer for International Negotiation and Mediation

6.1 Cognitive Psychotherapy and International Negotiation: Historical Features

A fundamental article written by Albert Ellis, published in the *Journal of Cognitive Psychotherapy* in 1992 and entitled "Rational-Emotive Approaches to Peace," set the first step toward a modern cognitive approach to international relations and to the utilisation of cognitive psychotherapy acquisitions in terms of "social psychotherapy." In 1994 Aquilar, following the path traced by Ellis, published an article entitled "Psychotherapy for Peace" in which he associated Bowlby's attachment theory (1969) and Liotti's cognitive-evolutionist theory (1994; see also Guidano and Liotti, 1983) with Ellis' strictly rational-emotional aspects, in order to aim at a direct intervention of psychotherapists in the field of peace building. In this field, it is also necessary to refer to Safran's contribution (Safran & Segal, 1990; Safran & Muran, 2000) on the study of interpersonal processes in communication.

The chain of negative, threatening, terrorist, and war events that have heavily involved the "western world" as never before since the end of World War II, induced even Aaron Beck – starting from 1999 with the important volume *Prisoners of Hate*, followed by a significant article in 2002 – to read the conflicts' reality, the word faces in this current historical period, with the instruments provided by cognitive psychotherapy.

Since the year 2000, Mauro Galluccio has been trying to constitute a task force of psychotherapists, negotiators, and mediators from the cognitive area interested in the project of building up a training structure for negotiators and mediators, aimed at providing a higher probability of positive results for peace efforts. Galluccio personally involved in the project Albert Ellis, Francesco Aquilar, Aaron Beck, and Jeremy Safran (at the beginning) and Michael Mahoney, Robert Leahy, and Paul Gilbert (to name but a few) at a later stage, interacting with them and providing a synthesis of possible contributions coming from different, but compatible, points of view (Galluccio, 2003).

In the year 2000 a fundamental volume was also published, edited by C.R. Snyder, *Handbook of Hope: Theory, Measures and Applications*, which uses the cognitive-emotional processes of hope not just for psychologically helping the survivors of trauma, an impairment, or a loss, but also for developing a socially functional hope directed toward the constitution of "hopeful governments" (Snyder, 2000; Snyder & Feldman, 2000).

These authors have provided a cognitive frame and a conceptual innovation to the interpersonal aspects of international negotiation and mediation. Lately, the contribution of metacognition researchers, who already implemented the comprehension of therapeutic relations (Semerari, 1992), allowed the making of a further forward step toward the comprehension of personal relations during negotiations. In particular, the description of five metarepresentational mind functions (Falcone, Marraffa, & Carcione, 2003), appears to be absolutely necessary in order to have a significant negotiation. Such functions are: identification, decentring, differentiation, integration, and mastery.

Finally, the relation between emotional norms and social order, studied by various cognitive sociologists, establishes a new conceptual bridge and an action sphere with the description of "emotional norms" which vary depending on the referring group, and which could be considered the basis of some thought rigidities processes and of "extreme" action projects (Thoits, 2004).

6.2 Critics of the Standard Cognitive Approach

In order to make a distinction between the cognitive revolution and cognitive science, some operative definitions could help us to understand better the influential context in which the cognitive approach was born. The cognitive revolution has been represented by that general method of perceiving the world in terms of knowing systems and information processing that has been widely applied to different sciences and disciplines in the second half of the twentieth century. A milestone of the cognitive revolution has been represented by the birth of cognitive science. This term has been referred to six specific disciplines, the so-called cognitive hexagon. This is constituted by: artificial intelligence, cognitive psychology, neurosciences, linguistics, anthropology, and philosophy.

These different disciplines participate in the development of a unitary science, thanks to the practice of interdisciplinary rapport, throughout the common project that has as a core interest the study of the structures and processes with which knowledge is organized and processed. A particular emphasis has been put on the methodology of validation of theories through the simulation of models. The cognitive revolution has posed basic questions on the nature of the mind and showed to the actors a high potential for a qualitative improvement. Taking into account this rich and influential context, the theory and principles of the standard cognitive approach suffered the rigidity of a framework potentially capable of watering down this innovative thought movement. Summarizing, we have had six basic critics to the standard approach as shown below (see Mahoney, 1991); to these we add two more recent critics (Semerari, 2000):

1. Unconscious processes' relevance is minimised, when not ignored by cognitive-behavioural therapy.
2. The cognitive-behavioural model considers emotions as a subproduct of beliefs. This is disadvantageous for two main reasons. Firstly, actors in the theoretical domain may be tempted to devalue the importance of the information; secondly, they may devalue the importance of emotions' roles in the knowledge process.
3. The cognitive-behavioural model, even if it sets cognitive processing between the stimulus and the behaviour, sees anyway the cognitive processes as processes of responses to a stimulus.
4. Automatic thoughts and beliefs, as they are explained in the cognitive-behavioural approach, have essentially the form of thoughts expressed in words. This way will decrease the possibility to express the experience with other modalities.
5. There is an emphasis on the rationality as a factor of adaptation.
6. This rationalization could weaken the perception of the complexity of relational events between people (and their role in the international negotiation context).
7. Aaron Beck stated that individuals can learn how to recognize and correct cognitive thinking errors that are the basis of their suffering. Why is the active help of a specialist needed then? Why does it also seem that there is resistance to a change process?
8. The last critic is represented by the relationship between unconscious and conscious processes we have already seen in the first point. The standard cognitive approach describes individuals/patients essentially in terms of mental contents, for example, automatic thoughts, and structure of contents, as schema. There is, however, an important need also to consider and evaluate the quality of mental functions (metarepresentation and metacognition).

6.3 Application Sphere

The contribution cognitive psychotherapy may be giving to the field of international negotiation is not limited just to the identification of cognitive and metacognitive processes useful for fruitful negotiations. It also regards the management of psychological consequences of war and terrorism as negative aspects of a failed negotiation. The work of numerous colleagues on post-traumatic stress disorders, on mourning, on depression caused by losses, and on depression caused by defeat, has provided an important contribution, as specified by Gillespie's, Duffy, Hackmann, Clark (2002), Karam's (2005), and Zikic's (2005) work.

The functions of cognitive psychotherapy as they have been evolving until now, in the sphere of a psychology for peace, can be summarised and grouped in some macrocategories, such as

1. *Prevention*, with a strong focus on identification and overcoming of "dysfunctional" beliefs ("irrational" ideas) and cognitive distortions. This category includes social communication actions aimed at discouraging possible terrorist organisations' flankers and/or adepts.
2. *Managing*, with focus on interpersonal processes and metacognitive function. This category includes dissuasive actions directed to already active, but dubious, flankers or adepts.
3. *Reparation*, with direct psychotherapeutic help for the victims, survivors of war experiences, and/or terrorism. This category includes the psychological recovery of repentant terrorists or flankers.

In addition to those sectors could be added the objective of constituting/setting up a cognitive school of negotiation and mediation,[1] which would develop in future negotiators the skills (cognitive, metacognitive, nonverbal, and verbal communication abilities) needed for the successful management of negotiations.

6.4 Contribution Synthesis

The negotiation process, at every level, implies the ability to comprehend the other's point of view and to respect it. Moreover, it implies a partial renunciation of one's own overall objectives and satisfaction for both sides.

Ellis' contribution (1992, 2002) could be synthesised as a methodology aiming at:

- Overcoming depression and desperation
- Overcoming prejudices and arrogance
- Overcoming semantic errors such as "labelling"
- Overcoming vulnerability and defensiveness
- Overcoming rage and hostility
- Overcoming rigid and absolutist thoughts
- Overcoming low tolerance frustration
- Overcoming communication difficulties
- Developing empathy
- Emphasising hope for the future
- Helping nonviolence and internationalism

In order to reach these objectives, Ellis proposes many operative strategies, without undervaluing the nonpsychological aspects of conflicts and wars.

---

[1] Continuing, amplifying and "psychologising" the work that former United States' President Jimmy Carter is doing in the Carter Centre, which is committed to advancing human rights and alleviating unnecessary human suffering.

Aquilar's contribution (1994, 1996, 2000, 2006a,b) is instead focused on:

- Developing others' mind comprehension abilities
- Developing thought process flexibility
- Understanding the fundamental role emotions play in the negotiation process
- Developing temporary ambiguity tolerance capacity
- Understanding the fundamental role played by verbal and nonverbal communication on more contemporary levels: explicit/implicit, co-operative/threatening, anxious-resistant/anxious-avoidant
- Implementing the knowledge of the other's anthropological-cultural context
- Developing hypotheses on "education" modalities received, from the point of view of Bowlby's attachment theory and Liotti's cognitive-evolutionist theory, for the forecast of emotional reactions of the counterpart facing negotiation difficulties
- Paying particular attention to the processes defined as "social psychotherapy" (which is explained further in the second part of the book).

Aaron T. Beck's contribution (1999, 2003) is mainly focused on:

- Development of a tolerance, that is at least strategic, in regard to beliefs colliding with one's own.
- Identification and immediate modification of cognitive distortions (overgeneralisation, selective abstraction, catastrophisation, magnification/minimisation, tunnel vision, etc.) of a cognitive-oriented negotiator, and empathic tolerance toward the interlocutor cognitive distortions' identification.
- Awareness of the consequentiality of hostile processes, with the description of three subprocesses: (a) predisposition to events; (b) precipitation of events; and (c) reaction to events.
- Avoidance of the upper hand of "primary thinking" in which the other is perceived as a negative monolithic category. Primary thinking implies an interpretation of other's behaviours as negative a priori, until it is falsified by abstract prejudices.

Safran's contribution (beyond the exquisitely technical aspects related to the therapeutic relation) can be applied to negotiation and to mediation through the identification of abilities that must be developed in a future negotiator. These abilities, as summarised by Galluccio (2003), are:

- Flexibility
- Adaptation
- Interpersonal sensitiveness
- Metacommunication
- Power of persuasion
- Creativity
- Patience
- Tenacity

The elements analysed up to now would require a deeper explanation, because each one of those demands, in order to be developed, specific training and a series of basic personal characteristics in the subjects.

6.5 Metarepresentation and Metacognition

A further valuable analysis step, to help us better understand those sitting at the negotiation table, will take not only comprehension of cognitive dynamics involved in the process, but also the metacognitive and metarepresentative abilities to incorporate intrapersonal and interpersonal skills, within negotiators' working relationships in order to reach the basic co-operation necessary for them to achieve the mutually desired outcome. When we attribute mental states to our interlocutor or someone in general terms, we build up a representation of a mental representation. Attributing to us the belief that if we go in a restaurant we can have a piece of cake at the end of our lunch (a mental representation) the observer builds the metarepresentation: "They think that there are cakes in the restaurant's kitchen." We will say that building explanations and mental previsions is the result of a metarepresentational capacity (Sperber, 2000). Therefore, a metarepresentation is the representation of a representation (Falcone, Marraffa, & Carcione, 2003). The ability to build and elaborate mental representations of mental representations is the object of various studies or disciplines of cognitive science. We briefly analyze two of them: metacognition and mind's theory.

Metacognition studies metarepresentations linked to basic cognitive processes (such as memory) in an advanced stage of a child's evolution (usually in the scholar age). Metacognitive contents shed light on the understanding/meaning of whole knowledge and beliefs through which the subject interprets and estimates her mental states/processes. This could be intended as a form of knowledge and identification of one's own mental state. The study of metacognitive functions helps us to understand/mean all cognitive activities related to control and regulation, through which a given actor, actively and with consciousness, walks and acts in his interactive environment. More specifically, we can have an input (knowledge) on his own mental states and his representations of others' mental states, conducive to solving cognitive tasks, ruling mental events, and forecasting and explaining other individuals' behaviours. The ability of an adult to monitor the contents of her conscious experience, in order to recognise them as mental states (emotions, feelings, thoughts, memories, opinions, expectations, fantasies) seems to be the implementation of the development of the mind's theory which starts in the childhood (Liotti, 2001).

Mind's theory's theoretical paradigm implies the hypothesis that an ingenuous psychology theory is at the core of the mind reading capacity. This theory is intended as a corpus of psychological knowledge leading to the explanation and forecasting of our behaviour and that of the others. This has been possible thanks to the development of a series of experimental works on the "false beliefs" from which it emerged that children around four years of age are capable of perceiving mental states as representations. They know that a psychological status is not a mere passive recording of reality but is instead a reconstruction of it, although eventually an incorrect one. To sum up, mind's theory studies the ability of identifying mental states, and the ability to think about them. Metacognition studies other functions, such as regulation and monitoring of cognitive activities. Di Maggio et al. (2007), Falcone, Marraffa, and Carcione (2003), and Semerari (2000) have been providing a frame and a conceptual innovation to the understanding of emotions in the interpersonal dimension that could be easily applied to the field of international negotiation. Moreover, the contribution of metacognition's researchers, who already implemented the comprehension of therapeutic relations, allows making a further forward step toward the comprehension of personal relations during the negotiation process.

At this point, a brief outline has to be dedicated to the metarepresentational functions, which future negotiators should necessarily develop, and these are (Falcone, Marraffa, & Carcione, 2003):

- *Identification*, that is, the ability to recognise one's own and others' emotions appropriately
- *Decentring*, that is, the ability of assessing interactive sequences, being able to assume (and remember) someone else's point of view in the relational context
- *Differentiation*, that is, the ability of understanding mental states as representations of reality, therefore potentially wrong and at least probabilistic
- *Integration*, which is the ability to connect coherently the different components of emotional and mental states, of organising them consciously in a sequence, of structuring a thought hierarchy keeping a precise/definite identity
- *Mastery*, that is, the ability to intervene deliberately in one's own thoughts, mental states, and emotional states, in order to face complex situations fairly

We may then look forward to defining some psychological "minimum training standards" for future negotiators and mediators and an efficient study programme that allow us to reach this goal. This could be done through the constitution of an international cognitive school of negotiation and mediation, which would develop in future negotiators, together with current techniques and strategies, the cognitive, metacognitive, nonverbal, and verbal communication abilities useful for the successful management of negotiations and mediations.

6.6 Concluding Remarks

Although emotional influences have been analysed by scholars in different areas of the political environment and the negotiation process, there has been little or no direct discussion of the applicability of these findings to the field of international negotiation, for example, how deep analysis and mastery of emotional competence may help to detect and reorganize breakdowns in the international negotiation context. Overall, after reading this insight into the international negotiation arena and the role of cognition and emotion thought processes, maybe one's perception could change if negotiators learn to listen and observe others in a manner that is outside their own mental states. Negotiations can span the spectrum of an international environment and delve deep into relationships people have with each other on a day-to-day basis. We negotiate in marriage. We negotiate at work. We negotiate with all children. We negotiate with friends. Take all of this and combine a different language, a foreign childhood in a faraway place from your own, and a burning issue where you have a vested interest whether personally, politically, monetarily, or otherwise and one will begin to realise the importance of understanding cognition and emotion during international negotiation.

6.7 Practical Guide: Cognitive Social Psychotherapy in Action

In this chapter we have introduced the story of the contribution that cognitive psychotherapy has been giving to the field of international negotiation and mediation. Until now it has fundamentally been a theoretical contribution, of understanding and planning lines of development. In this volume we try to make a further step ahead in proposing a concrete modality of application of the principles of cognitive psychotherapy (and particularly of cognitive-evolutionist or cognitive-attachment psychotherapy) to the training of the negotiators and to the more articulated redefinition of the political questions/matters giving greater space to the psychological variables and above all the emotional ones. The concept of interpersonal motivational systems represents an input for understanding the powerful emotions that push individuals, groups, people, and governments to action.

The application of the research and clinical experiences regarding metacognition and metarepresentational functions allows the understanding of some of the causes for which individuals are unable to learn from experience how to modify their own dysfunctional way of thinking: for the lack of mental functions that regulate thought, exactly organized on "meta" level. Only with this basis can communicative difficulties (and difficulties on the communication of the communication, that is to say, metacommunicative) be adequately interpreted. Those difficulties, even if they have been identified for many years by researchers specialised in the matter, have not operationally been overcome in a satisfying way. Such aspects are not only considerable for the realm of international negotiation and mediation, but also in the management of emotions and of relationships in daily life: beginning from parent–children relationships, to career counselling, and up to better management of romantic love relationships.

On the other side, studies on cognitive training may bring to the preparation/setting up of a program useful to train negotiators (but also the more sensitive politicians and the more illuminated leaders and rulers) to understand and to master emotions, motivations, and communication in a way also to overcome problems linked to cognitive, emotional, and of agonistic-competition difficulties exasperated by the potential and possible negotiating "other part": the abilities of understanding other people's minds (that belongs to metacognition), in fact, could be strengthened up to the point of acquiring the ability of being able "to reassure" the negotiating other part (on condition that, naturally, the negotiation does not subtend a deception or an overpowering).

All that has been stated up to now in this book belongs to the object of study and application of cognitive social psychotherapy (Aquilar, 1996, 2006a), of which this volume represents a determinant element, in proposing itself two fundamental objectives:

a) To make available and operational the acquisitions of psychotherapy for a broad number of people (and of cognitive psychotherapy in particular), so that they are not a privilege of the few but, as happened with the hygienic norms at the end of the nineteenth century, to allow social use of it at least in its broad aspects. This with the purpose to allow a better development of individuals' potentials, for a more balanced development of life as "happy" and "meaningful" as possible, in line with the inevitable problems life loves to propose.
b) To contribute to raising awareness among governments, people, and negotiators on new, creative, and more "pacific" conflict solutions, not based on utopian generic philosophies, but on the psychobiological basis of an affective neuroscience which can be applied to the defence (and to the harmonic development) of humankind, safeguarding the specifications, legitimate and fundamental differences among persons, groups, and people, that represent an evolutionary resource.

This could seem a too ambitious objective, above all because it passes through an apparently simple, rapid program of training for negotiators (and for politicians and government officials) of three intensive weeks for the first level, which we outline in the second part of this volume. Nevertheless, the perception of a perspective change of reality does not require a lot of time, as the structure of all scientific revolutions, beginning from the so-called Copernican revolution, has shown throughout the last centuries.

7
Further Directions: Toward a Cognitive-Oriented Post-Graduate School of Negotiation and Mediation

International negotiation may typically advance in tandem with the actual or threatened use of power, whether military, economic, or of other sorts. The respective powers of the actors and the resulting *rapports de force* (balance of power) may condition the process and the results for those involved in the negotiation process and consequentially for international actors behind them (with whom they work in tandem). Because the actual or threatened use of force may also provoke conflict spirals and escalation, a psychological perspective of this kind of strategic thinking is highly useful. As Harold Nicolson stated in his famous book, *Diplomacy* (1963): "Because the psychological vigilance is a vital factor of the negotiation process, if a diplomat becomes so presumptuous to lose interests for the psychology of the counterpart he goes in hibernation and, in the field of the negotiation, he becomes useless." Rubin (1991–2002), instead, paid a tribute to a multidisciplinary perspective: "The challenge is to find ways to co-ordinate psychological expertise with the expertise afforded through other disciplinary perspectives and to renew the role of psychology."

The theory of games was developed in order to provide a logically consistent framework for analysing interdependent decision-making processes. It shows through logic–mathematical experiments that co-operation is the best rational and most efficient strategy if both parties at the negotiating table jointly take into account the utility of co-operation (see also Avenhaus, 2002; Axelrod, 1984). It would be a safer and far more rational world if we could apply with diligence the strategies detected by game theory! Unfortunately, in reality the co-operative solution is not automatically adopted by parties. It is rather a long process in which situational/contextual, as well as cognitive, emotional-motivational, and relational factors come into play. A number of studies have brought to the attention of scholars the evidence of the role played by people's plans, goals, understandings, and expectations in determining their reactions to the situations in which they find themselves.

As we have seen, cognitive scientists, cognitive and behavioural psychologists and psychotherapists, sociologists, and political scientists have been studying and producing results on the influence of particular human cognitive thinking errors in the evaluation of information. The negotiation process may be affected by negotiators' predictions, perceptions, and expectations of the events as well as negotiators' prediction of a certain behaviour that may be assessed through the lens of these cognitive distortions, dysfunctional beliefs, and consequential emotional disturbance. Moreover, those authors have been able to detect the influence of the belief systems of leaders and negotiators on the representation of conflictual situations, and on the consequential adoption of negotiating strategies and tactics (see also Van den Assem, 2000). Hence, standardised theoretical normative models can be enriched and sometimes substituted by models produced by descriptive or psychological (cognitive) approaches.

Yet when decision making is interactive – as is true in negotiation, where each party's anticipated choices affects the other's – assessment of what the other side will probably do is important in order to limit natural uncertainties. Negotiators may also be conditioned by their individual characteristics which modify their perception of situations and may influence their strategic choices, hence their results. As matter of fact, our research has been aimed at obtaining a better grasp of the impact of personality and characteristic traits on the interaction of powers in a specific international negotiation process where the asymmetry of powers undoubtedly represents a *fait accompli* of the real negotiating context.

The negotiation process is nurtured by the exchange of arguments/topics, information, messages, signals, and emotions designed to make a common or cognitively shared binding interpersonal experience. A particular negotiating transaction can prepare a script for the emotional communication and the consequent counterpart's responses to it. In our conceptual framework emotion is intended from a social functional perspective, to be a management tool in conflicting situations in order to better co-ordinate the interpersonal dependence that binds negotiators together. The best way to manage emotions is represented by the ability to identify, express, and modulate them in response to external and internal stimuli. This ability could be a tool or on the other hand a dangerous and harmful handicap for actors in their capacity to resolve problems.

Emotions appear to play a number of roles in addition to contributing to solving adaptive problems. For example, emotions are functional in forming social relationships and smoothing social interactions, and also in cognitive functioning, as is illustrated by research on moods (Isen, 2004). Hence, emotion research could penetrate international relations and international negotiation theory precisely because of these functional consequences. Briefly stated, emotional exchanges belong to the social fabric and regulate interpersonal relationships. This is so by virtue of capacities for empathy, and by sensitivity to sympathy and the detection of suffering in others (Beck, 1999).

Careful analysis of the role emotions play in social interaction shows that such interaction is shaped both by one's own emotions and by how others perceive one's emotions (Mahoney, 1995). Social interaction depends on the manner and degree to which emotions are appraised and regulated by the individuals concerned, which in turn depend on their awareness and mastery of their own emotions (Saarni, 1988, 1999). These abilities and knowledge constitute what is termed "emotional intelligence" (Salovey et al., 2004). Forgas (1998) and Isen (1987, 2004) have been giving importance to positive affects in the negotiation process. They, with regard to positive emotions and information processing, have elaborated a theoretical perspective based on empirical data in which it has been remarked that effective negotiation requires creative cognitive information processing that in turn is guided by positive, rather than negative emotions.

Recent affective neuroscience empirical research and clinical experience refer to the observation that in human interactions, each person tends in nature to synchronise her behaviour in accordance with the behavioural and emotional states of the other person because of inner interpersonal motivational systems (Bowlby, 1988; Gilbert, 1989; Liotti, 2001, 2005b; Panksepp, 1998). The negotiator who deliberately adopts a poker face strategy may contribute to the "pollution" of the interaction[1] between parties.

Affective neuroscience is one of the domains that have shown impressive progress over the last 30 years. Neuroscience research has demonstrated important functional differentiations in emotion-relevant brain processes. Evidence shows distinctions between areas more involved in triggering or organizing emotions and areas more involved in the execution of responses, and still others that are pertinent to feelings. Evidence has also concluded that certain brain circuits fulfil a key role in more or less specific emotions, such as fear, anger, separation distress, or joy and play (Panksepp, 2003). Moreover, brain processes have been identified that are essential to social feelings, thus corroborating a biological basis for such feelings.

How best to conceive the functional nature of the various brain processes is one of the current concerns that may lead to linking brain processes more closely with behavioural, physiological, and experiential phenomena. Certain emotional response mechanisms appear to be context-sensitive whereas others are not; some are responsive to attention, whereas others cannot be influenced in such a way. Moreover, neuroscience research is extending toward the study of feelings. It supports the psychological distinction of levels of subjective experience (more immediate or diffuse, and more reflexive or articulate) and provides evidence for the role of body information and information integration in feelings.

We think it would be important to apply concepts of affective neuroscience to the study of international negotiation because the modern study

---

[1] For instance, to pretend not to be disgusted or angry or sad (when in fact you are) could be dangerous, because the active suppression of an emotional experience will deprive us of important information and awareness of pieces of reality and consequently will facilitate the deterioration of important skills to cope with events the negotiating contexts propose to us.

of neuroscience is helping us in exploring the biological bases of consciousness and mental processes, by which we perceive, learn, remember, and act (Damasio, 1994, Liotti, 2001, Panksepp, 1998). Damasio (1994) has been demonstrating the interplay between emotion and feeling in the decision-making process. This provides an interesting neurobiological underpinning of our research and studies in the field of international negotiation.

In our view, it is rather interesting to underline the importance of emotional competence, the way in which one identifies, expresses, and modulates emotions, to help manage working relationships and to pave the way for positive and maybe successful negotiations. Emotional competence is an ability that negotiators and mediators should master in order to try to have peaceful relationships in planning long-term sustainable interactions. We are confident that future and continued work will pay more attention to the intertwined effects among psychological variables and the political and strategic conditions under which they have the greatest impact on international relations' interactions and international negotiation.

It is true that psychological models alone may not provide a complete picture for international relations because they may not address how international and domestic conditions/constraints shape preferences, ideas, and beliefs; or how the policy formulation process aggregates individual preferences and beliefs to produce policy outputs for the state (Keohane, 2005). Cognition and affect mediate between international and domestic structures and processes of the international relations decisions of political leaders, and we hope to explain the nature of those interdependent relations by integrating psychological variables into more comprehensive theories of international negotiation and strategic interaction.

Cognitive psychology and cognitive-behavioural psychotherapy may contribute to open a new perspective from which to assess and widen deeper awareness into the international negotiation realm. It can certainly complement, in a multidisciplinary perspective, approach theories on negotiation, but it cannot substitute for them. A cognitive approach can shed light on individual and group dynamics on how people feel, perceive, and process information, have expectations, and set up their reality. However, the contextual scenario becomes of major importance. In fact, our research project has been aimed at obtaining as much as data we could collect through the tool of the interview process in order to disclose clusters that in the context of international negotiations are usually under a "benign secrecy." Dr. Galluccio's personal capacity to talk individually with so many distinguished negotiators for at least two hours added value to our research project, permitting us to collect valuable data and trying through a benign Socratic method to sensitize our interlocutors to cognitive processes and emotional responses in themselves and in their counterparts (through the tool of personal characteristics to come up safely during the interactions of actors within the international negotiation contexts).

We talked and we observed attentively the intimate links between action and reactions and the perpetual maintenance of vicious circles in human interactions within the context of international negotiations. For example, we saw from their talks and responses how fragmentary information, presented below the threshold of awareness, may suffice for certain emotional reactions, or prepare the ground for the response to more complex information. At the same time, in many elementary and automatic reactions, information from context and from an individual's history did (and does) play a role.

The observations of previously mentioned eminent scientists centred on the relations between individuals' problematic thoughts – or cognitions – and their feelings and behaviour brought them to the development of a cognitive therapy of human psychological disorders.

There is increasing evidence that people respond very rapidly to new stimuli or changes in their immediate environment (that A. Beck calls "events"). These new pieces of information are subjected at first to an immediate crude evaluation that attaches a positive or a negative value to the stimulus. Translated into language, the evaluation conveys the notion of "good for me" or "bad for me," or "right" or "wrong." This initial process occurs very rapidly (within one-third of a second) and is unconscious (Beck, 2002). A more complete processing is achieved when additional information from the environment (or from bodily sensations) is taken into consideration. This allows for an evaluation of the total context of the event and a determination of whether the initial evaluation was relevant to the individual's interests and was significant. If this second appraisal indicates that the event was significant and relevant, then a more elaborate response, in the form of an image or in words occurs (Beck, 1999). The imagery or verbal experience conveys the more complete meaning of the event.

These are the famous automatic thoughts and images that are at the periphery of awareness, and people can become more aware of them with training and can describe them in detail (Beck, 1988). With psychotherapy these cognitions provide the basic material used to understand the personal meaning of an event. Through cognitive psychotherapy negotiators could be trained not only to identify these cognitions but also to reality-test them. If the cognitions do not appear to be valid reasonable interpretations, the patient can learn to reframe them. One can raise a significant question regarding the validity of the various cognitive techniques. Over the past two decades, different studies incorporating a huge number of angry subjects treated with cognitive therapy were analysed and it was found that the average individual treated with cognitive behaviour therapy had a better outcome than more than 70% of untreated subjects in terms of anger reduction (Beck, 2003).

Throughout all these years the therapy application showed practically that helping people to modify their cognitions resulted in improvement. Such cognitive therapy addresses individuals' problems in a number of different ways.

1. Beck and Ellis have always been attempting to give the people with whom they have been working more objectivity toward their thoughts and beliefs by encouraging them to question their interpretations. Do your conclusions follow from the facts? Are there alternative explanations? What is the evidence for your conclusion? Similarly, they evaluated the underlying beliefs and formulas. Were they so rigid or extreme that they were used inappropriately and excessively? These therapeutic strategies helped receivers not to overreact to situations.
2. It has been observed and scientifically proved that these findings were not restricted to people with serious psychiatric disorders. The same kinds of erroneous beliefs influenced the feelings and behaviour of people experiencing daily normal life problems (Beck, 1995; Ellis, 1995; Mahoney, 1995; Robins & Hayes, 1995; Haaga & Davison, 1995).
3. It has been observed through different applications of cognitive therapy that there is a common denominator across these various forms of harmful behaviours: namely, that the victim is perceived as the enemy, and the aggressor sees himself as an innocent victim.
4. There is a scientific certainty that people have the same mental processes when they are engaged in either individual or group violence. Ellis (1992, 2002) and Beck (1999, 2002) explored the literature on such social ills as prejudice, persecution, genocide, and war. Although there are large differences in the sociological, economic, and historical causes, the final common denominator is the same: aggressors have a positive bias regarding themselves and a negative bias toward their adversary, often conceived as the enemy.
5. Sharpening our insight into the cognitive factors (interpretations, beliefs, images) can provide some leads in remediating the intrapersonal, interpersonal, and social problems of modern society (Beck, 1999).
6. There is a need to expand our knowledge of the aberrations of power-driven leaders and their naïve followers. In the words of Beck (1999: 287),

> We know a great deal about the nature of prejudice, but we have not yet been able to convert this information into effective programs to prevent large-scale massacres. The most successful form of intervention to date has been in the superimposition of controls from above by supranational organisations like NATO and the United Nations.

7. We have seen that Ellis (1992, 2002) and his disciples hypothesised that psychotherapy often helps people to become less disturbed and especially less hostile and more peaceful, and when it is individualised and/or presented through the mass media it can have a significant effect on helping people relate better to others, to become more co-operative and pacific, and to encourage the groups and countries in which they reside to abjure war and encourage peace.
8. Negotiators are human beings made of flesh and blood, they have a brain, and they perceive and process information in order to assess their own

reality. The reality is not the same for any two people but it can change slightly according to their perceptions. Hence, our cognitive approach could be a useful tool to try to better assess cognitions, emotions, and motivations appraisal within the international negotiation realm.

9. Last but absolutely not least, we have seen that even if many authors have remarked and studied the errors in the thinking of national leaders, this knowledge has not yet been put to practical use. Similarly, only rudimentary steps have been taken to modify the thinking of members of warring ethnic groups (Ellis, 1992; Beck, 2002).

7.1 The Project of a European Cognitive School of International Negotiation

Emotions typically arise because of the evaluations of events in relation to a person's individual concerns and expectations. Being conscious of emotions offers you flexibility of responses based on the particular history of your interactions with the environment. The negotiator should then learn how to identify, express, and modulate emotions which have been generated and acquire meaning because of the interpersonal process that binds negotiators together. This would be of the utmost importance bearing in mind that all the actors in the negotiation process are interpersonally linked and play an active role in shaping relationships.

An implemented awareness of thinking strategies could be promoted in negotiation schools through activities that require reflection (Aquilar & Galluccio, 2005). Group work or discussion time can also regularly include a "process observer," namely a participant who agrees to pay attention to how the interaction progresses and to report to the group an analysis of its process. Activities like these, which require negotiators to make the sometimes invisible work of thinking visible and explicit, may help negotiators to understand that as thinkers, they are in charge of the situation in that particular context. More purposeful, flexible, and creative problem-solving in the negotiation field may be the result.

A joint multidisciplinary effort appears vital in order to aim at a European Cognitive School of International Negotiation. It would be necessary to come to the definition of some psychological minimum training standards for future negotiators, and of an efficacious study programme, and – above all – of a guided practice of negotiation which answers to the principles and supplies the abilities listed above. The initial subjects of this minimum study programme and of guided practice could be the following.

- The building of knowledge and architecture of the mind
- Mechanisms of thought and behaviour modification
- Evolutionary factors in co-operation and competition development
- Dysfunctional beliefs ("irrational" ideas) and cognitive distortions

- Verbal and nonverbal communication processes: homogeneous and differentiation/discrepancies aspects
- Persuasion processes
- Tolerance of frustration and diversity
- Metarepresentational functions: identification, decentring, differentiation, integration, mastery
- Management of negotiation's interruptions/breakdowns
- Recovery/rediscovery of a common aim
- Management of relations with governors

Each of the above-mentioned points requires further specifications, with the description of precise "exercises" for the evaluation of the abilities/skills acquired and improved (this is the aim of the second part of this book). The experience of group training for future psychotherapists, which is the patrimony of the cognitive training/formation schools, will play a determinant role not only in the conceptualisation, but also in the practice, of those previously listed principles and applications.

7.2 Practical Guide: Group Cognitive Training and Trainees' Characteristics

Familiarization with and acquisition of a mastery of cognitive and emotional processes requires the activation, during the training period, of emotions that promote learning, and of a cooperative context among the trainees. For this, despite the seriousness and the responsibility implicit in the objective, the strategies of learning may pass through a combination of theoretical "lessons" (in the morning) and a series of experiential and expressive situations cognitively used that belong to the circle of art therapies. Art therapy uses, in therapeutic-didactic interventions, techniques which are mediated through music, sketch, dance, theatre, and poetry.

This is the "secret" of the speed of learning: the confidence with emotions, motivations, and metacognition is not only communicated through theoretical communication but is developed through direct experience that is tightly connected to the cognitive-emotional apparatus of each participant. The exercises of "reading other people's minds" (fundamental metacognitive ability) are not carried out in an abstract fashion but are concretely proposed, taking into account the problems that every single individual has had to face during his personal life, and then generalized as greater political and negotiation questions. The negotiation that develops as an interpersonal process in the life of every human being since infancy (with parents, schoolmates, teachers, figures of authority, romantic relationships) is ontogenetically repeated over and over again in order to develop awareness of it and to strengthen its abilities of use.

The fundamental objective is to allow people to learn how to manage intense emotions (which are systematically present as a central component of the motivation to action) and to overcome (often subconscious) auto- and heterodestructive habits. It is a matter of an extensive application of psychotherapeutic treatments of groups set up for those people who have this emotional disregulation in a more serious form. Moreover, it is a matter of providing in a short time operational information which concerns sociological and anthropological-cultural elements linked to the intrinsic aspects of the negotiation. We aim to provide for consequential elements derived from the negotiated experience already carried out until now, in order to learn from past experiences through concretely applied historical analysis. We aim to increase the level of understanding of nonverbal language and of persuasion modalities (with particular reference to the innovation-decision processes or the change of idea-emotions on a topic, or on a relationship).

To this extent, the teaching staff requires numerous abilities and competencies. That which we refer to as the hypothesis that we propose is established by a director of the training, three cognitive psychotherapists, a sociologist-anthropologist, and a political scientist negotiator. The six teachers should develop their program in groups composed of 6 to 20 persons, with a preference for the smallest group, which would be in a situation where six teachers and six participants are in close contact for three weeks, as further specified.

Access to the groups could be reserved to currently serving professional negotiators, and also to subjects (figures) from the political world, who intend to widen their abilities of understanding negotiation and mediation problem resolution.

8 Practice and Exercises for Negotiators and Mediators

8.1 Concrete Objectives

After the articulated treatment of the theoretical and historical issues presented so far, concerning both international negotiation and psychology and psychotherapy applications, especially cognitive ones, we now introduce a possible scheme of intervention for the training of future negotiators which considers what has been described above, and has been mentioned in the sections titled "Practical Guide."

Summarizing what we have developed in the first part of the volume, the first possible conclusion is that it would be important to teach the negotiators (both actual and future) the principles and utilizations of psychology and of psychotherapy applied to negotiation with the purpose of increasing their abilities; and all this in the shortest possible time, and with the maximum operational effectiveness we can obtain.

We do not forget, of course, that political problems and balance of power between negotiators and governments represent decisive constraints, which can make success impossible in spite of all the good intentions. What we want to remember, however, is that suitable and adequate training could reduce the difficulties inherent in the negotiation process independently of those constraints, and that a mentally more open position toward a "negotiation without losers" could increase the possibility that the same negotiators can push their own governments toward a perspective of peace and civil cohabitation between people and nations (Ellis, 1992).

The psychological-professional specific training that we propose derives from a diligent integration of two types of processes: those of group psychotherapy and those of the training of individual functions. Numerous studies have been carried out in the last years in both the above-mentioned fields of application, and the purpose of this chapter is to provide for a possible exemplification of it. Nevertheless, in the field of international negotiation and of mediation, the applicative information, the techniques, and the knowledge concerning the transmission of the techniques, are particularly delicate tools. In this sense, as is often done for the training of future psychotherapists, a part of the information (and the bibliography that documents it) are reserved to the persons that indeed develop the training journey.

In this session, therefore, we proceed to delineate a training program, which concerns the first level of training for negotiators, and is composed of 15 meetings of eight hours every day (four hours of frontal lesson and four hours of practical exercise), so that it could be possible to complete the job in three intensive weeks, from Monday to Friday. The dimension of the group to which we refer varies from 6 to 20 subjects, with a preference for the smallest group, with a staff composed of a director of training (psychotherapist or political scientist), three cognitive psychotherapists, a sociologist-anthropologist, and a political scientist.

So we sum up the functions that the program aims to teach, and the motives for the utility of such learning with respect to negotiation.

8.2 Improving Comprehension of Processes: How to Negotiate

The understanding of processes represents the first step in promoting a personal and professional awareness in the mind of the future negotiator: for this it is necessary to train the subjects to an articulated and driven auto-observation and to a renarration of the story of their own lives, with the purpose of reducing the negative and nonapparent influences of one's own past. To reach an understanding of interpersonal processes it appears important to promote an understanding of intrapersonal processes, of the emotional and behavioural functioning mechanisms of everyone, through different phases of the lifecycle until the present state.

At first sight, negotiation apparently requires knowledge of the interaction processes between people and competence in reaching effective problem-solving strategies. Consequently, a development of personal creativity appears to be an inevitable complement of effective negotiation. However, a theory of individuals' development that is sufficiently complex to incorporate updated scientific knowledge on the matter and at the same time sufficiently simple to be learned quickly and be concretely applied (Guidano & Liotti, 1983; Liotti, 2001; Aquilar, 2006a,b), and that could allow negotiators to identify their own cognitive organization and above all that of the interlocutors (and eventually of the rulers) would be able, in addition to the apparent level, to allow them "to read" the negotiation on a deeper level and to be able to draw proposals that are acceptable to the counterpart more easily.

8.3 A Three-Dimensional Theory of Individual Knowledge: Cognitive-Emotional Organization, Attachment Modality, Meta-Cognition Development

In order to answer the issues which have been brought to our attention since the beginning of the book, it could be useful to draw on a three-dimensional theory of individual knowledge, which would allow negotiators (as it allows psychotherapists and as it is taught to postgraduate students of psychotherapy), a rapid assessment/evaluation of oneself and, if it is possible, of the interlocutors, as well.

The three dimensions considered in this theory, which at this point are simplified and summarised in order to avoid heavy conversation, are cognitive-emotional organization, attachment organization, and personality organization. Four principal modalities for each dimension, to which the majority of people could be referred, are examined. In total there are therefore 12 elements, enough to "frame" the individuals for operational purposes, and also in order to interact in a more effective way with them (including their "own" individual variables that, if they are known, could be examined to positively understand and modify the interactions).

All three dimensions derive from the studies of psychopathology and clinical psychology, considering "pathology" as an alteration of "physiology," and using it as a "widening" of physiology, which makes its understanding easier.

8.4 The Cognitive-Emotional Organizations and Their Evolutionary Meaning

An articulated conceptualization of the individual's development, that could allow people to find their way in order to value themselves and others, is based on the consideration of the presence of four fundamental cognitive-emotional organizations, to which each individual could belong. It would be particularly complex, and inadequate in comparison to the objectives of the present volume, to deliver an accurate description of the functional modalities (or more often dysfunctional) of every organization. In synthesis, the organization of the thoughts and emotions of human beings could have structured itself in such a way during evolution with the purpose of guaranteeing humankind four fundamental characteristics necessary for survival and development: creativity, to resolve problems; verification, in order to eliminate inadequate creative solutions and to select those that are effective; the search for meaning, to give pleasure and sense to vital experience and pass it on; protection from danger, to systematically structure a "defence" of single individuals, of different groups, and consequently of the whole of humankind, with the purpose of preserving it in maintaining a wealth of evolutionary alternatives.

In this hypothesis, the imbalance of the cognitive-emotional organizations decisive for the development of humankind, could be at the basis of the main psychopathological disorders which do not compromise the sense of reality (those that once were called disorders of the "neurotic" area, to differentiate them from those of the "psychotic area" broadly characterized by a substantial fracture of one's sense of reality).

Thus, the evolutionary meaning of each cognitive-emotional organization could be graphically represented, as if each of them represented one of the cardinal points, as shown in Figure 8.1.

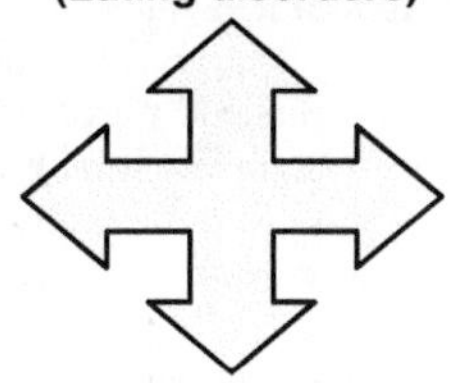

FIGURE 8.1. The cognitive-emotional organizations.

TABLE 8.1. Organization of eating disorders type.

1. Evolutionary value	Creativity
2. Central level	Expectations/judgement
3. Bodily attention	Body, weight, food, stomach
4. Underlying states of mind	Disappointment, indefiniteness, anger
5. Attachment	Disorganized, frightened, wavering
6. Family system	"Gold cage"
7. Main worry	Abandonment
8. Problematic sentences	It is better not to expose oneself, not to define oneself; I don't know; It depends (from indefiniteness)

TABLE 8.2. Obsessive organization.

1. Evolutionary value	Verification
2. Central level	Responsibility/certainty
3. Bodily attention	Gastrointestinal system/skin
4. Noticed states of mind	Uncertainty, doubt, alarmed "worry"
5. Attachment	Disorganized double in prevalence avoiding
6. Family System	Detached, severe, alarmed, based on duties, perfectionist
7. Main worry	To be mistaken in persisting
8. Problematic sentences	I am not sure, I have a doubt/dilemma

The imbalance of every organization could prefigure and thus lead to psychopathology, thanks to which it has been possible to study and define such organizations.

To synthesize the fundamental characteristics of each cognitive-emotional organization (even eventually with the purpose of autodiagnosing within each of them, as exemplification), they are reported in Tables 8.1 to 8.4, on the basis of some intuitively comprehensible categories.

TABLE 8.3. Depressive organization.

1. Evolutionary value	Search for meaning
2. Central level	Onerous engagement, effort (useless)
3. Bodily attention	To be wounded by a general painful state; generalized exhaustion; eventually alternated to: polisensorial hyperactivation; hyperenergy
4. Noticed states of mind	Lack of meaning, of desires, of joy; dejection; anger; eventually alternated to: hyperactive enthusiasm
5. Attachment	Avoiding/rejecting
6. Family system	Elevated level of expressed negative emotions/silence
7. Main worry	To survive even for a little minute in a sadly unbearable state of mind
8. Problematic sentences	I can't go on

TABLE 8.4. Phobic organization.

1. Evolutionary value	Protection from danger
2. Central level	Conflict between freedom-loneliness and company-oppression
3. Bodily attention	Breath, breast, heart
4. Noticed states of mind	Fear, anxiety, alarm, "impressionistic" worry
5. Attachment	Anxious-resistant
6. Family system	Hyperprotection, limitation, intrusiveness
7. Main worry	Endless solitary agony
8. Problematic sentences	I am afraid of, And if then…, If I am alone I need help

8.5 The Attachment Modalities and the Internal Working Models

Attachment theory, initially elaborated by John Bowlby, and developed by his collaborators and followers, is substantially a space-temporal theory (Holmes, 1993): if I am next to (or in harmony with) whom I love, I feel calm, cheerful, and I explore the world; if I am away from (or in disharmony with) whom I love, I feel anxious, sad, and lonely/alone, and this can make me furious and/or become detached and/or revengeful, if each one of my attempts to restore a proximity with the person has failed or has been unheard. From the repeated interaction with meaningful figures (also called "attachment figures"), one can derive some tacit unexpressed "conclusions," which underlie the development of the relational-emotional system of each of them: such conclusions can be denominated "internal working models" (Bowlby, 1969).

Attachment theory, initially devised for describing the mother–child interaction, has found a series of experimental confirmations and a notable range of applications not only in the field of clinical psychology but also in understanding adults' attachment processes (especially in romantic relationships). The different identifiable forms of attachment therefore have gotten different denominations, depending upon the type of research on childhood or on adulthood, but the categories are substantially similar.

Every cognitive-emotional organization seems to introduce a different order of the interpersonal motivational system of attachment, related to past vicissitudes suffered in relationships with figures of childhood attachment, and a related internal working model, with a possible diversification in the following categories.

1. *Avoiding attachment* (or dismissing): the desire for proximity, nearness/closeness, to receive help, or to have contact with meaningful others is predominantly inhibited; the internal working model describes oneself as deeply (and often unconsciously) unworthy of real care or of affection and the others as unworthy of trust, because they are hostile and/or indifferent, but the explicit behaviour appears "dismissing," in the sense that the subjects prefer to keep the other at a distance; the subject appears to feel at ease with autonomy but not with intimacy.
2. *Anxious-resistant attachment* (or "preoccupied"): the desire for proximity, nearness/closeness, to receive help from, or to have contact with meaningful others is particularly strong and problematic; the internal working model describes oneself as deeply (and often unconsciously) unworthy of real care and of affection, and the others as unworthy of trust because they are intrusive and/or unpredictable (in principle and by definition), and the explicit behaviour appears preoccupied with the fear that the others do not desire the close proximity that the subjects would like to get and to maintain; the subject appears to feel at ease with intimacy but not with autonomy.
3. *Secure attachment* (or "free"): the desire for proximity, nearness/closeness, to receive help, or to have contact with meaningful others is considered legitimate and does not develop into sensations and emotions that are considered problematic; the internal working model describes oneself as worthy of real care and of affection, and the others trustworthy because capable to love; there appears to be present a rapid ability of discrimination between other humans "capable to love" and humans "incapable to love" and this discrimination appears to be permanently active; the subject appears to feel at ease both with intimacy and autonomy.
4. *Disorganized-disorientated attachment* (or "fearful"): the desire for proximity, nearness/closeness, to receive help, or to have contact with meaningful others is considered scary, frightening, and dangerous; so the behavioural conduct appears incongruent and contradictory, with alternation of phases in which one desires "to melt" with the attachment figure and phases in which one desires "to mark oneself out" at all costs from this figure; the internal working model describes oneself as deeply (and often unconsciously) unworthy of real care and of affection, and the others untrustworthy because they appear as suffering too much and needy of help to be reliable; the subjects appear uneasy both with intimacy and with autonomy, and they tend to go through in a recursive way phases of socially avoiding behaviour.

8.6 The Personality Behind Types of Cognitive Egocentrism, Problematic Interpersonal Cycles, Levels of Metacognition, Organization of Aims, Control/Discontrol of Impulses

Some aspects linked to the structuring of thought and to the management of emotions can be relevant for the understanding of oneself and of the interlocutor, and of the relationship between two people. Among the numerous theories available in the literature, particularly useful appear to be those deriving from the clinical study of so-called "personality disorders" of current psychopathological classification, for a complete description of which we refer to the *DSM-IV-TR* (American Psychiatric Association, 2000), and for a therapeutic treatment of which we refer to the volume of Di Maggio, Semerari, and collaborators (2007).

The study of some elements appears particularly interesting for its possible applications to international negotiation, particularly:

1. Cognitive egocentrism, in all its subtypes, is a central mechanism of all personality disorders (Liotti, 1992, 2001).
2. Problematic interpersonal cycles are the processes described in Chapter 3, in which the negative forecasts (which include an emotional-sensorial memory) unintentionally activate a relational (or social) dynamic that confirms them (Safran & Muran, 2000).
3. Metacognitive functions, that include autoreflexivity, understanding of other peoples' minds and "mastery," and that in the personality disorders appear absent or reduced (Semerari, 2006).
4. The organization of aims in the mind of every human being (and their possible modification, which happens with respect to beliefs and experiences), is particularly problematic in some disturbed personalities (Castelfranchi, Mancini & Miceli, 2002).
5. The control of impulses (Liotti, 2001, 2007), that if uncontrolled, as in some personality disorders, may lead to dangerous behaviour for oneself and for others (this behaviour, if coupled with good persuasive abilities, could bring whole groups to perform socially harmful actions).

Except in rare cases, it is unlikely that professional negotiators (and the rulers who name them) are affected by real personality disorders of psychopathological importance. Nevertheless, a "lighter" form of the same problematic could be present in them, with the presence of thick cognitive egocentrism (often in a covert form), with the absence or the reduction of some metacognitive functions, with a disorganization of the purposes/aims, and with poor control of impulses. Referring to the classification of personality disorders, the following problematic forms could be identified, each characterized by a specific metacognitive disfunctionality, disorganization of the purposes/aims, and lack of control of impulses (evident or hidden).

1. Narcissistic egocentrism, characterized by an apparent sense of "grandeur," a particular lack of real empathy, a hypersensitivity to the opinions of the others, with a sense of extreme vulnerability to suffered carelessness
2. Borderline egocentrism, characterized by the presence of manifold representations of oneself and the world, contradictory and not integrated; by a disregulation of the whole emotional system; by a reduced ability of management of the impulses
3. Paranoid egocentrism, characterized by a continuous worry regarding deception and betrayal, and by preventive lack of basic trust, with a representation of reality that is raw, divided in a dichotomous way between "good" and "bad," not openly shown but cleverly dissimulated

To recognize these forms of cognitive egocentrism in oneself and in others, and to graduate her own behaviour toward the meaningful others (as, for instance, the negotiators of the counterpart) with the purpose of reducing the negative effects of the dysfunctions described above, it is possible to effect specific exercises, some of which are proposed later.

From this follows a possible scheme of autoevaluation/assessment (and of evaluation/assessment of the counterparts) that could be condensed as shown in Table 8.5.

TABLE 8.5. Possible scheme of autoevaluation/assessment (and of evaluation/assessment of the counterpart).

Types of Egocentrism	Interpersonal Schemes/ Cycles	Metacognition	Aims	Impulses
Borderline	Me humiliated/ the other humiliating	Lack of identification	Evident: to negotiate; Hidden: to prevent the humiliation (in fact activating myself to confirm it)	Immediate to preventive aggression (false mastery, preparatory to attack)
Narcissistic	Me neglected/ the other neglecting	Lack of decentring	Evident: to negotiate; Hidden: to prevent feeling neglected and of little importance	Immediate to the "seduction" with fantasy of active abandonment following immediately
Paranoid	Me betrayed/ deceived; the other traitor/deceiver	Lack of differentiation	Evident: to negotiate; Hidden: to identify the betrayal and to punish the guilty one	Initial hypercontrol, for then to let himself "free" in private with his "faithful" entourage, dreaming about a revenge

8.7 Diagnosis and Self-Diagnosis of the Three Dimensions

Thus far, in the model that we propose, during the training course the participants could learn to identify (both in their self and in the others):

1. The cognitive-emotional organization of affiliation
2. The structuring of the attachment (including the internal operational models and the analysis of the emotions inside the different interpersonal motivational systems)
3. The type/kind of egocentrism eventually present in oneself (including the functional analysis of metacognition)

Once you establish these basis competencies, which allow one to widen one's own limits and to understand eventually "circumventing" or "containing" other people's limits, one would need to increase the other consequent abilities.

8.8 Improving Cognitive Skills and Overcoming Cognitive Distortions

The basis cognitive abilities are composed of numerous mental functions, which in the development of each individual could have been more or less encouraged or inhibited by relational and environmental factors. As previously mentioned, the main cognitive processes are the following.

1. Perception, that is, the individual organization of sensory data, which constitutes an active process, not a passive one as it would seem; perception moves on information that derives from the five senses, and every sense has one "bodily memory" that is activated by its same activation. Among the five traditional senses (sight, hearing, touch, taste, smell), each characterized in an idiosyncratic way in every individual, a remarkable meaning is represented by the so-called "inside touch" or proprioceptive, which derives from the level of greater or smaller tension of the internal bodily organs, and which is often representative of an emotional state. The anger that "takes to the stomach," as a sense of recurrent gastric constraint, is just one of the examples of this type of sensation, which is interpreted by everyone in a perception strongly influenced by states of mind and beliefs (more or less immediately conscious).
2. Consciousness, considered as the "memory of the present," that is, the mental activity of each of us, which monitors our thoughts and emotions, and presides over behavioural decisions in the light of those emotions and motivations. The most recent studies on consciousness describe numerous alterations of the state of consciousness as linked not only to psychopathological troubles but also to certain/determinate social situations; the so-called consciousness disorganization, for instance, could be a prelude to aggressive actions, or also to cruel actions.

3. Attention, that is, a particular state of consciousness in which the subjects are focused on a task, with a consequential reduction of the level of vigilance over other bodily and mental functions. An elastic alternation between the focusing and the generalisation of the abilities to pay attention appears a necessary ability in such complex tasks as the negotiation, in which it is necessary to be focused on the specific negotiated task, but on the other hand to continuously keep in mind even information *a latere* deriving from the observation of nonverbal behaviour (and from the decoding of the verbal one) of the negotiating counterparts.
4. Memory, that is, a process much more active and elastic than might seem to the naïve observer. The processes of memory often regulate the attribution of meaning to reality; a vast quantity of information that is present in the memory carries out an important role in the ability of persuasion vis-à-vis the interlocutor. One can distinguish between "episodic" and "semantic" memory, and the negotiator could profit from learning "not to trust" in the semantic memory.
5. Learning, that is, a process constituted by the modalities, rhythms, and vivid and colourful emotionality with which new information and abilities are acquired and mastered.
6. Language, that represents the skeleton of thought and communication, and has to be distinguished in its verbal and nonverbal forms and in language for "inside" and "external" dialogue.

The cognitive distortions, of which we have already spoken in the text, represent the most common and frequent thinking errors people can commit. Numerous exercises have been fine-tuned by cognitive psychotherapists to identify cognitive distortions in persons, in order to help people to modify their structural presence in their own thought processes. An example could be to invite a subject to describe in three minutes one of his own negotiated experiences, in helping him to identify cognitive distortions of his same experience representation (built up on the basis of narration), in re-examining in the light of cognitive distortions described in Chapter 3 of the book.

8.9 Improving Behavioural and Social Skills

The behavioural repertoire concerns the quantity, the quality, and the flexibility of the behaviours which an individual possesses. A series of mechanisms, which establish and modify behaviours (both one's own and other people's behaviours) has been identified from the research and practice of cognitive-behavioural psychotherapy. Learning these principles and application of modalities of conditioning and deconditioning of behavioural nature appears necessary for a correct understanding of an activity as complex as that of negotiation.

Social abilities, and the consequent social competence, concern instead the complex of actions that allow a subject to successfully interact in the environment, and to deduce from it not only "external" objectives but also a sense of personal satisfaction. Particularly, in the training of negotiators it is necessary to aim at a certain sophisticated level of social ability: if an individual has been selected to carry out the delicate role of negotiator she has a social ability that is superior to the average person's (besides having really remarkable cultural-specific training). However, for the "slim/subtle" aspects of the negotiation this may not be enough. Social abilities also shine through performing rigid formal protocols of behaviour, to which negotiators have surely been already trained. The level of social competence therefore can aim at influencing the opinion that the negotiating counterpart will be forming. In addition to this, a socioanthropological-cultural knowledge could allow for "unconscious personal approval" even from negotiators that belong to cultures radically different from the western one.

8.10 Improving Communicative Skills

Communication within the negotiation context is considerably complex because of multiple problems of meaning attached to every single interaction, and because of the continuous dialectic between the formal/apparent, substantial levels and (foreseen/unforeseen) derived consequences.

One may not only be able to adequately transmit the information, but also be able to "really" understand those transmitted by the counterpart and to decode (adequately modulated) the "not-said," the "subtly threatened," and the "really-feared-but dissimulated."

Communicative abilities (and metacommunicative, that is to say regarding the capacity to communicate on that which has been previously communicated) include a correct decoding not only of verbal language, but also and above all of nonverbal language (paying particular attention to discrepancies between that which has been "said" and the nonverbal apparatus to what has been said, sometimes confirming what has been said, but sometimes disconfirming it). Moreover, numerous systems exist for the evaluation/assessment of the implications (evident or hidden) present in the communication, in particular in crossing the theoretical possible implications with the analysis of the possible aims of the interlocutor.

Moreover, it is necessary to have overcome cognitive egocentrism, which concerns not only the personal aspect of what we have previously talked about, but also that which is tightly linked to the cultural anthropology reference of every people or group.

8.11 Improving Emotional Competence and Metacognitive Functions

Even if we only consider the high number of divorces and separations and the remarkable increase of romantic-sentimental unhappiness present in the globalised society, this testifies in favour of a reduced emotional competence of people in general, more than research projects, however numerous and well done, can show.

Therefore, it appears necessary to devise a system that would give to emotional competence the capacity to be described, measured, and teachable, and we need a learning methodology which would allow the subjects to really develop their emotional competence, not just to abstractly learn its characteristics.

8.12 Improving Mindfulness and Concentration

Recently, within the globalisation process not only of markets but also of resources available for humanity, an interesting fusion between east and west has been pursued by theorists and clinicians of so-called "mindfulness," a technique originating from the oriental disciplines, operationally translated by western researchers in a program of training on the awareness of oneself that has revealed itself as particularly useful for the prevention of relapses of depression (Segal, Williams, & Teasdale, 2002). Such practice appears also particularly effective in promoting the abilities of concentration on a determined task, and in reducing the aspects of stress and generalized anxiety.

8.13 Improving Frustration Tolerance and Hope Processes

Among the long-studied aspects of human behaviour which are useful for the practice of negotiation, tolerance toward frustration, which since the 1960s has increased thanks to rational-emotive, cognitive, and behavioural techniques, appears particularly meaningful. Instead, a more recent development in this sector is represented by the possibility to measure, to use, and to strengthen the ability to hope, intended not only as an antidepressant content/tool but also as a determining factor for better planning of the future, both personal and social (Snyder, 2000).

9 Features of a Training Program Organised in 15 Meetings: Frontal/Face to Face Lessons, Art-Therapeutic Techniques, Microanalysis of Negotiation Sequences, Emotional and Metacognitive Awareness, Overcoming of Egocentrism, and Renarration of Experience

To assemble and make operational information and abilities described up to now in a brief period, verifying the real mastery acquired by the participants, appears a complex assignment and impossible task if we only use a methodology based on academic lessons. In this sector, the contribution obtained from the application of techniques derived from the art therapies (Liebmann, 1986; Aquilar, 1996, 2000, 2002; Schaverien & Odell-Miller, 2005), a modality of use of sketch, painting, music, dance, narrative/fiction, poetry, and theatre for the determination (and modification) of the psychological apparatus of individuals, divided in groups which foresee a program for a limited time, appears particularly effective. This approach allows for faster learning, in a cooperative context, which is potentially amusing despite the seriousness of the faced problematic. The contents of the theoretical lessons have been partly outlined in the first part of the book. Some of the proposed techniques are analysed instead in detail to provide a good example.

9.1 First Day

Theoretical lesson: Introduction to cognitive and behavioural psychotherapy

Group seminar: Diagnostic self-presentation, badge of resources and limits, first grid of emotional-motivational analysis according to the above-mentioned model.

The self/auto-presentation diagnostic derives from the techniques of formation for personal growth and for the education of adults, and it initially consists in inviting every participant to freely introduce himself or herself in a maximum time of three minutes (subjects may also, in a first instance, confine themselves to saying only their name and city of origin: even this information will also be subsequently interpreted). The conductor of the experiment records the autopresentation of everyone, and emphasises differences between different modalities (making neither inferences nor interpretations, in this phase) and asks for a second in-depth autopresentation in which every participant is invited to intuitively describe how his own emotions work and in particular what makes him outraged and what calms him down.

The second auto-presentation is also recorded. In listening to it again the conductor lets every participant note (also involving all the other participants, and inviting them to make a preliminary hypothesis) what hypothesis of cognitive-emotional organization can be considered, what attachment structuring and which internal operational models are to be considered, how aggressiveness and territoriality of everybody works/functions, and which interpersonal problematic cycles she could unintentionally tend to activate with her behaviour and above all with her expectations.

The badge of the resources and the limits derives from the technique of the coat of arms (*blasone*) of de Peretti and consists in inviting subjects to fill out one's own "badge" listing some personal characteristics, according to the model shown in Figure 9.1 (of which a hypothetical example is presented).

Thanks to these elements it is possible to draw, in choosing even the form, one's own badge, which is then critically examined by the other participants ("naïve" examination) and by the trainer ("professional" examination), which is useful in order to allow a gathering of data about different implications on the adequacy/inadequacy of one's own self-assessment and on the possible individual vulnerability in the negotiation situation/context. Also the graphic form that everybody is going to choose for his or her own badge and the relation between size and distribution within different elements will be assessed and interpreted.

9.2 Second Day

Theoretical lesson: Introduction to the psychology of negotiation (generic and international).

Group seminar: Generic negotiation role playing, that is, simulated execution of "neutral" negotiations, that regard all daily life practices: to start to ask for an appointment for a romantic-sexual meeting; to negotiate an increase of salary with the director of human resources of a firm; up to negotiating a divorce, with critical examination of behavioural errors/mistakes, possible cognitive and communicative errors, and generation process of possible alternatives; Metacognitive analysis grid, examination of some personal experiences of suffered humiliation/injustice and of cognitive and emotional effects for a short

Motto	**"Remember to always dare"**
Symbolic image	
3 Abilities that I possess	Intelligence, culture, patience
3 Limits, problems or failings that I think I have	Touchiness, overweight, doubtfulness
3 Types of intelligence that intuitively I hold as prevailing in me (between those described by Gardner: linguistics, logical-mathematics, musical, spatial, bodily-kinaesthetic, interpersonal, intra-personal, naturalistic, existential)	Linguistics, musical, intra-personal
Type of cognitive-emotional organization	Alimentary disorders
Type of cognitive-emotional organization with which I prefer to deal with, and why	Phobic: Because I like to reassure who is afraid.
Sentence that I am often repeating to myself	"In the end I will do it"
Other people's sentence which drive me crazy (outraged)	"I cannot do it"
Sentence that I keep repeating to myself when I am relaxed	"This is wonderful! "

FIGURE 9.1. Hypothetical example of a technique of the coat of arms (*blasone*).

or a long time period, through the psychotheatre techniques of the emotions (Aquilar, 1996).

The psychotheatre of the emotions is an expressive technique adjusted, tuned, and finalised by Aquilar (1996) who has been re-elaborating the concepts of Moreno's psychodrama and of different forms of theatre therapy present in specialist literature on this topic. The procedure is simple: participants are invited to identify an episode characterized by a strong emotion, for instance in this case of suffered humiliation/injustice, and to write a short "storybook" of that episode, of a maximum duration of three minutes, selecting the characters that will develop the role of actors from other members of the group. The subject can choose to personally personify himself or to play the role of another participant, or also decide just to be the director of the scene.

Then this should be put in action by selected participant-actors, and substantially "be relived" by his creator, who may then describe felt emotions both in his memory and while observing the stage representation of it. The other participants of the group are invited to express the emotions felt during the scene and to express alternative opinions on the assessment/evaluation that the subject had of his experience. Moreover, they could suggest to him behavioural alternatives (which could also act as a "corrective experience of the past"), and of eventual different interpretations (or more articulated) of the scene and of its meanings and implications.

Every selected scene is used for a detailed examination in terms of cognitive-emotional organization, of interpersonal motivational systems, of activated emotions (and of their succession or copresence), of made conclusions, of activated interpersonal problematic cycles, of recognizable cognitive egocentrism modalities (or hypothesized), of nonverbal communication analysis, and of conclusions in terms of a widening of the possible behavioural repertoire, of the development of interpretative alternative proposals, of interruption and reparation/recovery of the dysfunctional interpersonal cycles, of cognitive distortion identification that is systematically present, and of practical implications for the use of every rereading in other contexts, in this case with particular importance given to generalisations useful for international negotiation.

9.3 Third Day

Theoretical lesson: Introduction to evolutionary psychology. How to gather, understand, and renarrate one's own story of personal development. Features attachment theory; individual reconstruction of attachment story done also in psychotherapy, and her reduced version for the group's work.

Group seminar: Laboratory of sketch, psychotheatre of the emotions on childhood emotions (family, school, social).

The drawing laboratory derives from the graphic techniques of art therapies, and it is used for allowing the participants and the teachers to have quicker access to some unconscious and unaware aspects of the representation of herself and of the world. Independent of the graphic abilities of every participant, in the proposed use for this type of objective, one is asked to draw a series of key elements: first of all, an autoportrait of her entire figure as she perceives it at present; then her own autoportrait of the past in a series of meaningful moments of development (for instance: 6 years, 11 years, 14 years, 18 years, undergraduate graduation ceremony, postgraduate graduation ceremony, etc.); then one is asked to search one's memory and to draw a meaningful episode of failed negotiation during childhood (for instance with one's own parents, or with teachers, with schoolmates, or with persons that were the first objects of sexual interest).

The drawings are interpreted and discussed in the light of cognitive-emotional analysis criteria, as referred to in the psychotheatre of the emotions. Moreover, the drawing laboratory allows us to have access to unconscious aspects of the representation of oneself, of others, of the world, and of the relation between oneself, the others, and the external world which follows from the graphic forms that the drawing shows to us: the proportion between characters, the different "strengths" of the sketch/line, the distances between the drawn persons, the underlined details or neglected ones; these are all elements taken into consideration when deciding which is favoured in the consciousness of every participant.

9.4 Fourth Day

Theoretical lesson: Introduction to social cognitive psychology. How attraction and personal repulsion work. How judgement mechanisms are established, maintained, and modified.

Group seminar: Laboratory of musical expression, poetry laboratory.

The musical expression laboratory derives from the techniques of cognitive psychology of music (Sloboda, 1987), of music applied to psychotherapy (Ellis, 1977; Aquilar, 2000), and of music therapy (for a review: cfr. Aquilar, 2002), and it allows us to learn how to use music in its components (rhythm, speed, melody, chords, lyrics, etc.) in a way to express emotions and to modify cognitive structures.

Initially, the participants are invited to familiarize themselves with some musical instruments (beginning with percussion), favouring actions of positive cooperation at the end of which, in small groups, it is possible to enjoy harmonic music in its entirety. Secondly, on the basis of known melodies, some of the "rational-emotional" songs of Ellis (1977) are taught to the participants. The songs are built by the author in a way to modify the recurrent errors of thought and the dysfunctional beliefs in a humourous and amusing way (albeit particularly effective). Then the "psychotherapeutic songs" of Aquilar (2000) are used to instil in the memory some fundamental principles of attachment theory and of cognitive psychotherapy applied to interpersonal relationships.

The poetry laboratory derives from the techniques of applied linguistics (Kovecses, 1991; Esposito, 1996), of applied creative writing (Zamponi & Piumini, 1988; Bisutti, 1991) and from those of semiotics (for a synthesis, cfr. Aquilar & Ferrante, 1994; Aquilar, 1996, 2000, 2006b; Gensini, 2004). Starting from some structured poetic forms (anagrams, haiku, rhymes, acronyms, logogrifs, metaphors, metonymies, synesthesia, calligrams, visual poetry), the participants are invited to express the emotions that they feel with respect to personal and professional interactions in ways different from the usual ones, guiding them to create a visual poetry that synthetically describes their own internal working models and the necessary operations to overcome their own identified limits in negotiating and mediating.

Visual poetry consists in the preparation of a self-portrait sketch in which, for every part of the body, the subject is invited to write a verse which contains personal and relational meaning. At the conclusion of the laboratory, the participants will compose a poem that would give them access to the unconscious implications of the concept of "negotiation" (in the different modalities in which everybody intends it) and of the concepts related to it. In such a way it is possible to reduce the level of cognitive egocentrism and to trace the cognitive and metacognitive errors possibly present in their mental schemas and initially inaccessible to the conscience.

9.5 Fifth Day

Theoretical lesson: Psychology of romantic love, adult romantic attachment, romantic emotions and aggressiveness

Group seminar: Psychotheatre of the emotions on romantic love; assessment of the first week's experience.

9.6 Sixth Day

Theoretical lesson: The interpersonal motivational systems

Group seminar: Emotional-motivational analysis grid

9.7 Seventh Day

Theoretical lesson: Metacognition and personality

Group seminar: First grid of metacognitive analysis ("the questions")

9.8 Eighth Day

Theoretical lesson: The metarepresentational functions

Group seminar: Second grid of metacognitive analysis ("the answers")

9.9 Ninth Day

Theoretical lesson: Awareness and unawareness

Group seminar: Psychotheatre of the emotions on cognitive unconsciousness: how to identify and restructure cognitive-emotional processes of which one is not aware

9.10 Tenth Day

Theoretical lesson: Negotiation techniques and negotiators' specific stress management

Group seminar: Negotiation role-playing; laboratory of expression and of bodily decoding; assessment of the second week's experience

The laboratory of expression and bodily decoding derives from the application of the techniques of communication and of nonverbal decoding and from those of dance therapy (Peserico, 2006). The objective is to render the participants able to appropriately appraise the "bodily" aspect of the emotions, both as postural expression and as proprioceptive sensation, as well as unintentional communication of the emotions and of hidden intentions. The subjects are trained in a way to acquire an improved awareness of the movement and to express their own emotions, above all those of frustration, sense of impotence, and negative resignation through movement, conceived as indirect modality to learn to tolerate negative emotions related to the uncertain and/or problematic course of the negotiation.

The interaction between persons typical of the negotiation process is expressed through simple techniques regarding the postures, and the meanings of different postures in movement are directly explored. Through this laboratory it is possible for the persons to modify the negative bodily sensations linked to the frustration of one's own aims, which often activate problematic and negative interpersonal cycles, beginning with the sensory memory. Moreover, a section of the laboratory is dedicated to the study and the decoding of facial expressions, with particular attention to the analysis of the signs of lying, deception, bluff, and of real or "strategic" threat (according to the schemes of "What the face reveals" (Ekman & Rosenberg, 2005).

9.11 Eleventh Day

Theoretical lesson: Persuasion techniques

Group seminar: Processes of innovation-decision; the structure of personal revolutions; exercises of taking of perspective: how to learn to see the reality from different points of view before taking decisions

9.12 Twelfth Day

Theoretical lesson: Nonverbal communication

Group seminar: Reading of postures and bodily poses, proxemics; aptica: psychodiagnosis and interpretation of movements and gestures

9.13 Thirteenth Day

Theoretical lesson: Metacommunication and invisible loyalties

Group seminar: Metacommunication exercises I: in family, in love, in the job; metacommunication exercises II: the practice of international negotiation and mediation: how to speak about the way we have previously spoken

The concept of "invisible loyalties" has been proposed by Borszomeni-Nagy & Spark (1973) and Spark within the environment of systemic family psychotherapy, and it has been developed in some aspects that are of particular importance in the context of the negotiation. The basic assumption is that in every individual there can be different systems of "loyalty" (familiar/family, social to a people or to a nation, to a religion, even to one "personal fairy tale") present, which weigh upon one's own aims and on one's state of mind, often in an "invisible" way. In this lesson the theoretical aspects of the model are treated. For the operational ones, a laboratory on invisible loyalties is foreseen, which is subsequently introduced in the training program on the intermediate level (in this part we have only been delineating the basic programme).

9.14 Fourteenth Day

Theoretical lesson: Compassionate mind, cruelty, competition, and cooperation

Group Seminar: Recalling of personal episodes of compassion acted, lived, or received; recalling of personal episodes of cruelty, acted, lived, or suffered; monitoring of negotiators' thoughts within the intervals between two negotiation sessions

The concept of "compassion" was proposed by Paul Gilbert (2005) not only as a methodology for overcoming some psychopathological disorders, but also as a key for the understanding of the mechanisms of cruelty, individual and political and social, in the light of a disproportion and deterioration of the psychobiological system of dominance–submission. In its elaboration, the author proposes an interesting model that makes clearer how cruelty develops itself in some social environments, how it is possible to identify it, and what mechanisms of leadership can spread it, in some historical periods and under certain economic conditions, until producing cruel governments endowed of a discrete popular support.

Some interactions, during the negotiations, could provoke in the negotiators a reduction of the compassion toward themselves, increasingly negative thoughts of autoattack and emergence of self-defeating counterproductive emotions of shame (psychobiologically consequential to sensations of defeat). The negative thoughts of autoattack (autoaccuses, excess sense of guilt, autocriticism, autosentence, autoinsult, etc.) could interfere with the mental lucidity of the negotiator, collocating him in a condition of inferiority compared with the interlocutor/counterpart. Regarding the application of the theory, Gilbert and Irons (2005) have proposed a "compassionate mind training" to establish and to maintain a compassionate attitude toward oneself, that would reduce autoattacks and shame. From this technique derives a model of auto-observation of the thoughts during the interval between one negotiation and another in order to favour a monitoring (and a reduction) of the thoughts of autoattack.

9.15 Fifteenth Day

Theoretical lesson: Evolutionary psychology, cognitive psychotherapy, specific training and international negotiation

Group seminar: Exercises in order to increase the frustration tolerance threshold and increase hope

10
Conclusion

In the discourse developed here, we have tried to establish a bridge between two apparently distant disciplines: international negotiation and cognitive psychotherapy. Such a bridge has been built in developing an analysis of the cognitive and emotional processes identifiable in international negotiation, and applying the results of this analysis to propose and to delineate a project of specific training for negotiators, which in a limited period of time would allow the negotiators to acquire the ability to understand their interlocutors and to master their emotions, useful in improving the quality and, one hopes, partially also the results of the negotiation.

The evolutionist and psychobiological approach to the matter appears particularly meaningful, which can reach even to the survival of humankind on earth. Wars, a consequence also of failed negotiations, are currently so potentially violent to put at serious risk the existence of humankind. Evolutionist psychology suggests strategies based on interpersonal motivational systems, which are mechanisms built precisely by the evolutionary process to favour and to protect the development and welfare of human beings. A planetary progression of "compassion" can help to avoid possible catastrophes, and also to reduce the use of violence in the interactions among persons, peoples, and nations. In this "biological" sense, negotiation in this historical phase constitutes, as never before, a fundamental resource for millions of people and in fact for the whole of humankind. Even if the negotiators do not represent themselves but their governments, they can, however, have a determinant role in the process that aims to favour peace and civil cohabitation on the planet.

Further research is necessary and urgent, from which one can derive new and more effective applications. We hope that this initial attempt, which can certainly still be improved, can represent a stimulus in this direction.

Appendix 1
Dangerous Human Characteristics in the Study of ACP–EU International Negotiations

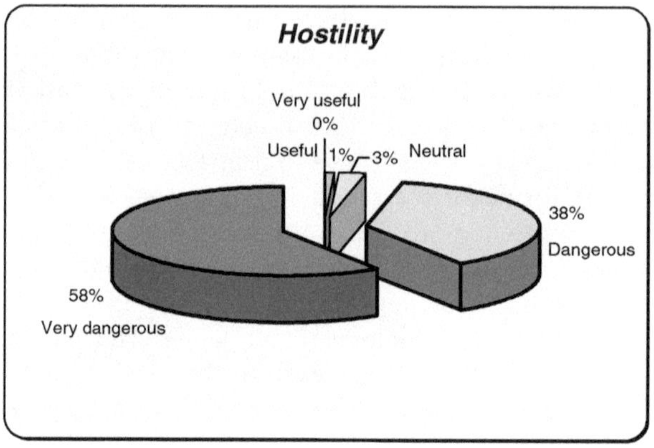

FIGURE A1.1. Hostility.

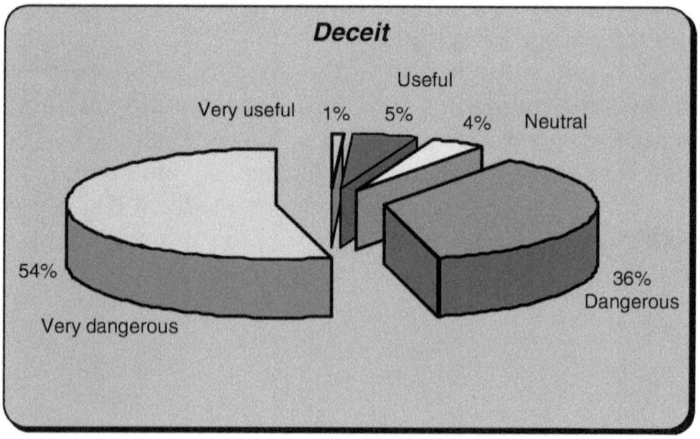

FIGURE A1.2. Deceit.

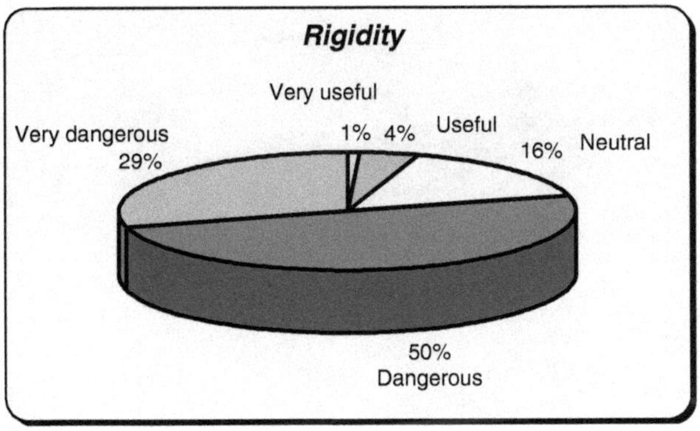

FIGURE A1.3. Rigidity.

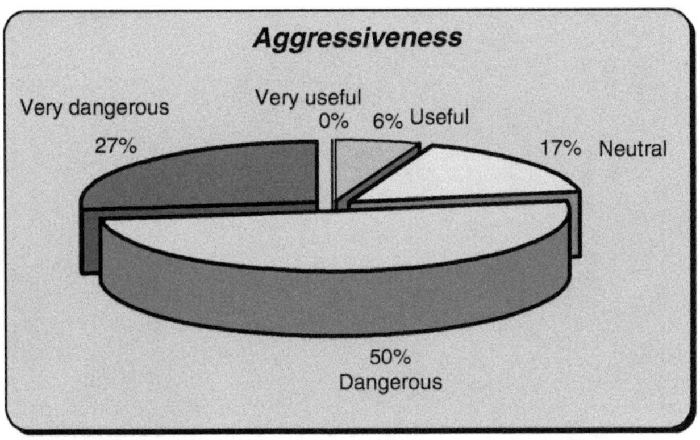

FIGURE A1.4. Aggressiveness.

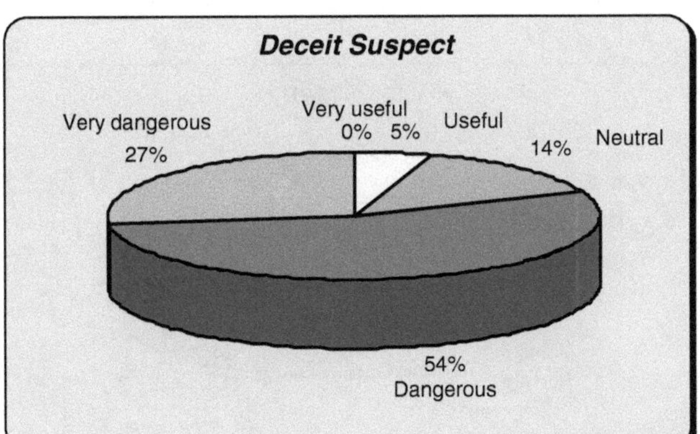

FIGURE A1.5. Deceit suspect.

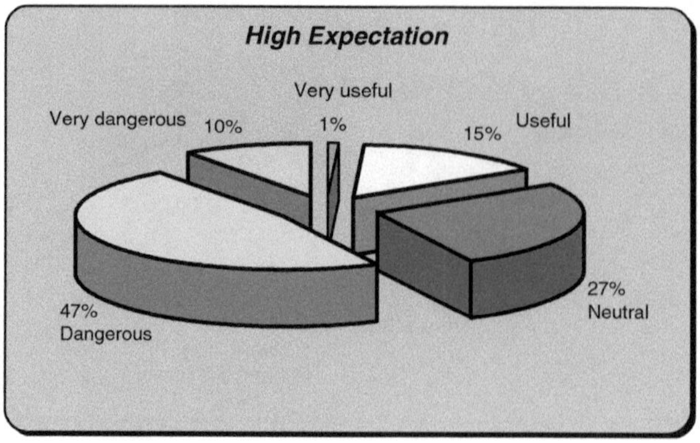

FIGURE A1.6. High expectation.

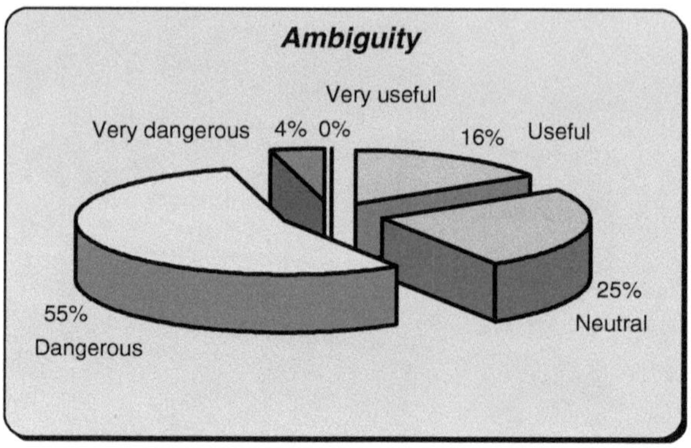

FIGURE A1.7. Ambiguity.

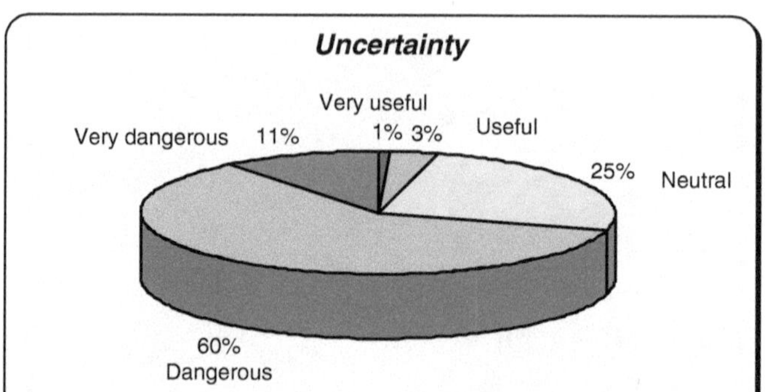

FIGURE A1.8. Uncertainty.

Appendix 2
Less Negative Factors (Depending on Different Perceptions) in the Study of ACP–EU International Negotiations

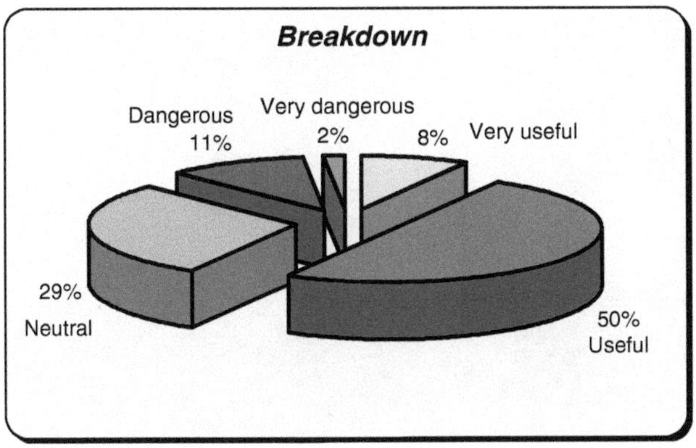

FIGURE A2.1. Breakdown.

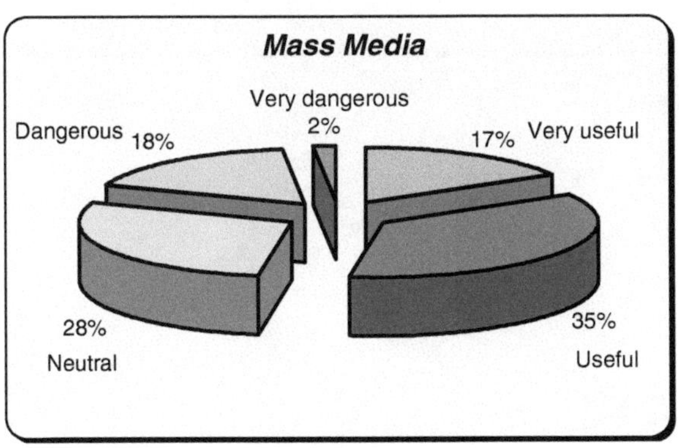

FIGURE A2.2. Mass media.

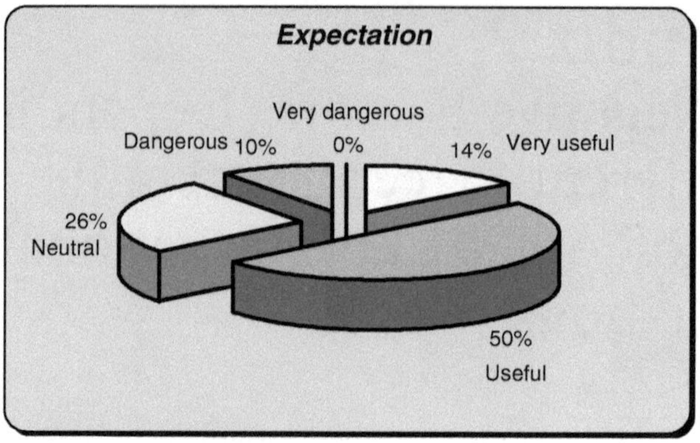

FIGURE A2.3. Expectation.

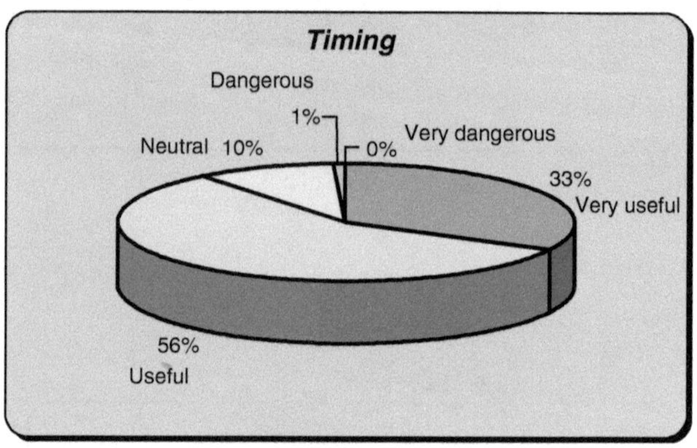

FIGURE A2.4. Timing.

Appendix 3
Positive Factors in the Study of ACP–EU International Negotiations

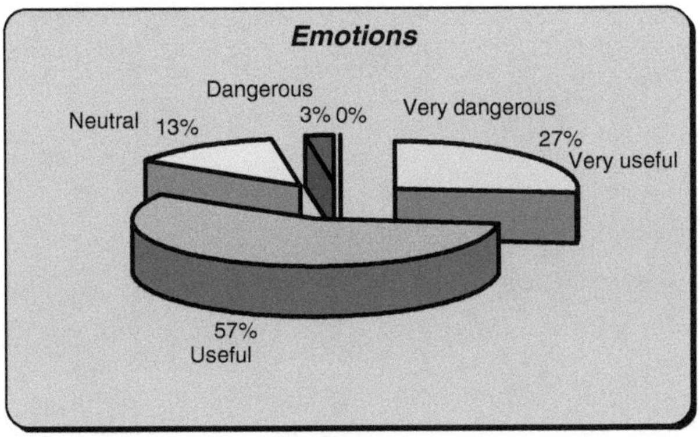

FIGURE A3.1. Emotions.

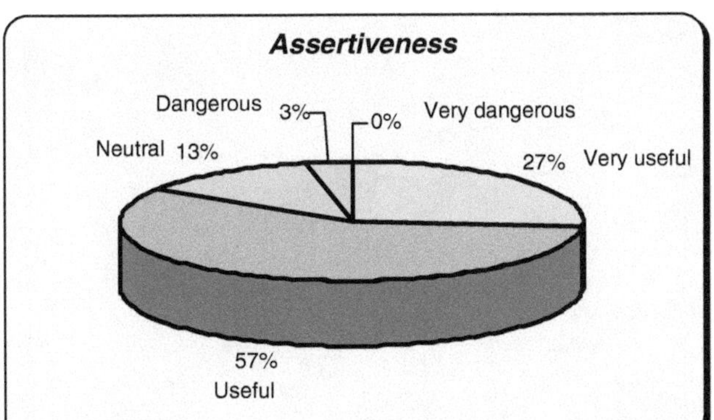

FIGURE A3.2. Assertiveness.

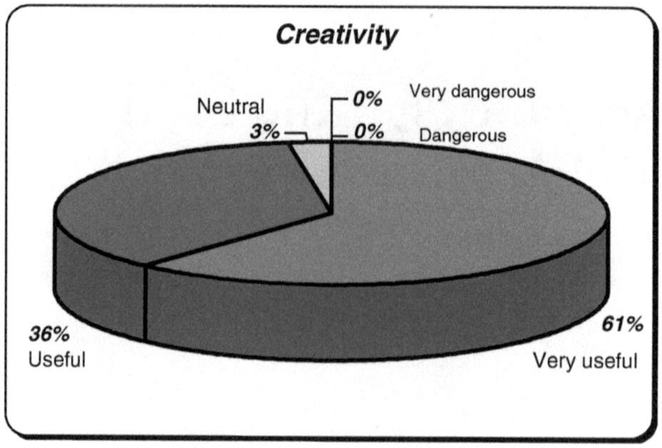

FIGURE A3.3. Creativity.

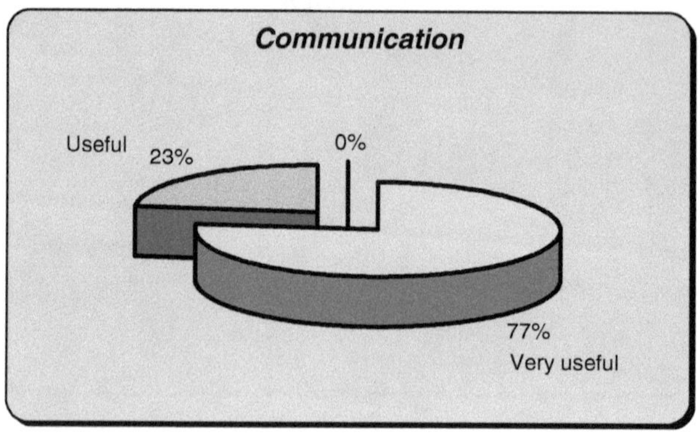

FIGURE A3.4. Communication.

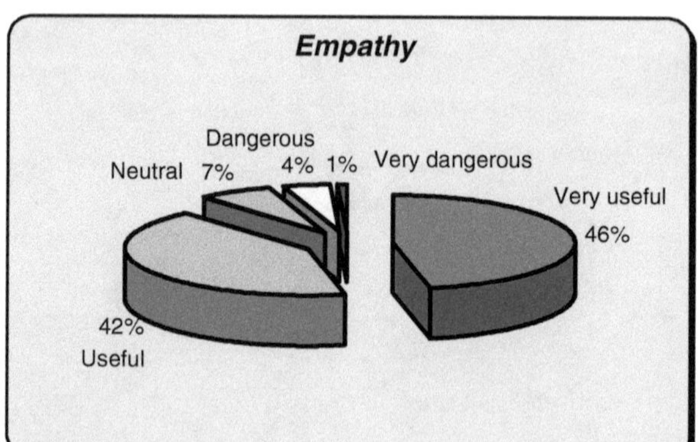

FIGURE A3.5. Empathy.

References

Adler, R.S., Rosen, B., Silverstein, E.M. (1998), Emotions in negotiation: How to manage fear and anger. *Negotiation Journal* **14**(2, April): 161–179.

Allred, K.G. (2000), Distinguishing best and strategic practices: A framework for managing the dilemma between creating and claiming value, *Negotiation Journal* (October) **16**(4): 387–397.

APA (American Psychiatric Association) (2000), *Diagnostic and Statistic Manual of mental disorders*, 4th edition, APA, Washington.

Aquilar, F. (1994), Psicoterapia per la pace. *Il tetto*. **31**(182): 158–169.

Aquilar, F. (1996), *La Coppia in Crescita*, Assisi: Cittadella.

Aquilar, F. (2000), *Riconoscere le Emozioni*. Milano: Franco Angeli.

Aquilar, F. (2002), An introduction to the psychology of music. In: Scarano, P., *Giocomusica*, Napoli: Simeoli.

Aquilar, F. (2006a), *Psicoterapia Dell'Amore e del Sesso*. Milano: Franco Angeli.

Aquilar, F. (2006b), *Le Donne dalla A alla Z*. Milano: Franco Angeli.

Aquilar, F., Ferrante, S. (1994) (Eds.), La coppia in crisi: istruzioni per l'uso. Assisi: Cittadella.

Aquilar, F. Galluccio, M. (2005), International Negotiation: A New Challenge for Cognitive Psychotherapy. Paper presented at the *35th Congress of the European Association for Behavioural and Cognitive Therapies (EABCT)*. Thessalonica, Greece, 21–24 September 2005.

Argyle, M. (1994), *The Psychology of Interpersonal Behaviour*. London: Penguin Books.

Argyle, M. (1995), *Bodily Communication, Second Edition*. London: Methuen.

Asch, S. (1952), *Social Psychology*. Englewood Cliffs, NJ: Prentice-Hall.

Avenhaus, R. (2002), Game theory. In Kremenyuk, V.A., *International Negotiation*. San Francisco: Jossey-Bass, pp. 202–228.

Axelrod, R. (1984), *The Evolution of Cooperation*. New York: Basic Books.

Bandura, A. (Ed.) (1995), *Self-Efficacy in Changing Societies*. Cambridge: Cambridge University Press.

Bandura, A. (1997), *Self-Efficacy: The Exercise of Control*. New York: John Wiley & Sons.

Bara, B.G. (1996), *Manuale di Psicoterapia Cognitiva*. Torino: Bollati Boringhieri.

Bazerman, M.H., Curhan, J.R., Moore, D.A., Velley, K.L. (2000), Negotiation. *Annual Review of Psychology*, 51, pp. 279–314.

Bazerman, M.H., Baron, J., Shonk, K. (2001), Enlarging the societal pie – A cognitive perspective. *Social Science Research*. Harvard NOM Research Paper No 02–17, pp. 1–37.

Beck, A.T. (1976), *Cognitive Therapy and the Emotional Disorders*. New York: International Universities Press. (It.Tr.: Principi di Terapia Cognitiva, (1984). Roma: Astrolabio).

Beck, A.T. (1988), *Love Is Never Enough*. New York: Harper and Row.
Beck, A.T. (1995), Cognitive therapy: Past, present, and future. In Mahoney, M.J. (Ed.), *Cognitive and Constructive Psychotherapies*. New York: Springer, pp. 29–40.
Beck, A.T. (1999), *Prisoners of Hate*. New York: Harper Collins.
Beck, A.T. (2002), Prisoners of hate, *Behaviour Research and Therapy*, **40**: 209–216.
Beck, A.T. (2003, 2004), Personal communication, London.
Beck, J.S. (1995), *Cognitive Therapy: Basics and Beyond*. New York: Guilford Press.
Beck, R. Fernandez, E. (1998), Cognitive-behavioral therapy in the treatment of anger: A meta-analysis. *Cognitive Therapy and Research* **22**(1): 63–74.
Bercovitch, J. (2002), *Studies in International Mediation*. New York: Palgrave Mcmillan.
Bisutti, D. (1991), *La Poesia Salva la Vita*, Milano: Mondatori.
Borgo, S., della Giusta, G., Sibilia, L. (2001), *Dizionario di Psicologia Cognitivo-Comportamentale*. Milano: McGraw-Hill.
Bosman, R., Sonnemans, J., Zeelenberg, M. (2001), Emotions, rejections, and cooling off in the ultimatum game. Working Paper of the University of Amsterdam, pp. 1–26.
Boszormenyi-Nagy, I., Spark, G.M. (1973), *Invisible Loyalties*. New York: Harper & Row.
Boulding, E. (1988), Image and action in peace building. *Journal of Social Issues,* **44**(2): 17–37.
Boulding, K. (1956), *The Image*. Ann Arbor: University of Michigan Press.
Bowlby, J. (1969), *Attachment and Loss: I. Attachment*, London: Hogarth Press.
Bowlby, J. (1988), *A Secure Base*. London: Routlege. (It.Tr.: Una Base Sicura (1989). Milano: Raffaello Cortina Editore.
Bowles, N.R., (2004), *The Diplomacy of Hope*. London: I.B. Tauris.
Burgoon, M., Hunsaker, F.G., Dawson, E.J. (1994), *Human Communication*. Thousand Oaks, CA: Sage.
Bush, G.W. (USA President), The President's state of the Union Address, January 29, 2002.
Carter, J. (2002), *Nobel Lecture*. Oslo, December 10.
Castelfranchi, C., Mancini, F., Miceli, M. (2002), Fondamenti di cognitivismo clinico. Milano: Bollati Boringhieri.
Colman, A.M., (2003), *Oxford Dictionary of Psychology*. New York: Oxford University Press.
Damasio, A. (1994), *Descartes' Error: Emotion, Reason and the Human Brain*. New York: G.P. Putnam's Sons.
Damasio, A. (1999), *The Feeling of What Happens. Body and Emotion in the Making of Consciousness*. USA Orlendo: Harvest Books.
Damasio, A. (2003), *Looking for Spinoza*. Orlando, FL:: Harcourt Brace.
Dattilio, F.M. (1998), *Key Studies in Couple and Family Therapy*. New York: Guilford Press.
De Rivera, J. (1968), *The Psychological Dimension of Foreign Policy*. Columbus, OH: Merrill.
De Rivera, J., Laird, J. (1988), Peace fair or warfare: Educating the community. *Journal of Social Issues,* **44**(2): 59–80.
De Silvestri, C. (1981), *I Fondamenti Teorici e Clinici della Terapia Razionale Emotiva*. Roma: Astrolabio.
Deutsch, M. (2002), Social psychology's contributions to the study of conflict resolution. *Negotiation Journal,* **18**(4): 307–320.
Deutsch, M., Coleman, P.T. (Eds.) 2000, *The Handbook of Conflict Resolution*. San Francisco: Jossey-Bass.
De Zulueta, F. (1999), *Dal Dolore alla Violenza*. Milano: Raffaello Cortina.

Dimaggio, G., Semerari, A. (Eds.) (2003), *I Disturbi di Personalità. Modelli e Trattamento.* Bari: Laterza.

Dimaggio, G., Semerari, A., Carcione, A., Nicolò, G., Procacci, M. (2007), *Psychotherapy of Personality Disorders*, New York: Routledge.

Dogana, F. (1993), *Le Piccole Fonti dell'Io*. Firenze: Giunti.

Dogana, F. (2000), Siamo angeli o diavoli: Il dilemma della natura umana. *Psicologia Contemporanea*. Firenze: Giunti Gruppo Editoriale, **159**(May–June): 4–11.

Druckman, D. (2002), Content analysis. In Kremenyuk, V.A. (Ed.), *International Negotiation*. San Francisco: Jossey-Bass, pp. 288–312.

Edelman, G.M. (1989), *Il Presente Ricordato: Una Teoria Biologica della Coscienza* (It. Tr.) Milano: Rizzoli, 1991.

Eibl-Eibelsfeldt, I. (1984), Die Biologie des Mensschlichen Verhaltens Grundiss der Human Ethologie. Hamburg: Piper.

Ekman, P. (1985), *Telling Lies. Clues to Deceit in the Marketplace, Politics, and Marriage*. New York: Norton. (It. Tr.: I volti della Menzogna, (1989). Firenze: Giunti).

Ekman, P. (1993), Facial expression and emotion. *American Psychologist* **48**: 384–392.

Ekman, P. (1999), *La Seduzione delle Bugie*. Roma: Di Renzo.

Ekman, P. (2003), *Emotions Revealed*. New York: Times Books.

Ekman, P., Davidson, R.J. (Eds.) (1994), *The Nature of Emotion*. New York: Oxford University Press.

Ekman, P., Rosenberg, E.L. (2005), *What the Face Reveals*, 2nd edition, Oxford, UK: Oxford University Press.

Ekman, P.A. (1984), *Expression and the Nature of Emotion: Approaches to Emotion*. New York: Erlbaum.

Ellis, A. (1962), *Reason and Emotion in Psychotherapy*. NJ: Lyle Stuart. New York.

Ellis, A. (1977), *A Garland of Rational Humorous Songs*, New York: RET Institute.

Ellis, A. (1992), Rational emotive approaches to peace. *Journal of Cognitive Psychotherapy*. **6**(2): 79–104.

Ellis, A. (1994), *Reason and Emotion in Psychotherapy. Revised and updated*. New York: Carol.

Ellis, A. (1995), Reflections on rational-emotive therapy. In Mahoney, M.J. (Ed.), *Cognitive and Constructive Psychotherapies*. New York: Springer, pp. 69–73.

Ellis, A. (2001), *Overcoming Destructive Beliefs, Feelings, and Behaviors*. New York: Prometheus Books.

Ellis, A. (2002), Personal communication, New York.

Ellis, A. (2004), *Emotional Disturbance and Its Treatment in a Nutshell*. New York: Albert Ellis Institute.

Ellis, A., Crawford, T. (2000), *Making Intimate Connections*. CA: Impact. Atascasero, California.

Ellis, A., Dryden, W. (1987), *The Practice of Rational-Emotive Therapy*. New York: Springer.

Ellis, A., Harper R.A. (1975), *A New Guide to Rational Living*. North Hollywood, CA: Wilshire Books.

Ellis, A., Young, J. (1987), Cognitive therapy and rational-emotive therapy. *Journal of Cognitive Psychotherapy*. **1**(4): 201–255.

Erzenzinger, Jr., E.R. (2002), *Conversations with Phineas Gage: A Neuroscientific Approach to Negotiation Strategies,* James Boskey ADR Writing Competition, pp. 1–17.

Esposito, M.R. (1996), Il linguaggio dei desideri. In Aquilar F. (Ed.), *La Coppia in Crescita*. Assisi: Cittadella.

Eysenck, M.W. (1990), *The Blackwell Dictionary of Cognitive Psychology*. Oxford, UK: Blackwell.

Eysenck, M.W., Keane, M.T. (2005), *Cognitive Psychology*. Hove, East Sussex: Psychology Press.

Falcone, M., Marraffa, M., Carcione, A. (2003), Metarappresentazione e psicopatologia. In *I Disturbi di Personalità. Modelli e Trattamento*, Dimaggio, G., Semerari, A. (Eds.). Bari: Laterza, pp. 43–76.

Faure, G.O. (2003), *How People Negotiate*. Amsterdam: Kluwer Academic.

Faure, G.O., Sjostedt, G. (1993), Culture and negotiation: An introduction. In *Culture and Negotiation*, Faure and Rubin (Eds.). pp. 1–13. Thousands Oaks, California: Sage.

Fessler, D.M.T., Pillsworth, E.G., Flamson, T.J. (2004), Angry men and disgusted women: An evolutionary approach to the influence of emotions on risk taking. *Organizational Behavior & Human Decision,* **95**: 107–123.

Festinger, L. (1957), A Theory of Cognitive Dissonance. Stanford: Stanford University Press.

Fifield, A. (2005, 30/31 July) N. Korea and US begin to close gulf over nuclear arms. *The Financial Times*, p. 3.

Fifield, A., Khalaf, R., Fidler, S. (2006, 4 October) US says NK weapons test would threaten peace. *The Financial Times*, p. 1.

Fisher, R., Kopelman, E., Schneider, A.K. (1994), *Beyond Machiavelli. Tools for Coping with Conflict*. Cambridge, MA: Harvard University Press.

Fisher, R., Shapiro, D. (2005), *Beyond Reason. Using Emotions as You Negotiate*. New York: Penguin Books.

Fisher, R., Ury, W., Patton, B. (1991), *Getting to Yes. Negotiating an Agreement without Giving In*. London: Random House.

Forgas, J.P. (1998), On feeling good and getting your way: Moods effects on negotiation cognition and bargaining strategies. *Journal of Personality and Social Psychology,* **74**: 565–577.

Forgas, J.P. (Ed.) (2001), *Feeling and Thinking*. Cambridge, UK: Cambridge University Press.

Frijda, N.H. (1986), *The Emotions*. New York: Cambridge University Press.

Frijda, N.H. (1987), Emotions, cognitive structure and action tendency. *Cognition and Emotion*, **1**: 115–143.

Frijda, N.H. (1993), Moods, emotion episodes, and emotions. In Lewis, M., Haviland, J.M. (Eds.), *Handbook of Emotions*. New York: Guilford Press, pp. 381–403.

Frijda, N.H. (2004), Emotion and action. In Manstead, A.S.R., Frijda, N., Fischer, A. (Eds.), *Feelings and Emotions*. Cambridge, UK: Cambridge University Press, pp. 158–173.

Frijda, N.H., Manstead A.S.R., Bem, S. (Eds.) (2000), *Emotions and Beliefs*. Cambridge, UK: University Press.

Frijda, N.H., Mesquita, B. (1994), The social roles and functions of emotions. In Kitayama, S., Markus, H.S. (Eds.), *Emotion and Culture: Empirical Studies of Mutual Influence*. Washington, DC: American Psychological Association, pp. 51–87.

Gabbard, G.O., Beck, J.S., Holmes, J. (2005), *Oxford Textbook of Psychotherapy*. Oxford, UK: Oxford University Press.

Gallucci, R. (2002), *Conversations with History*. Institute of International Studies, UC Berkeley. Interview given on February 2002. E-mail address: http://globetrotter.berkeley.edu/people2/Gallucci/gallucci-con0.html.

Galluccio, M. (2003), A multidisciplinary approach to international negotiation: cognitive, emotive and communicative aspects. Paper presented at the European Congress of Latini Dies. Liege, 1–4 April, 2003. An excerpt of this paper has been published in *The Revue Francophone de Clinique Comportamentale et Cognitive*. Belgium: Afforthecc & Aemtc. **VIII** (1, March).

Galluccio, M. (2004), International negotiation: Cognitive, emotional and communicative aspects. Paper presented at the *27th Annual Scientific Meeting of the International Society of Political Psychology*. Lund, Sweden, July 15–18, 2004.

Galluccio, M. (2005a), Addressing cognition and emotion in international negotiation and co-mediation practice: A research project. Paper presented at the *28th Annual Scientific Meeting of the International Society of Political Psychology*. Toronto, Canada, July 3–6, 2004.

Galluccio, M., (2005c), Theoretical elements of international negotiation. Paper presented at the *35th Congress of the European Association for Behavioural and Cognitive Therapies (EABCT)*. Thessalonica, Greece, 21–24 September 2005.

Galluccio, M., (2005d), Emotional competence as a compass to facilitate the negotiation process. Paper presented at the *Second International Biennale on Negotiation. Paris*, November 17–18, 2005.

Galluccio, M., (2006), Processo di negoziazione e mediazione internazionale. Paper presented at the *XIII National Congress of the Italian Association for Behavioural and Cognitive Therapies (SITCC)*. Naples, Italy, 27–29 October 2006.

Galvani, P. (2004), Il blasone, elementi per una metodologia esplorativa dell'autoformazione. In Quaglino, G.P. (Ed.), *Autoformazione*, Milano: Cortina.

Gambini, P. (2006), Introduzione alla psicologia. Volume secondo: i processi cognitivi, Milano: Franco Angeli.

Gardner, H. (1985), *Frames of Mind: The Theory of Multiple Intelligences*, New York: Basic Books.

Gardner, H. (1999), *The Disciplined Mind*, New York: Simon & Shuster.

Gardner, H. (2000), Using multiple intelligences to improve negotiation theory and practice. *Negotiation Journal*, **16**(4): 321–324.

Gardner, H. (2006), *Multiple Intelligences*. New York: Basic Books.

Gawronski, J. (2005, 27 July), *Corea del Nord: "Come possiamo fidarci degli USA?"* La Stampa, p. 8.

Geller, D.S., Singer, J.D. (2000), *Nations at War*. Cambridge, UK: Cambridge-University Press.

Gensini, S. (2004), *Manuale di Semiotica,* Roma: Carocci.

George, C., Solomon, C. (1999), Attachement and caregiving: The caregiving behavioral system. In Cassidy, J., Shaver P.R. (Eds.), *Handbook of Attachment*. New York: Guilford Press. It. Tr. *Manuale dell'Attaccamento,* (2003), Roma: Givanni Fioriti, pp. 649–671.

George, J.M., Jones, G.R., Gonzalez, J.A. (1998), The role of affect in cross-cultural negotiations. *Journal of International Business Studies,* **29**(4, Fourth Quarter): 749–772.

Geva, N., Skorick, J.M. (2003), The emotional calculus of foreign policy decisions: Getting emotions out of the closet. Paper presented at the *Shambaugh Conference*, March 6–9, 2003.

Gilbert, P. (1989), Human Nature and Suffering. London: Erlbaum.

Gilbert, P. (Ed.) (2005), *Compassion. Conceptualisations, Research and Use in Psychotherapy*, New York: Routledge.

Gilbert P., Irons C. (2005), Focused therapies and compassionate mind training for shame and self-attacking. In: Gilbert P., *Compassion*, New York: Routledge.

Gilbert, P., Leahy, R.L. (2007), *The Therapeutic Relationship in the Cognitive Behaviour Psychotherapies*. London: Routledge.
Gillespie, K., Duffy, M., Hackmann, A., Clark, D.M. (2002), Community based cognitive therapy in the treatment of post-traumatic stress disorder following the Omagh bomb. In Behavior Research and Therapy 40(2002), pp. 345–357.
Goldstein, J., Keohane, R.O. (1993), *Ideas and Foreign Policy*. London: Cornell University Press.
Greenberg, L.S. (2002), *Emotion-Focused Therapy*. Washington, DC: American Psychological Association.
Greenberger, D., Padesky, C.A. (1995), *Mind over Mood*. New York: Guilford Press.
Guidano, V.F. (1987), *Complexity of the Self*. New York: Guilford Press.
Guidano, V.F. (1991), *The Self in Process*. New York: Guilford Press.
Guidano, V.F., Liotti, G. (1983), *Cognitive Processes and Emotional Disorders*. New York: Guilford Press.
Haaga, D.A.F., Davison, G.C. (1995), An appraisal of rational-emotive therapy. In Mahoney, M. (Ed.), *Cognitive and Constructive Psychotherapies*. New York: Springer, pp. 74–86.
Harrison, S. (2004, 4 May), Inside North Korea: Leaders open to ending nuclear crisis. *The Financial Times*, p. 3.
Haselton, M.G.; Ketelaar, T. (2006), Irrational emotions or emotional wisdom? The evolutionary psychology of affect and behaviour. In Forgas (Ed.), Hearts and minds: Affective influences on social cognition and behavior, pp. 21–40. New York: Psychology Press.
Herrmann, R. (2003), Image theory and strategic interaction in international relations. In *Political Psychology*. New York: Oxford University Press, pp. 285–314.
Holmes, J. (1993), *John Bowlby and Attachment Theory*. London: Routledge.
Holmes, J. (2001), *The Search for the Secure Base. Attachment Theory and Psychotherapy*. London: Brunner-Routledge.
Holsti, O.R. (1965), The 1914 case. *American Political Science Review*, **58**: 365–378.
Holsti, O.R. (1967), Cognitive dynamics and images of the enemy: Dulles and Russia. In Finlay, D., Holsti, Ole, Fagen, R., *Enemies in Politics*. Chicago: Rand McNally.
Holsti, O.R. (1971), *Crisis, Escalation, War*. Montreal: McGill–Queens University Press.
Holsti, O.R. (1976), Foreign policy formation viewed cognitively. In Axelrod, R. (Ed.), *Structure of Decision*. Princeton, NJ: Princeton University Press.
Houghton, D.P. (1998), Historical analogies and the cognitive dimension of domestic policymaking. *Political Psychology*, **19**(2): 279–303.
Huddy, L. (2003), Group identity and political cohesion. In Sears, D.O., Huddy, L., Jervis, R. (Eds.). *Oxford Handbook of Political Psychology*. Oxford, UK: Oxford University Press, pp. 511–558.
Isen, A.M. (1987), Positive affect, cognitive processes, and social behaviour. In Berkowitz, L. (Ed.), *Advances in Experimental Social Psychology*, Vol. 20, pp. 203–253. New York: Academic Press.
Isen, A.M. (1993), Positive affect and decision making. In Lewis, M., Havilland J.M. (Eds.), *Handbook of Emotions*. New York: Guilford Press.
Isen, A.M. (2004), Some perspectives on positive feelings and emotions. In Manstead A.S.R., Frijda, N., Fischer, A. (Eds.), *Feelings and Emotions*. Cambridge, UK: Cambridge University Press, pp. 263–281.
Isen, A.M., Rosenzweig, A.S., Young, M.J. (1991), The influence of positive affect on clinical problem solving. *Medical Decision Making*, **11**: 221–227.
Janis, I.L. (1982), *Groupthink*. Boston: Houghton Mifflin.
Janis, I.L., Mann, L. (1977), *Decision Making: A Psychological Analysis of Conflict, Choice, and Commitment*. New York: Free Press.

Jervis, R. (1976), *Perception and Misperception in International Politics*. Princeton, NJ: Princeton University Press.

Jervis, R. (1978), Cooperation under the security dilemma. *World Politics,* **30**: 167–214.

Jervis, R. (1985), Perceiving and coping with threat. In Jervis, R., Lebow, R.N., Stein, J.G. (Eds.), *Psychology and Deterrence*. Baltimore, MD: Johns University Press.

Jervis, R. (1989), Rational deterrence: Theory and evidence. *World Politics,* **41**: 183–207.

Jones, T.S., Bodtker, A. (2001), Mediating with heart in mind: Addressing emotion in mediation practice. *Negotiation Journal*. **17**(3, July): 217–244.

Jones, W.S. (1997), *The Logic of International Relations*. New York: Longman.

Jonsson, C. (2002), Cognitive theory. In Kremenyuk, V.A. (Ed.), *International Negotiation*. San Francisco: Jossey-Bass, pp. 270–287.

Kahn, R.L. (1991), Organizational theory. In Kremenyuk, V.A. (Ed.), *International Negotiation*. San Francisco: Jossey-Bass, pp. 148–163.

Kahn, R.L. (Addendum by Lewicki, R.J.) (2002), Organizational theory. In Kremenyuk, V.A. (Ed.), *International Negotiation*. San Francisco: Jossey-Bass, pp. 159–185.

Karam, A.N. (2005), Cognitive therapy a new challenges: Conflict resolution in national and international negotiation, Paper presented at the *35th Congress of the European Association for Behavioural and Cognitive Therapies (EABCT)*, Thessaloniki, Greece.

Kelly, J.R. (1988), Entrainment in individual and group behaviour. In McGrath, J. (Ed.), *The Social Psychology of Time: New Perspectives*, Vol. 91, pp. 89–110. Newbury Park, CA: Sage.

Keohane, R.O. (2005), After hegemony. Cooperation and discord in the world political economy. New Jersey: Princeton University Press.

Kelman, H.C., Fisher, R., (2003), Conflict analysis and resolution. In *Political Psychology*. New York: Oxford University Press, pp. 315–353.

Kissinger, H. (1979), *White House Years*. New York: Little, Brown.

Kissinger, H. (1994), *Diplomacy*. New York: Touchstone.

Kissinger, H. (2002), *Does America Need a Foreign Policy?: Toward a Diplomacy for the 21st Century*. New York: Touchstone.

Kovecses, Z. (1990), *Emotion Concepts*, New York: Springer.

Kovecses, Z. (1991), A linguist's quest for love. *Journal of Social and Personal Relationships*, **8**(1): 77–98.

Kremenyuk, V.A. (Ed.) (2002a), *International Negotiation. Analysis, Approaches, Issues*. San Francisco: Jossey-Bass.

Kremenyuk, V.A. (2002b), The emerging system of international negotiation. In Kremenyuk, V.A. (Ed.), *International Negotiation*. San Francisco: Jossey-Bass, pp. 22–39.

Labroo, A.A., Isen, A.M., Stanteau, J. (2000), The influence of positive affect on strategic decision-making in prisoner's dilemma situations. Paper presented at the annual meeting of the *Society for Judgement/Decision-Making*, New Orleans.

Lake, R. (2000), *L'Arte della Negoziazione Interculturale*. Milano: Franco Angeli.

Lambert, R. (2003), Misunderstanding each other. *Foreign Affairs*. **82**(2, March–April): 62–74.

Laney, J.T., Shaplen, J.T. (2003), How to deal with North Korea. *Foreign Affairs*. **82** (2, March–April): 16–30.

Larson, D.W. (1997), Trust and missed opportunities in international relations. *Political Psychology*. **18**(3): 701–734.

Lau, R.R. (2003), Models of decision-making. In Sears, D.O., Huddy, L., Jervis, R. (Eds.), *Oxford Handbook of Political Psychology*. Oxford, UK: Oxford University Press, pp. 19–59.

Lax, D.A., Sebenius, J.K. (2002), Dealcrafting: The substance of three-dimensional negotiations. *Negotiation Journal* **18**(1, January): 5–28.

Lazarus, R.S. (1993), Thoughts on the relations between emotion and cognition. *American Psychologist* **37**: 1019–1024.

Leahy, R.L. (2005a), *The Worry Cure*. New York: Harmony Books.

Leahy, R.L. (2005b), A social-cognitive model of validation. In Gilbert, P. (Ed.), *Compassion. Conceptualisations, Research and Use in Psychotherapy*. New York: Routledge.

Leahy, R.L. (2007), Schematic mismatch in the therapeutic relationship. In Gilbert, P., Leahy, R.L. (Eds.), *The Therapeutic Relationship in the Cognitive Behaviour Psychotherapies*. New York: Routledge.

Le Doux, J. (1998), *Il Cervello Emotivo*. Milano: Baldini & Castoldi.

Levy, J.S. (2003), Political psychology and foreign policy. In Sears, D.O., Huddy, L., Jervis, R. (Eds.), *Oxford Handbook of Political Psychology*. Oxford, UK: Oxford University Press, pp. 253–284.

Lewis, M., Haviland-Jones, J.M. (Eds.) (2000), *Handbook of Emotions*. New York: Guilford Press.

Liebman, M. (1986), Art therapy for groups. London: Routledge.

Lindskold, S. (1978), Trust development, the grit proposal and the effects of conciliatory acts on conflict and cooperation. *Psychology Bulletin* **85**: 772–788.

Liotti, G. (1992), Egocentrism and the cognitive psychotherapy of personality disorders. *Journal of Cognitive Psychotherapy*, **6**: 43–58.

Liotti, G. (1994), *La Dimensione Interpersonale della Coscienza*. Roma: La Nuova Italia Scientifica.

Liotti, G. (1999), Disorganization of attachment as a model for understanding dissociative psychopathology. In Solomon, J., George, C. (Eds.), *Attachment Disorganization*, New York: Guildford Press, pp. 291–317.

Liotti, G. (2001), *Le Opere della Coscienza*. Milano: Raffaello Cortina.

Liotti, G. (2005a), Una teoria per la pratica. Attaccamento disorganizzato e psicoterapie a setting multipli. In Liotti, G., Farina, B., Rainone, A. (A cura di), *Due Terapeuti per un Paziente*. Bari: Laterza, pp. 19–48.

Liotti, G. (2005b), I sistemi motivazionali interpersonali. In Liotti, G., Farina, B., Rainone, A. (A cura di), *Due Terapeuti per un Paziente*. Bari: Laterza, pp. 225–228.

Liotti G. (2007), Internal working models of attachment in the therapeutic relationship. In Gilbert P., Leahy R.L. (Eds.), *The Therapeutic Relationship in the Cognitive Behavioral Therapies*. New York: Routledge.

Liotti, G., Farina, B., Rainone, A. (A cura di) (2005), *Due Terapeuti per un Paziente*. Bari: Laterza.

Liotti, G., Mollon, P., Miti, G. (2005), Dissociative disorders. In Gabbard, G.O., Beck, J.S., Holmes, J. (Eds.), *Oxford Textbook of Psychotherapy*. Oxford, UK: Oxford University Press, pp. 203–211.

Luttwak, E.N. (1999), Give war a chance. *Foreign Affairs* **78**(4, July–August): 36–44.

Mahoney, M. (Ed.) (1995), *Cognitive and Constructive Psychotherapies*. New York: Springer.

Mahoney, M.J. (1974), *Cognition and Behavior Modification*. Cambridge, MA: Ballinger.

Mahoney, M.J. (1991), *Human Change Process*. New York: Basic Books.

Manstead, A.S.R. (1991), Expressiveness as an individual difference. In R.S. Feldman, B. Rimé (Eds.), Fundamentals of nonverbal behavior (pp. 285–328). Cambridge: Cambridge University Press.

Manstead, A.S.R., Frijda, N., Fischer, A. (Eds.) (2004), *Feelings and Emotions*. Cambridge, UK: Cambridge University Press.

Marcus, G.E. (2003), The psychology of emotion and politics. In D.O. Sears, L. Huddy, R. Jervis (Ed.), Oxford Handbook of Political Psychology. Oxford: Oxford University Press.

Maturana, H. (1990), *Autocoscienza e Realtà*. (It. Tr.) Raffaello Cortina, Milano 1993.

McCauley, C. (1989), The nature of social influence in groupthink: Compliance and internalization. *Journal of Personality and Social Psychology* **57**(2): 250–60.

McCauley, C. (1998), Group dynamics in Janis' theory of groupthink: Backward and forward. *Organizational Behaviour and Human Decision Processes,* **73**: 142–162.

McLean, I., McMillan, A. (2003), *Oxford Concise Dictionary of Politics*. New York: Oxford University Press.

Meichenbaum, D. (1977), *Cognitive-Behavior Modification*. New York: Plenum.

Meichenbaum, D. (1995), Changing conceptions of cognitive behavior modification: retrospect and prospect. In Mahoney, M. (Ed.), *Cognitive and Constructive Psychotherapies*. New York: Springer, pp. 20–26.

Moffitt, M.L., Bordone, R.C. (Eds.) (2005), *The Handbook of Dispute Resolution*. San Francisco: Jossey-Bass.

Morris, M.W., Keltner, D. (2000), How emotions work: An analysis of the social functions of emotional expressions in negotiations. *Research in Organizational Behavior*, **22**: 1–50.

Moscovici, S., Zavalloni, M. (1969), The group as a polarizer of attitudes, in Journal of Personality and Social Psychology, **12**: 125–135.

Nelson, D., Wheeler, M. (2004), Rocks and hard places: Managing two tensions in negotiation. *Negotiation Journal* **20**(1, January): 113–128.

Nesbitt-Larking, P. (2004), Social theory and political psychology. Paper presented at the *27th Annual Scientific Meeting of the International Society of Political Psychology*, Lund, Sweden, July 15–18, 2004.

Nicolson, H. (1963), *Diplomacy*. Oxford, UK: Oxford University Press.

Nye, J.S. (2002), *The Paradox of American Power*. New York: Oxford University Press.

Nye, J.S. (2003a), U.S. power and strategy after Iraq. *Foreign Affairs*. **82**(4, July–August): 60–73.

Nye, J.S. (2003b), *Understanding International Conflicts*. New York: Pearson.

Nye, J.S., (2004), *Soft Power*. USA: Public Affairs. New York.

O'Connor, K., Arnold, J. (2002), The shadow of the past: How bargaining histories shape negotiated outcomes. Center for Leadership in Dynamic Organizations. Johnson Graduate School of Management. Cornell University Working Paper Series.

O'Connor, K.M., Arnold, J.A. (2003), *Walking Away from the Table: How Negotiator Self-Efficacy Affects Decision Making*. Paper presented at the IACM 15th Annual Conference, June, 9–12, 2002.

O'Connor, K.M., De Dreu C.K.W., Bazerman, M.H., et al. (2002), What we want to do versus what we think we should do: An empirical investigation of intrapersonal conflict" in Negotiation, Organizations and Markets Research Papers. Harvard NOM Research Paper No. 02–18. Published in the same year in the *Journal of Behavioral Decision Making* **15**(5, May): 403–418.

Oppenheim, A.N. (1984), Psychological processes in world society. In Banks, M. (Ed.), *Conflict in World Society,* UK: Wheatsheaf Books. Brighton, Sussex.

Panksepp, J. (1998), *Affective Neuroscience: The Foundations of Human and Animal Emotions*. Oxford, UK: Oxford University Press.

Panksepp, J. (2001), The neuro-evolutionary cusp between emotions and cognitions. *Evolution and Cognition*. **7**(2): 141–163.

Panksepp, J. (2003), An interface of the affective, behavioral, and cognitive neurosciences: Decoding the emotional feelings of the brain. *Brain and Cognition* **52**: 4–14.

Parkinson, B., Fischer, A.H., Manstead, A.S.R. (2005), *Emotion in Social Relations*. New York: Psychology Press.

Parsi, V.E. (1998), Oltre il confine: Psicologia politica e relazioni internazionali. In *Nuove Questioni di Psicologia Politica*, Assunto Quadrio Avitarchi (a cura di). Milano: Giuffrè, pp. 274–314.

Peretti A. de (1986), Gamme du blason. *Les Amis de Sèvres* **123**(September): 78–85.

Peretti A. de (1992), *Organiser des Formations*, Paris: Hachette.

Peretti A. de (1994), *Techniques pour Communiquer*, Paris: Hachette.

Peserico M. (2006), *Danzamovimentoterapia*, Roma: Carocci.

Pettigrew, T.F. (1998a), Applying social psychology to international social issues. *Journal of Social Issues*, http://www.findarticles.com, pp. 1–15.

Pettigrew, T.F. (1998b), Influencing policy with social psychology. *Journal of Social Issues* **44**(2): 205–219.

Pinker, S. (1997), *How the Mind Works*. New York: Harper Collins.

Planalp, S.; Fitness, J. (1999), Thinking/feeling about social and personal relationships. *Journal of Social and Personal Relationships*. **16**(6): 731–750.

Pruitt, D.G. (2002), Strategy in negotiation. In Kremenyuk, V.A. (Ed.), *International Negotiation*. San Francisco: Jossey-Bass, pp. 85–96.

Quaglino, G.P. (A cura di) (1999), *Leadership*. Milano: Raffaello Cortina.

Quaglino G.P. (2004), *Autoformazione*, Milano: Cortina.

Raiffa, H. (1982), *The Art and Science of Negotiation*. Cambridge, MA: Harvard University Press.

Raiffa, H. (2002), Contributions of applies systems analysis to international negotiation. In Kremenyuk, V.A. (Ed.), *International Negotiation*. San Francisco: Jossey-Bass, pp. 5–21.

Ramstad, E., Moffett, S., Fairclough, G. (2006,4 October), *North Korea plans nuclear-bomb test. The Wall Street Journal*, p. 11.

Reda, M.A. (1986), *Sistemi cognitivi complessi e psicoterapia*. Roma: NIS.

Reed, S.K. (1989), *Psicologia Cognitiva*. Bologna: il Mulino.

Robins, C.J., Hayes, A.M. (1995), An appraisal of cognitive therapy. In Mahoney, M.J. (Ed.), *Cognitive and Constructive Psychotherapies*. Washington, DC: Springer, pp. 41–66.

Rotblat, J., Daisaku, I. (2006), *A Quest for Global Peace*. New York: Tauris and Co. Ltd.

Rubin, J.Z. (2002), Psychological approach. In Kremenyuk, V.A. (Ed.), *International Negotiation*. San Francisco: Jossey-Bass, pp. 256–269.

Rubin, J.Z., Brown, B.R. (1975), *The Social Psychology of Bargaining and Negotiation*. Orlando, FL: Academic Press.

Rumiati, R., Pietroni, D. (2001), *La Negoziazione*. Milano: Raffaello Cortina.

Russell, J.A., Fernàndez-Dols, J.M. (Eds.) (2002), *The Psychology of Facial Expression*. Cambridge, UK: Cambridge University Press.

Saarni, C. (1988), Emotional competence: How emotions and relationships become integrated. In Thompson, R.A. (Ed.), *Socioemotional Development*. Nebraska Symposium on Motivation, Vol. 36. Lincoln: University of Nebraska Press.

Saarni, C. (1993), Socialization of emotion. In Lewis, M., Haviland, J. (Eds.), *Handbook of Emotions*. New York: Guilford Press, pp. 435–446.

Saarni, C. (1997), Coping with aversive feelings. *Motivation and Emotion*, **21**: 45–63.

Saarni, C. (1999), *The Development of Emotional Competence*. New York: Guilford Press.

Safran, J.D. (1984), Assessing the cognitive-interpersonal cycle. *Cognitive Therapy and Research*, **8**: 333–348.

Safran J.D. (1998), *Widening the Scope of the Cognitive Therapy*. NJ:Jason Aronson.

Safran J.D. (2002), Personal communication. New York,.

Safran J.D., Muran J.C. (2000), *Negotiating the Therapeutic Alliance*. New York: Guilford Press.

Safran J.D., Segal Z.V. (1990), *Interpersonal Process in Cognitive Therapy*. New York: Basic Books.

Salovey, P. et al. (2004), Emotional intelligence. What do we know? In *Feelings and Emotions*. Cambridge, UK: Cambridge University Press; pp. 321–340.

Sampson, E.E. (1989), The challenge of social change in psychology. Globalization and psychology's theory of the person. *American Psychologist* **44**: 914–921.

Sanderson, C.A., Karetsky, K.H. (2002), Intimacy goals and strategies of conflict resolution in dating relationships: A mediational analysis. *Journal of Social and Personal Relationships* **19**(3, June): 317–338.

Sandole, D.J.D (1984), The subjectivity of theories and actions in world society. In Banks, M. (Ed.), *Conflict in World Society*, pp. 39–55. UK: Wheatsheaf Books.

Sang-Hun, C. (2006, 4 October), North Korea planning nuclear weapons test. *The International Herald Tribune*, p. 1/7.

Sawyer, J., Guetzkow, H. (1965), Bargaining and negotiation in international relations. In Kelman, H.C. (Ed.), *International Behaviour: A Social-Psychological Analysis*. New York: Holt, Rinehart & Winston, pp. 466–520.

Schlesinger, A.M., Jr. (1965), *A Thousand Days*. Boston: Houghton Mifflin.

Scoggin, F., Jamison, C., Gochneaur, K. (1989), Comparative efficacy of cognitive and behaviour bibliotherapy. *Journal of Counseling and Clinical Psychology,* **57**: 403–407.

Sears, D.O., Huddy, L., Jervis, R. (2003a), *Oxford Handbook of Political Psychology*. Oxford, UK: Oxford University Press.

Sears, D.O., Huddy, L., Jervis, R. (2003b), The psychologies underlying political psychology. In *Oxford Handbook of Political Psychology*. Oxford, UK: Oxford University Press, pp. 3–16.

Sebenius, J. K. (2002), International negotiation analysis. In Kremenyuk, V.A. (Ed.), *International Negotiation*. San Francisco: Jossey-Bass, pp. 229–255.

Segal, Z.V., Williams, J.M.G., Teasdale, J.D. (2002), Mindfulness-based cognitive therapy for depression. New York: Guilford.

Semerari, A. (1992), Cognitive therapy in Italy: The debate on therapist-client relationship. *Journal of Cognitive Psychotherapy*, **6**(2): 145–147.

Semerari, A. (2000), *Storia, Teorie e Tecniche della Psicoterapia Cognitiva*. Bari: Laterza.

Semerari, A. (2006), I cicli interpersonali e i disturbi metacognitivi nella relazione terapeutica. In Sassaroli S., Lorenzini R., Ruggiero G.M., (Eds.) *Psicoterapia Cognitiva dell'Ansia*. Milano: Cortina.

Semerari, A., Carcione, A., Nicolo, G., Falcone, M. (2002), L'approccio metacognitivo. In Castelfranchi, C., Mancini, F., Miceli, M. (A cura di), *Fondamenti di Cognitivismo Clinico*. Torino: Bollati Boringhieri.

Schaverien, J., Odell-Miller, H. (2005), The art therapies, in: Gabbard G.O., Beck, J.S., Holmes, J. Oxford Textbook of Psychotherapy, Oxford: Oxford University Press.

Sloboda, J.A., (1987), The musical mind. The cognitive psychology of music. Oxford: Oxford University Press.

Smith, S. (1985), Groupthink and the hostage rescue mission. *British Journal of Political Science* **15**(1, January): 117–123.

Snyder C.R. (Ed.) (2000), *Handbook of Hope: Theory, Measures and Applications*. San Diego: Academic Press.

Snyder, G.H., Diesing, P. (Eds.) (1977), *Conflict Among Nations: Bargaining, Decision Making, and System Structure in International Crisis*. Princeton, NJ: Princeton University Press.

Snyder, C.R., Feldman, D. (2000), Hope for the many: an empowering social agenda, in: Snyder, C.R. (ed.), Handbook of hope. San Diego: Academic Press.

Sperber, D. (Ed.) (2000), *Metarepresentation*. Oxford, UK: Oxford University Press.

Stolorow, R.D., Atwood, G.E. (1992), *I Contesti dell'Essere*. It.Tr. Torino (1995): Bollati Boringhieri.

Tetlock, P.E. (1996), Dimensioni psichologiche della politica internazionale: processi cognitivi, influenza e identità. In Legrenzi, P., Girotto, V. (A cura di), *Psicologia e Politica,* Milano: Raffaello Cortina.

The Economist (2002, 2 February), George Bush and the axis of evil. *The Economist,* pp. 13–14.

Thoits, P.A. (2004), Emotion norms, emotion work, and social order. In Manstead, A.S.R., Frijda, N., Fischer, A. (Eds.), *Feelings and Emotions*. Cambridge, UK: Cambridge University Press, pp. 359–378.

Thompson, L.L. (2005), *The Mind and Heart of the Negotiator*. Princeton, NJ: Pearson Education.

Thompson, L.L., Medvec, V.H., Seiden, V., Kopelman, S. (2001), Poker face, smiley face, and rant'n' rave: Myths and realities about emotion in negotiation. In Hogg, M.A., Tindale (Eds.), *Blackwell Handbook of Social Psychology: Group Processes*. London: Blackwell.

Trevisani, D. (2005), *Negoziazione Interculturale*. Milano: Franco Angeli.

Ury, W. (1992), *Getting past NO*. London: Century Business.

Van den Assem, A. (2000), The perseverance of beliefs: The reaction of Kissinger and Brzezinski to the end of the cold war. *ActaPolitica* **35**(Summer): 169–195.

Van Kleef, G.A., De Dreu, C.K.W., Manstead, A.S.R. (2002), The interpersonal effects of anger and happiness on negotiation behavior and outcomes. Paper presented at the *15th Annual Conference of the International Association for Conflict Management*, June, Park City, Utah.

Van Kleef, G.A., De Dreu, C.K.W., Manstead, A.S.R. (2004), The interpersonal effects of emotions in negotiations: A motivated information processing approach. *Journal of Personality and Social Psychology* **87**(4): 510–528.

Watkins, M. (1999), Negotiating in a complex world. *Negotiation Journal* **15**(3, July): 245–270.

Watkins, M., Rosegrant, S. (2001), *Breakthrough International Negotiation*. San Francisco: Jossey-Bass.

Watzlawick, P., Beavin, J.H., Jackson, D.D. (1967), *Pragmatica della Comunicazione Umana*. It.Tr.: (1971), Roma: Astrolabio.

Wells, A. (2000), *Emotional Disorders and Metacognition. Innovative Cognitive Therapy,* Chichester: John Wiley & Sons.

Zajonc, R.B. (1980), Feeling and thinking: Preferences need no inferences. *American Psychologist* **35**: 151–175.

Zamponi E., Piumini R. (1988), *Calicanto*, Torino: Einaudi.

Zartman, I.W. (2003, 2005), Personal communications, Paris.

Zartman, I.W. (2005), *Cowardly Lions*. CO: Lynne Rienner.

Zartman, I.W., Faure, G.O. (Eds.) (2005), *Escalation and Negotiation in International Conflicts*. Cambridge, UK: Cambridge University Press.

Zikic., O. (2005), International negotiation: A new challenge for cognitive psychotherapy. The Serbian experience, Paper presented at the *35th Congress of the European Association for Behavioural and Cognitive Therapies (EABCT)*, Thessalonika, Greece.

Index